Contents

Acknowledgments

Writing can be a very rewarding, but also a frustrating process. Without the help of family and friends, it would have been impossible to balance the highs and lows of research. My deepest gratitude for his extraordinarily generous help, guidance and support for this book (and *many, many, many* previous drafts) goes to Randall Germain.

My students at the University of Sussex were a wonderful audience and their questions and comments provided many useful insights into the direction of this book. I am most grateful to my fellow colleagues, for stimulating intellectual exchange and constructive criticisms: Duncan Wigan, Sam Knafo, Johnna Montgomerie, Kees van der Pijl, Or Raviv, Phil Cerny, Dick Bryan, Avinash Persaud Susanne Soederberg, Peter North and many others. Many special thanks to Hazel Woodbridge, Shirley Tan and the rest of the production team at Palgrave Macmillan for their hard work and efficiency. I am indebted to Virot Ali, for his excellent research support and expertise on East Asia. And to Ronen Palan, for patient help with editing and much more.

List of Abbreviations

ADB	Asian Development Bank
AFC	Asian Financial Crisis
BIS	Bank for International Settlements
BoP	Balance of Payments
EBRD	European Bank for Reconstruction and Development
EMT	Efficient markets theory
EU	European Union
FDI	Foreign Direct Investment
FIDF	Financial Institutions Development Fund
FIG	Financial Industrial Groups (Russia)
FIH	Financial Instability Hypothesis
FT	Financial Times
G-7	Group of seven highly industrialised countries
GDP	Gross domestic product
GKO	Russian government short-term bonds
GNP	Gross national product
IFIs	international financial institutions
IMF	Intentional Monetary Fund
IT	Information technology
LLR	Lender of last resort
LTCM	Long Term Capital Management (fund)
LPT	Liquidity preference theory
M&As	Mergers and acquisitions
MNC(s)	Multinational Corporation(s)
NIFA	New International Financial Architecture
OECD	Organisation for Economic Cooperation and Development
OFZs	Russian government long-term bonds
OPEC	Organisation of Petroleum Exporting Countries
OTC	Over the counter
PPP	Purchasing power parity
SAPs	Structural adjustment programmes
UNCTAD	United Nations Conference on Trade and Development

USSR   Union of Soviet Socialist Republics
WTO   World Trade Organisation

Note: Dollars are in US dollars.

Introduction

The research that has culminated in this book was prompted, I now realise, by an incident that took place on one dreary October morning in 1997 in Minsk, capital of Belarus. It was my first day at work in one of the city's young investment firms. As a graduate student in economics, I was thrilled to have secured the post of financial analyst (whatever that might mean) in one of the city's thriving new financial institutions. Yet as I turned up at the smart office in the centre of Minsk, I was rather disappointed to learn that my new colleagues were distinctly uninterested in the new addition to their team. They were instead glued to computer screens, repeating ominously 'Asia is falling!'

Earlier that year, a frantic panic engulfed several of the world's most successful economies: the so-called East Asian 'tigers'. Having performed spectacularly well in attracting foreign investment and sustaining high economic growth for about 20 years, the small, export-oriented economies collapsed like a stack of domino chips under the pressures of currency speculation, asset bubbles and bank runs. The crisis that started on 2nd of July in 1997 in Thailand soon spread to neighbouring economies – the Philippines, South Korea, Malaysia and Indonesia. The scale and scope of the financial disaster was terrifying: for a long while, the 'tigers' had been widely perceived as 'miracle' economies, equipped with the necessary economic and human capital, and guided by pro-active, development-oriented governments. The financial collapses of summer–autumn of 1997 not only ruined many lives in the crisis-hit economies, but sent shock waves through the global financial markets. By October 1997, several of the affected countries had been forced to approach the IMF for emergency finance, and the ensuing crisis management programmes, centred on restrictive economic measures, exacerbated the consequences of the financial collapses even further.

Back in the small Minsk-based financial firm, anxiety about falling Asian markets was puzzling. The firm that I have joined was engaged mostly in speculative trade on the Russian securities market, and in the centre of Belarus, 'Asia' seemed remote and quite irrelevant. Things were made much clearer however, when three months later, the firm filed for bankruptcy and staff were made redundant. As it transpired, a fall of the distant Asia has had a direct, and very tangible, impact on the young financial markets in Russia and some of its neighbours, costing hundreds of managers and financiers their prestigious jobs.

It was this experience that prompted me to embark on a study of financial crises. Although the historical record of financial booms and busts goes a long way, it seems that financial crisis became a curse of the 1990s. The devastating wave of financial implosions in Mexico, East Asia, Russia, Brazil, Argentina and other emerging economies have thrown millions of people into poverty and misery. Unlike earlier outbreaks of financial instability, in the late 1990s, the crises were not confined to the peripheral regions of the global economy. To the bewilderment of many, distress soon spread to the seemingly well-governed, advanced capitalist world. The scandals of high-profile firms like LTCM, Enron, WorldCom, Parmalat, Fannie Mae and Freddie Mac, along with the burst of the Nasdaq bubble itself, have accentuated the fragility of finance, and compromised many conventional views on crisis and its management. What, then, are the causes of fragile finance today? How can we better understand the nature of financial crisis in the age of globalisation? And what lessons can be drawn from the recent experience? Exploring various approaches to understanding financial fragility and crisis, this book seeks to provide an answer to each of these questions.

A classic of financial history, Charles Kindleberger, once said: 'Financial crisis is like a pretty girl: difficult to define, but recognisable when seen' (in Kindleberger and Laffargue 1982: 2). Kindleberger's metaphor reflects the powerlessness that analysts and observers, both from the academe and in the policymaking community, encounter in the face of financial volatility. While it is easy to search for triggers of a crisis once it erupts, it is far more difficult to discern the warning signs of a looming collapse of a currency, a bank, or a stock market. It is even more difficult to see the warning signs in time when all three elements – currency, the financial sector and the banking system – are intertwined in a complex chain of global credit. And yet most of the financial implosions of the late 1990s–early 2000s occurred precisely at the juncture of foreign exchange pressures, banking sector strains and speculative manias in the financial market, pulling individual corporations, national economies and in the case of East Asia, a region, into the trap of over-indebtedness, illiquidity and ultimately, bankruptcy.

In the wake of the financial dramas of the last decade, a plethora of analytical perspectives on the nature of crises and possible remedies emerged in the academic literature and in the policymaking community. Conventional economic approaches have tended to treat the crises as a series of unfortunate but isolated events, only marginally related to each other, and caused mostly by peculiar problems of the economies concerned: crony capitalism in the case of East Asia; bad governance in the cases of Russia and Argentina; greed or 'irrational exuberance' in the case of LTCM, Enron and the 'dotcom' bubble. The perspective underlying such readings implies that the origins of crises lay not so much with the system as such, but with certain actors or market segments.

The study proposed in this book, on the contrary, seeks to demonstrate that there is a dangerous, yet still often overlooked connection between the crises of the past decade. It lies at the nexus of the increased opportunities for speculation offered by liberalised and globalised financial markets; and the ability of financial institutions and other market participants to continually generate and employ new instruments of credit. Being intimately interlinked, these tendencies shape the global financial system today and constitute a paradox of deregulated credit. As this study explains, on the one hand, the ability of financial institutions and other borrowers to generate new credit instruments and trading techniques facilitates the dispersion of risks in the markets, as well as the globalisation of finance. On the other hand however, the new channels of borrowing lead to a build-up of large structures of credit and thus, massive volumes of debt in a pyramid-like fashion. This tendency, I argue, is a major factor contributing to the present-day fragility of finance. Disturbingly, the effects of the liberalisation of financial markets, as well as the nature of credit itself, translate these institutional tendencies into crises of insolvency for private corporations, economic sectors, countries and even regions. Thus this book develops a vision of financial fragility that centres on three entrenched and intimately interrelated, yet poorly understood, products of deregulated credit: financial innovation, deficit financing, and progressive illiquidity of financial structures. With these premises, the book examines the role of subjective assessments, progressive illiquidity and deficit financing in the events that defined the global financial system during the past decade, and draws some implications for the emerging design of global financial governance.

Since the collapse of the Bretton Woods regime in 1971–1973, financial volatility has become a well-rehearsed theme in various branches of the social sciences. The events of the 1990s have fuelled the debate between various schools of thought further. In particular, the issue of the long-term implications of the crisis wave for world economic stability became a point of contentious debate. Some believe that the increased frequency of financial crises is a normalising element within a cyclical evolution of the global economy and that crises and bubbles can, in fact, be useful for the economic system as a whole (e.g. Kapstein 1996; Pollin 1996; Eatwell 2004; Allen and Gale 1999). Others are less optimistic, noting disturbing parallels between heightened financial fragility and recession tendencies today, and the Great Depression of the 1930s (e.g. Krugman 2000; Stiglitz 2004; Bonner and Wiggin 2005; Rowbotham 2000).

This book aims to understand the inner workings of crisis and the nature of financial fragility itself, and thus strives to remain open-minded rather than prescriptive in its message. Financial crisis is always destructive for those who are hit by it, but in many ways, crises turn out to be 'cleansing' events for the economic system: they do away with many of the preceding excesses, both in finance and production, reveal political mistakes and strategic miscalculations, and act as corrective devices for economic agents and policy-makers. For the East Asian 'tigers' and for Russia, the crises of 1997–1998 became a watershed. Millions of jobs were lost in the wake of post-crisis restructuring; poverty levels shot up, reminding many ordinary people that the otherwise obscure world of 'high finance' can have a very direct link to their livelihoods. Many political careers were crushed; in some cases, as in Malaysia, Russia and later in Argentina, the crisis brought an end to the political rule of the country's leaders.

In the advanced industrial countries, the collapse of the 'new economy' bubble in 2001, along with corporate scandals involving firms like LTCM, Enron, WorldCom and others, saw billions of dollars vanish from the markets, putting financial speculation and engineering under public scrutiny. Yet, although some predicted a deep global depression, the world seems to have escaped, at least so far, a recurrence of the 1930s-type of economic devastation. Ten years onwards, most of the crisis-hit economies have managed to recover from the traumas and outperform their pre-crisis growth. Across the world, the emerging markets, having suffered from the exhaustion of capital inflows in the wake of the 1997–1999 crises, are yet again receiving large inflows of capital. Furthermore, securitisation, credit derivatives and structured finance may help explain why the world financial markets have remained robust and were able to absorb individual shocks, most recently in the guise of rating downgrades of General Motors, the implosions of Refco and Parmalat, as well as the continuing slowdown of the US housing market (Assassi *et al.* 2007: 8–9). Global financial system, it seems, tested by the crises of 1997–1999 and reformed in their wake, has regained its resilience and stability.

At the same time, however, this book contends that it would be too short-sighted to forget the experience of the late 1990s. The caution does not only come from the long history of recurring financial implosions, but crucially relates to one of the most perplexing, and precarious, tendencies in finance and credit. In financial markets, where, according to Keynes, investment is largely about predicting how others will behave, *stability itself can be destabilising*. Indeed, in liberalised markets, periods of economic optimism and stability tend to invite excessive risk taking by financial operators. Monetary and financial policies aimed at supporting the markets also contribute to a build-up of investments. While some of these investments are sound, others are driven by pure speculation. As a period of growth continues, the proportion of speculative investments rises and finance become increasingly fragile: once expectations about the future are shaken, distress cascades through the system, often ending up in a systemic crisis. In other words, the inner mechanics of a financial crisis are rooted in the complex dichotomy between individual choices and aggregate outcomes: perceptions of individual financiers about the resilience of their portfolios and stability of market segments often translate into adverse dynamics at a systemic level. While an individual economic agent may perceive her portfolio to be safe, diversified and liquid, the system as a whole is not: the aggregate outcome of individual beliefs and strategies is a progressively fragile state of the financial market, industry or, as in the case of emerging markets, a national economy (Keynes 1936; Minsky 1977, 1982a, 1986, 1991a; Mehrling 2001; Savona 2002).

In analysing the manifestations of this in-built paradox of financial fragility today, this book draws inspiration from the scholarship of Hyman Minsky (1919–1996), an American economist who devoted his life to the study of the evolution of finance in capitalism. Minsky is perhaps the most prolific heterodox scholar of financial instability. Yet, within the discipline of global political economy, his name until recently has been somewhat overshadowed by the likes of Keynes, Kindleberger, Polanyi and Marx. At the same time, the wave of the recent crises has sparked a renewed interest in Minsky's scholarly legacy: his followers among the post-Keynesian economists provide some of the most illuminating insights into theories of financial crisis and financial regulation (Arestis and Sawyer 2001; Arestis 2001; Bellofiore and Ferris 2001; Davidson 1992, 2001, 2004; Dymski 2003; Toporowski 1999, 2001; Portes 1998). Remarkably, though perhaps less explicitly, analysts in key regulatory institutions (European Central Bank, Bank of England, Bank for International Settlements, the IMF), today address the policy challenges of asset inflation, financial fragility, liquidity cycles and systemic risk, drawing on the ideas of financial Keynesianism.

This book revisits Minsky's insights into financial fragility from the perspective of the globalised credit of today. It places Minsky's analytical framework in the context of the ongoing changes in the global financial system. Drawing on his, as well as on his followers' work, this study critically elaborates on central themes in Minsky's theory of financial fragility in the context of the 'investment bubble' crises in East Asia, Russia and other emerging markets, as well as in some segments of advanced financial markets. Notwithstanding important institutional and structural differences within the affected countries and companies, at the centre of each of the recent implosions lay the dangerous cocktail of financial speculation, progressive illiquidity and debt. Such observation brings out a further question about the significance of the recent wave of financial fragility: Is today's heightened financial fragility a blip of history, or, more disturbingly, is it an outcome of a structural shift within global capitalism?

Hyman Minsky was a pessimist. He believed that as long as capitalism is governed by sophisticated financial institutions and inter-linkages, it is inherently, and unpredictably, unstable. Analysing the post-war American economy, Minsky maintained that the basic source of financial fragility lies in the disproportionate development between real profit opportunities and debt commitments of major participants in the economic system. A major premise of the study presented in this book, is that speculation and over-borrowing still remain at the core of most financial imbalances and crises today; however the processes of private financial innovation and globalisation make it dangerously easy for today's financiers to disguise their growing share of borrowings as investments and often, misrepresent their liabilities as profits.

Disturbingly, the logic of 'borrow today to pay off the debts of yesterday' has come to pervade among individual investors, institutional funds, corporations and even governments. Ironically, the method of 'honest rip-off', famously employed by Charles Ponzi for the construction of numerous pyramid schemes in the 1920s America,[1] has become institutionalised in the age of global markets, turning much conventional economic wisdom on its head. The privatisation of credit and the liberalisation of financial markets offer guidelines for evaluating collateral that only subsist

---

1 Charles (Carlo) Ponzi (1882–1949) was born in Parma, Italy. He immigrated to the USA in 1903. Ponzi became the most famous (though not the only one) architect of a pyramid scheme: borrowing money off wealthy people for purposes of an 'enterprise'; than repaying the interest by borrowing more money from another round of 'investors'. Ponzi's schemes ripped off more then 40 million Americans during the 1920s economic boom. He was convicted of financial fraud several times, and died in poverty.

as long as the expectations underpinning them allow. When these subjective expectations reverse, the entire credit structure is altered and a crisis ensues. These dynamics, as this book argues, were clearly at work in the global political economy during the past decade, pulling individual institutions like LTCM, national economies (Russia, Brazil, Argentina), and even regions (East Asia) into the trap of illiquidity and bankruptcy. In all these episodes, the effects of financial liberalisation, the proliferation of derivative trading and new forms of financial intermediation made it particularly difficult to diagnose the trap of illiquidity and the seeds of crisis in time.

Minsky confessed, however, that he had underestimated the flexibility of financial capitalism. The apparent stability of profit flows, even in the face of great stress, supported the financial expansion further; while the emergence of large institutional investors has shifted the centre of the system from industry and banks of Minsky's time to complex and diversified financial markets of today (Mehrling 1999: 149). As a result of the proliferation of global financial markets, new techniques of borrowing and new channels of credit expansion, capitalism is increasingly driven by a highly complex, often hidden, web of financial dealings. Given the absence of an explicit anchor to this growing web of credit, it is tempting to see the world of today's finance as a giant Ponzi pyramid: indeed Minsky once noted that 'Ponzi finance is a usual way of financing investment in capitalism' (1986: 328). Such vision prompts us to raise the ultimate question: Does the ever-growing sophistication of finance enhance the resilience of the global economy, or conversely, is this sophistication only a disguise for the deepening structural fragility of global finance?

The parallels between the 1920s financial boom and the subsequent Great Depression, and the current period marked by financial sophistication and 'new economy' are disturbing: both periods were marked by a cycle of euphoric expectations, technological innovations, asset price bubbles and financial liberalisation. Confusingly, at the time of writing, key emerging markets seem to have buffered themselves from a recurrence of a 1997/98-type crisis and global capital markets are apparently awash with liquidity. Yet, as Minsky warned, *financial stability is always destabilising*, and current tranquillity can be deceptive.

1
The Rise of Fragile Finance

Not so long ago, finance and credit were considered to be a 'service' economy, supporting what many still consider to be the 'real' economy – manufacturing, labour, trade, tourism and so on. However, from the late 1960s onwards, perceptions about the role and functions of credit and finance have begun to change dramatically. To begin with, it appeared that on its own, financial system was able to generate massive, and relatively easy, profits, and that a growing proportion of the GDP of many advanced capitalist countries was generated by the financial sector alone. In the UK for instance, by the 1990s, the share of the financial sector in the economy as a whole surpassed 20% of the country's GDP. More importantly, the financial sector has acquired a far more prominent role in the political economy as a whole, especially when compared to the 'golden age' of capitalism – the economy of the Bretton Woods regime. Increasingly, the success or failure of an economy was related to the success or failure of the financial system. What were the causes of such a dramatic shift?

This chapter provides an introductory overview of the major changes that have driven the transformation of finance and facilitated its ascendance to the leading role in the global economic organisation it has assumed today. Specifically, as it is argued below, the rise of today's finance has been shaped by three interrelated processes: deregulation (liberalisation), privatisation, and financial innovation. = neo - liberalism

9

The post-World War II international financial regime

Finance is one of the perennial candidates for the title of the 'second oldest profession in history'. The origins of money and financial instruments go back thousands of years and are as old as history itself. The modern system of finance, however, has its roots in the re-emergence of market economy in Western Europe, from around the 11th century onwards.

Various instruments of credit evolved gradually over the centuries, but are strongly linked to the rise of the modern state system (Braudel 1982). By the late 19th century, many of the modern instruments of monetary policy and financial control had been developed (Germain 1997; Helleiner 1994; Knafo 2006). That period also saw the rise of immensely powerful financial houses such as J.P. Morgan and the Rockefellers in the USA joining the powerful European financial houses such as Barings or Rothschild which have been established earlier. These large financial houses were truly dominating the core capitalist economies. The early 20th century will be remembered by many as the rise of finance capital (Hilferding 1981) or banker's capitalism (Commons 2003). This period was the heyday of largely unregulated, highly mobile, politically powerful financial empires. It also witnessed one of the most famous financial booms in modern history: the 1920s stock market rise in the USA, driven by the euphoria associated with the new technological advances, new financial instruments and post-war recovery. The boom of the 1920s ended up with an infamous 'big bang': the Wall Street crash of October 1929, followed by the Great Depression of the 1930s.

What emerged in the wake of the Great Depression was an entirely new regime of financial regulation: a system characterised by tight governmental control over capital flows within and between nations, supported by a regime of fixed exchange rates. The immediate post-war structure of financial regulation is often described in financial literature as the period of *financial repression* – a regime of government policies and controls over the process of private financial intermediation (McKinnon 1973; Shaw 1973). Domestically, controls included interest rate ceilings, requirements for banks to hold government bonds to finance government budget deficits, targeted credit schemes to support 'selective' industries, high reserve requirements, and gold-anchored foreign exchange rates. Internationally, the regime of financial repression was accompanied by capital control restrictions on access to foreign financial markets (Korosteleva and Lawson 2005). Formally guided by the Bretton Woods international agreements, the system functioned for a quarter of a century (1944–1971), remarkably, without a major outbreak of financial volatility or crisis.[1]

The Bretton Woods era also saw the emergence of today's key international economic institutions such as the IMF, the World Bank and the WTO (formerly GATT). Although their role was not especially prominent during the years of the Bretton Woods regime itself, these bodies came to the forefront of world economic and financial integration in the post-Bretton Woods period. The tranquillity of the Bretton Woods era, associated primarily with financial stability, high post-war growth rates in major capitalist countries, as well as socio-economic balance, is conventionally attributed to the implementation of Keynesian economic policies. This period is often nostalgically referred to as 'the golden age' of capitalism. This age of financial and economic tranquillity, however, was about to be shaken by the breakdown of the Bretton Woods system in 1971–1973.

Deregulation and privatisation

August 15, 1971 will be remembered by many as the day when 'money' died. On that day, as one brilliant study has put it, US president Nixon 'transformed it [the dollar as a symbol of real, tangible wealth] into something totally new, a currency without any underlying value whatsoever and without any limitations on the government's (or private sector's) ability to create it' (Kurtzman 1993: 60–1). The abolition of the fixed exchange rate regime anchored in gold parity entailed many far-reaching consequences for the world economy; in this book, it is the effect on the nature of finance and credit that interests us.

The gold-dollar parity that had served as the foundation for the financial system under the Bretton Woods effectively meant that exchange rate risks were assumed, and controlled, by the state. Once

---

1 The crisis of 1966 is a notable exception and according to many accounts, marks the beginning of the period of world financial volatility.

the gold standard was abolished and exchange rates were floated however, the risk of exchange rate fluctuations was transferred to the markets. Exchange rate risks were, in other words, privatised (Eatwell and Taylor 2000: 2).

The removal of the fixed dollar-gold anchor to world finance introduced an additional factor of risk which needed to be managed, a task that was taken up by the financial system itself. The early 1970s therefore, witnessed the rise of the financial risk-management industry. Not only did large trading platforms for trafficking in foreign exchange appeared in the world's key financial centres – New York, London, Frankfurt, Tokyo – but a whole new industry of managing various financial risks began to evolve (Germain 1997; Langley 2002).

Critically underpinning this process of privatisation of credit and financial risk was a concomitant process of financial deregulation, or liberalisation. According to Palan (2003), the term financial deregulation describes a medley of regulations that contributed to the reduction, and often, complete elimination of barriers in domestic and international financial markets. Again, in stark contrast to the nationalised, tightly monitored and controlled world of finance under the Bretton Woods, the post-1971 financial system has been shaped by the removal of capital controls, deregulation of interest and exchange rates, institutional reforms of the financial sector which allowed the formation of many new institutions and channels of financial intermediation to develop. Importantly, deregulation and liberalisation entailed not only institutional and structural transformations within the financial sector. Freed from state control, the financial system was able to stretch far beyond national boundaries of Western capitalisms and reach the terrain of developing countries.

Already in the 1960s, commercial banks and other financial companies, exploiting national regulatory loopholes in order to expand their business, introduced new credit instruments and channels that circumvented national financial controls (Guttman 1994: 157). The emergence of the Eurodollar market, the rise of offshore financial centres, as well as the deepening of private financial innovation generally, have been attributed to these developments (Burn 1999, 2006; Palan 1998, 2002, 2003). At the international level, if the decades of the 1950s and 1960s were the era of foreign aid and FDI;

the 1970s became the heyday of commercial bank lending. Western commercial banks, awash with petrodollars, were looking for new clients. Having identified the investment needs of industrialising countries, they advanced loans to many sovereign borrowers, particularly to Latin American economies. As a result, for most of the 1970s, the international investor euphoria was driven not only by the growth prospects offered by these industrialising economies, but also by the eagerness of Western commercial banks to lend overseas in search of higher profits (Rowbotham 2000; Frieden 1981). If in 1960, bank lending to developing world was close to zero, in 1973 syndicated bank loans totalled $9.7 billion; in 1975 the figure rose to $12 billion. Altogether, in 1978 commercial banks accounted for 30.4% of the total accumulated debt of the developing economies (Woodward 2001).

The 1970s boom in lending to developing countries ended with a 1982 Mexican default that became generalised as the Third world debt crisis. The 1980s saw a drop in the volume of foreign investment flows into the developing countries, or became what has also been termed a 'lost decade' for Latin America (Corbridge 1993; Griffith-Jones and Sunkel 1989; Congdon 1988). Yet following painful debt restructurings and the implementation of structural adjustment programmes (SAPs) in the crisis-hit countries, by the early 1990s, the global investment cycle had been restored. According to Krugman, the fall of the Berlin Wall in 1989 made investing outside the Western world seem less risky than before. The 1990s economic reforms in China also offered the financial sector new avenues for global expansion, and thus the former communist world supplemented the investment opportunities presented by the existing 'clients' – Asian 'tigers' and Latin American markets. International movements of capital became so immense that investment funds coined a new name for what previously was mostly called Third world: now they became 'emerging markets', the new promising frontier of finance (Krugman 2000: 84–5). Across the economies of Latin America and the former socialist bloc, privatisation programmes and economic restructuring implemented under the auspices of the paradigm of the Washington Consensus provided new opportunities for direct and portfolio investment, while the policies of financial deregulation, such as capital account liberalisation, the deregulation of the banking system and the opening of national financial markets added to a sense of a new political and legal framework, accommodative to foreign capital (Kahler 1998: 4; Armijo 2001: 1; Eatwell and Taylor 2000, etc.).

Regional differences persisted, however, during the lending boom of the 1990s. In East Asia, despite the rapid growth in portfolio investment, FDI remained dominant. In the 'tiger' economies of East Asia, the success of state-led developmental models and export-led industrialisation contributed to the widely held vision of the 'Asian miracle', encouraging massive inflows of foreign investment (see World Bank 1993; Wade 1990). In contrast, portfolio flows were more significant in Latin America. There, a considerable portion of inward capital flows fuelling the rise of the emerging markets, was in reality indigenous capital previously held in offshore accounts. Together, East Asia and Latin America attracted the bulk of FDI and portfolio investment. South Asia, the Middle East, and sub-Saharan Africa lagged far behind (Kahler 1998: 4).

Although the volume and nature of foreign investment differed across the emerging markets, the 1990s financial boom was marked by one notable common feature. In contrast to the lending boom of the 1970s, when international capital flows were dominated by syndicated bank loans and the major recipients of money were Third world governments, in the 1990s, private capital flows have replaced multilateral and bilateral aid to developing countries. Between 1984–1989 and 1990–1996, net official flows fell by nearly 50%, while net private flows rose by approximately 700% (Armijo 2001; Woodward 2001).

According to Armijo (2001: 1), the change in the composition of capital flows entailed several political ramifications for the emerging markets. First, the greater share of private credit meant that borrowing countries were somewhat less subject to the political demands of creditor/donor states, but nonetheless were constrained to implement a package of neoliberal economic reforms. As this book will detail in Chapters 6–8, international financial institutions such as the IMF and the World Bank, global credit agencies and large institutional investors have assumed great influence over national political-economic programmes in emerging markets, and a good record on neoliberal economic restructuring was crucial to keep the country's favourable position in the global financial arena (Harmes 1998; Sinclair 2005). Second, the shift from public to private investment flows implies that while the governments in the emerging markets may now be less able to attain the political benefits from capital inflows, the political and economic influence of domestic big business increases (Haley 2001). Third, the shift towards more flexible and fluid forms of international investment has sharply accentuated the risk of balance-of-payments (BoP) crises for the borrowing country:

> As liquidity sloshes about the global financial system, seeking the highest returns, a nation may find itself inundated with 'hot money' from abroad that can ignite a giddy boom – or abruptly starved for credit when the foreign money decides, for whatever reason, to leave (Greider 1997: 263).

Despite differences in the composition, nature and geography of international capital flows, the investment cycles of the 1970s and the 1990s shared certain traits. For example, during the 1990s, like many smaller banks in the 1970s, many institutional investors were 'sucked' into markets they did not fully understand by the prospect of higher returns, as well as by the desire not to fall behind their shrewder competitors (Woodward 2001; Congdon 1988). Emerging markets in turn, keen to restore their economic growth but often lacking domestic investment funds, welcomed financial inflows in the 1990s, just as they did in the 1970s. Therefore, if in the 1970s, the 'recycling' of OPEC oil surpluses served as a means of easing the burden of adjustment to higher oil prices, in the 1990s, the increase of FDI and portfolio investment reflected emerging markets' access to the global pool of private credit. In this process, just like in the 1970s, data processing and accounting systems often remained underdeveloped and inadequate in measuring the build-up of liabilities accurately and on time; while efforts to improve them remained insufficient (Woodward 2001: 202).

Among the many reasons why, despite the advance of financial and IT technologies, these and other problems within the structure of global financial flows persisted, in the context of this book, one issue stands out in particular. Not only did the breakdown of the Bretton Woods regime in 1971–1973 see the rise of private finance and credit, but the end of national control over the exchange rate, interest rates and other monetary instruments provided the momentum to another defining feature of global finance: the spiral of financial innovation.

Financial innovation

Financial innovation is as old as credit and money itself. In fact, the different forms that money had taken throughout history – from barley in ancient Babylon to gold, silver, plastic cards and mobile phones today – are examples of innovation in credit instruments. Although it is difficult to agree on a precise definition of financial innovation, it is clear that it differs from invention and innovation in other markets and industries in several important ways. First, due to the very nature of finance (unlike in product markets, in financial markets, money is exchanged for a future promise), innovations in finance do not normally require large capital inflows and can be introduced relatively quickly (Guttman 1994: 157). Second, financial innovation involves finding new ways of borrowing, lending and investing. As such, it not only leads to the invention of various new financial instruments, but also to the emergence of new financial practices and institutions. Third, the invention and establishment of new credit instruments fundamentally relies on investors' expectations, confidence and credibility, and much less on 'underlying' economic variables, or what is often called 'fundamentals' (Eatwell and Taylor 2000). This makes finance and credit particularly sensitive to fluctuations in moods and other subjective factors.

And although, as mentioned above, financial innovation has existed for centuries, it was the breakdown of the Bretton Woods regime that spurred the acceleration of its most recent wave. According to Guttman (1994) the first wave of innovation in finance took place in the 1960s, when rising inflation levels made low-yielding savings deposits less attractive for investors. Experiencing erosion of their traditional deposit base, the banks faced growing demand for loans. To bridge this gap between sources and use of funds, US commercial banks began to rely on a variety of borrowed funds. This shift in the industry in the 1960s, from asset management to liability management, marks an important point in the evolution of the credit-based economy (Guttmann 1994: 157–8; Henwood 1997). Or what is also often called, the debt economy.

An additional structural factor that underpinned the current rise of financial innovation has been the privatisation of foreign exchange risk mentioned earlier in this chapter. Freed from state control, fluctuations of currency rates became a risk that investors across the world have to take into account when conducting their operations. Thus exchange rate became a variable, and hence a risk and a product, tradable in financial markets. Monitoring, managing and controlling the risk quickly became a highly profitable industry in itself. Profits are attractive, and easy profits especially so. From its inception therefore, the financial risk management industry has attracted not only the traditional financial institutions like banks, but provided the market niche for younger companies, more flexible and willing to engage in risk trading. Thus, the deregulation of financial markets and the privatisation of exchange rate risk in particular, gave rise to a variety of institutional innovations within the financial sector itself.

The political, economic, financial and technological changes of the post-Bretton Woods period have facilitated the emergence of many new participants in financial markets, whose functions stretch far beyond the traditional realm of activity of commercial banks, insurance companies or building societies. Rather than simply serving as means for intermediation – connecting savers and borrowers (like a typical commercial bank) – new financial players target risk generally, and more specifically, changes in macroeconomic fundamentals, prices of underlying commodities (like corn or oil), market indices (exchange rates, prices of shares or bonds), financial indicators (e.g., interest rates) or aggregate indicators (e.g., stock market indices). The instruments designed to quantify, manage and trade in these risks are known as derivatives, or secondary financial instruments. Importantly, these secondary instruments can be based on underlying commodity markets, as well as financial markets themselves. As a result, the financial industry today is a complex, tightly interconnected, plethora of participants, including, among others, financial branches of transnational corporations, banks (commercial and investment), non-bank financial intermediaries, such as hedge funds, insurance funds, mutual funds, investment and pension funds, private equity funds, as well as individual retail investors.

The variety of instruments and techniques that financial investors and traders adopt and develop is changing rapidly, and any attempt to summarise the products of innovation is likely to become obsolete very quickly (see Finnerty 1992, in Henwood 1997: 51; also Miller 1986; Mishkin and Strahan 1999). At the same time, it is notable that along with the institutionalisation of financial innovation – i.e., the emergence and establishment of large institutional funds – some financial practices have become quite standardised and centralised. For example, futures, options and swaps have become standard and widely used derivative contracts, while some of the newer instruments, like synthetic and structured derivative contracts[2] – are customised products, which are tailored to the needs of a particular client or a transaction.

The participants of the global financial market trade on organised platforms, such as stock or currency exchanges; they can also conduct their operations face-to-face, or over the counter (OTC); or *via* the offshore financial centres. The worldwide deregulation of financial markets and the continuing advance of financial innovation makes today's finance incredibly complex, sophisticated and often, simply murky. For instance, in parallel to the rise of new trading techniques and products, financial innovation has been closely paralleled by the process of securitisation. Securitisation is a technique of converging assets that would serve as collateral for a bank loan into securities which are more liquid and can be traded at a lower cost than the underlying assets (Steinherr 2000: 291).[3]

Across many financial markets, securitisation has united many previously unconnected participants into a tightly interwoven chain of global credit. Yet along with making credit networks more fluid and interconnected, the securitisation and sophistication of today's financial techniques often make it particularly difficult to identify the 'ends' of a financial transaction. Specifically, while securitisation makes assets highly tradable, the 'bundling together' of such assets makes the task of evaluating price exposures, the nature of risks involved, as well as the very identity of borrower and lender, extremely difficult. This complexity, or obscurity, of finance, is one of the main outcomes of the post-Bretton Woods spiral of financial revolution (see Best 2005).

---

2 Structured finance – the creation of debt instruments by securitisation or the addition of derivatives to existing instruments.

3 As Steinherr notes, the largest category of securitised assets is real estate mortgage loans which serve as collateral for mortgage-backed securities. Car loans and credit card obligations are also securitised.

What drives financial innovation? As noted above, it is the privatisation of foreign exchange risk in 1971–1973 and the rise of the post-Fordist mode of economic organisation that account for the rise of the latest spiral of financial innovation (Eatwell and Taylor 2000, 2002; Strange 1997, 1998; Germain 1997), yet at least two other factors have facilitated the revolutionary transformations in the post-Bretton Woods finance. Both of these factors originate in science and scientific progress: one is related to the implementation of technological progress and its popularisation; another stems from the advances in fundamental science. Perhaps the most crucial of these factors has been the advance of information and communication technology (ICT). In a market economy, the ultimate effect of technological advances is to intensify competition and make the economic system more efficient. Yet it is common for a new idea and technology to take some time to be tested, adopted and find its customers. As Shiller (2003: 101–2) notes, the device as banal as a wheeled suitcase has taken more than 20 years to be invented, patented, produced and perfected to its today's version.

Similarly, the productivity benefits from the introduction of new IT techniques for the industrial economy were relatively slow to establish and measure. A 2002 OECD study reported that in the first half of the 1990s, IT contributed to a mere 0.2–0.5 percentage points per year of economic growth in the OECD economies. During the second half of the 1990s, the figure rose to 0.3–0.9 percentage points per year, with the US economy being the main beneficiary (Colecchia and Schreyer 2002). In contrast to this somewhat disappointing record of IT innovation in raising productivity, the financial sector adopted and implemented new technological instruments with great appetite and speed.

In the financial sphere, the rise of mobile telecommunication networks, the development of Internet and satellite technology, along with many other inventions which facilitate the flow of information and money have been employed and advanced with astonishing ease and speed. In a fascinating story of the rise of megabyte money, Kurtzman (1993: 169) observes: 'the volume of information travelling on Internet is growing by 25% a month. Most parts in the system can send 2 million bits of information a second; some parts can move 1 billion bits a second...The average speed of transmission is half the speed of light.' Supported by economic and political globalisation, the IT sector has raised the efficiency of financial institutions tremendously. The capitalisation of the new financial companies has far outreached the value of the 'old' economy-manufacturing giants. A powerful combination of financial and virtual technologies has created a colossal pool of funds that were central to the new economy's advance. This pronounced disparity of dynamism between industrial and financial accumulation is believed to mark a new epoch in the trajectory of capitalism (Fine *et al.* 1999: 71–2).

Finally, the rise of the new financial risk industry would not have been possible without advances in science, and in particular, discoveries in financial mathematics and physics. Managing financial risk – a process known as financial engineering – involves building sophisticated financial portfolios, in which price and risk exposures of various assets needs to be carefully weighted and projected into the future. The evolution of financial derivatives markets is thus intimately linked to developments in finance theory, financial mathematics and physics (Saber 1999). As a result, theoretical approaches to finance based in mathematics, such as the capital asset pricing theory (CAPT) or Black-Scholes option pricing model, became a powerful engine of financial innovation and engineering, facilitating the spread of portfolio selection and diversification models, arbitrage trading and leverage techniques at the global level.

Finance as a global system

The combination of the processes outlined above – the deregulation of financial markets, the privatisation of financial risk, the advance of financial innovation and sophistication – have contributed to the complexity of contemporary finance. Global financial ascendance does not only rest on rapid internationalisation of capital markets and a growing pool of financial capital. Today's financial capitalism came about through disintermediation, increased securitisation, arbitrage activities and 'over the counter' trading, critically endorsed by the policies of deregulation and liberalisation (Bello *et al.* 2000: 2–5). The complexity of credit that is the result of such transformations makes it difficult for an outside observer to penetrate into the internal workings of the financial market, for several reasons.

At a conceptual level, one of the difficulties in analysing the transformations within finance today stems from the fact that the dominant mode of thinking about economic and financial processes remains grounded in neoclassical economics and methodological individualism. Mainstream economic theory, despite being challenged from various angles, continues to hold that the trade in goods and services determines international capital flows and foreign exchange rates. Already in the 1980s, Peter Drucker (1986: 787) observed that while the economic theory teaches that exchange rates are determined by the comparative-advantage factors (such as comparative labour costs and labour productivity, raw materials costs, energy costs, transportation costs and the like), in reality it is the exchange rates that determine how labour costs in country A compare to labour costs in country B. With financial deregulation and privatisation advancing further, it became clear that today, financial variables and dynamics are determined not by economic 'fundamentals' (e.g., Eatwell and Taylor 2000; Best 2005) but by arbitrage opportunities and investor confidence. Another consequence of financial liberalisation and privatisation is that in the post-Bretton Woods world, capital account dominates the current account *via* the exchange rate. Thus, often the country's trade balance and general macroeconomic stability are influenced by the inflows and outflows of capital, adding to a risk of exposure to external shocks and a sense of fragility in the national economy.

The obscurity of modern finance aggravates this risk of fragility further (see Best 2005). Following the breakdown of barriers between financial markets, the consolidation of financial conglomerates and the spread of securities markets worldwide, all segments of the credit system are now tightly interdependent. At the global level, the continuous emergence and growth of new and largely secretive financial products means that regulatory authorities have not yet found a way to get companies to account for derivatives in their balance sheets (Allen 1999: 3). As the spiral of financial innovation evolves,

> ... its use, which was initially seen as a way of economising on money, becomes more and more difficult to distinguish from 'real' monetary use. The perspective then switches round, and

the instrument is soon recognised as money. The hierarchy of money forms is thus evolutionary and the limits of money somewhat blurred; some instruments may be analysed both as means of accelerating the circulation of money and as fully-pledged monetary forms (Levy-Garboua and Weumuller 1979, in Lipietz 1983: 90).

The technique and practice of managing financial risks allows new forms of risk to be generated and elevates volatility both in space and time; which is now both necessary in order to make money, and itself creates more risks (Leyshon and Thrift 1997: 294). In the words of Susan Strange, 'far from stabilising the system by damping its ups and downs the devices such as futures markets – developed to deal with uncertainty – have actually served to exaggerate and perpetuate it' (1997: 119). This apparent ability of financial markets to generate new forms of money is particularly alarming on a global scale. The opening of new credit lines and the 'bundling up' of assets into deeper and yet increasingly narrow pools of capital intensifies the debt structure of many financial institutions and countries. This, in turn, makes them more susceptible to herd-like behaviour of investors in times of financial strain or panic. Yet this new source of huge risks remains poorly understood and not fully captured by existing monitoring models (Eatwell and Taylor 2000: 45–7).

Another consequence of the ascendance of the tightly interconnected, privatised credit system has been the notably uneven pattern of growth in the financial sphere and in the industrial economy (Brenner 1998, 2000). The rise of the financial risk management industry has led to a long period of financial ascendance, which in turn, obscures the long-term growth rates in most OECD countries, which have remained lower than in the 'golden age' of the 1950s and 1960s. In the booming currency markets, more than 1.5 trillion dollars change hands daily; the creation of new types of financial derivatives stretches the global pool of credit further. For instance, the market for credit derivatives continues to grow at a fast rate; in 2004 it reached nearly $3 trillion (BIS 2005a; Fitch Rating, 15 November 2004). Between 2002 and 2005, the rate of growth of global trade in financial derivatives averaged around 30% per year, while the growth of world gross product stayed at around 3.9% (IMF 2005b).

Risk, therefore, is far from being an incidental factor in the world of finance. Rather, the global financial system has come to manifest an 'institutionally structured risk environment' (Giddens 1991). In this system, access to new financing almost overwhelmingly depends not on existing equity, but on the commodification, or numerification, of past debt. As Strange and others argue, today, it is the ability to tap credit, more than profits earned in the last cycle of production that determines a firm's ability to expand (Aglietta and Breton 2001; Germain 1997: 126; Strange 1997).

The realities of this vast, complex and sophisticated web of credit and hence inevitably, debt, pose serious challenges to various participants of the global economy. One of the most significant of such challenges is the marked increase in financial volatility. Financial instability has many causes and can be quite indiscriminate, as this book shows further. Yet a major consequence of the institutional and structural changes in the nature and organisation of finance outlined above relates to knowledge and thus, power differential, that exists between private markets and public authorities. Nowhere is this discrepancy more evident than in the emerging markets.

The creators of novel financial instruments and techniques – institutional funds and financial companies – typically know much more about the behaviour of these products, and therefore, can benefit from their use. Firms, financial institutions and governments in the emerging economies, although now active players in the global capital market, are still constrained by their conditional access to credit, availability of hard currencies and previous historical records. They remain at a distinct disadvantage when having to discern the specific conditions of a market segment and critically, when trying to avert panic or a looming crisis. In this regard, despite the worldwide deregulation of financial markets and credit networks, financial institutions in the emerging markets who borrow through them tend to take higher risks than their counterparts in the advanced capitalism (Surin 1998; Haley 2001; Horowitz and Heo 2001; Armijo 2001: 3). And although, as I argue in this book, the global interconnectedness of credit also facilitates the spread of financial contagion across the world, it is the emerging markets, dependent on foreign capital inflows, export markets and the availability of foreign exchange, which are particularly prone to recurrent financial instability and crises. As illustrated by recurring crises throughout the post-Bretton Woods period and in particular, during the last decade, the explosion in new financial instruments and markets, supported by highly sophisticated systems of financial coordination on a global scale entails alarming repercussions. Difficulties of individual institutions can quickly translate into large-scale collapses of industries, national economies and even regions. As this book will detail below, it is the hazards of financial expansions that typically contain crisis tendencies. Trouble is, the murky nature of the process of private credit expansion also makes it difficult to discern crisis potential in time.

2
A Theory of Fragile Finance

The number of large-scale financial crises the world has witnessed since the early 1970s is daunting: beginning with the Southern Cone financial crisis of the late 1970s; followed closely by the so-called Third World debt crisis of the early 1980s; the savings and loan debacle in the US in the late 1980s; the near-defaults of many 'second-world' states in the late 1980s–early 1990s, the Exchange Rate Mechanism (ERM) crisis in 1992, the Mexican 'Tequila' crisis of 1994–1995; the East Asian crisis of 1997; the Russian meltdown of 1998; the collapse of the Brazilian Real in 1999, the Turkish crisis of 2000–2001; corporate bankruptcies in the US in 1999–2002, the Argentine default of 2001–2002... (Bello *et al.* 2000: 10). Not to speak of an ongoing financial crisis of many so-called 'collapsed states', which is not the subject of this investigation. In light of such a long and disturbing list, the question must be asked: Why have financial crises become so prevalent today? Can it be the case, as Drucker (1986) intuited, that an overblown financial sector is finally 'colliding' with the real economy, provoking crises of peripheral and semi-peripheral economies? Or is it the case that crises affect only poorly governed nations, incompetent or otherwise unwilling to handle the rational principles of economic organisation and the requirements of the changing market conditions?

According to Paul Davidson (2001), broadly speaking, 20th century history of economic thought has produced two competing – and, some argue, incompatible – theories of financial markets: the efficient market theory (EMT) of finance and Keynes's liquidity pref- erence theory (LPT). In time, both theories have outgrown their

original formulations and have incorporated different methodo-
logies and insights. They remain, however, fundamentally different
in their view of financial markets in general. The EMT and its followers prioritise the liberalisation of financial markets and progress
of financial intermediation as the means to economic efficiency. In
contrast, LPT calls for vigilant regulation of finance, with institutions and rules constraining and monitoring the behaviour of
market participants (Davidson 2001: 15). The two formulations are
distinguished in their understanding of the role new forms of
financial intermediation and non-economic factors play in the
global capital markets. This and the following chapters review the
two theories of financial markets and analyse their distinct contribution to a theory of financial crisis and instability.[1]

Efficient market theory of finance: Crisis? What crisis?

In one way or another, financial crises always result from some
policy miscalculation or governmental ineptness, plain corruption
or a severe external shock to the economic system, such as the oil
price hike in the early and late 1970s, or the rise of US interest rates

---

1 A word of qualification is in order at this point. IPE analyses tend to
   discuss economic processes and problems through the prism of three
   intellectual traditions: neoliberalism (neoclassical economics), institutionalist and Marxist (radical) political economy (see for instance, Gilpin
   2000). This book deviates from this convention, avoiding recourse into
   an explicitly Marxist discussion of financial crisis. The major reason for
   such an omission is that Marxist political economy does not appear to
   have a designated theory of financial crisis as such. It is quite odd, given
   the otherwise central position of crises to Marxist critique of capitalism,
   yet as Clarke observes, efforts to elaborate on crisis theory in Marx's own
   works remain scant. At various times Marx appears to associate crises with
   the tendency of the rate of profit to fall, with capitalism's tendency to
   overproduction, underconsumption, disproportional and over-accumula-
   tion with respect to labour, without ever clearly championing one or the
   other theory (Clarke 1994: 5, 9). And although Chapter 3 of this book
   (pp. 45–51) does draw on some works originating in Marxist political
   economy, a thorough analysis of the radical theory of finance and credit
   in capitalism lies beyond the scope of this publication. For a good sense
   of this scholarly current, see for instance, Altvater 1997; Harvey 1999;
   Itoh and Lapavistas 1998.

in 1982, or the spread of financial panic from the East Asian markets in late 1997. (The reverse, however, is not necessarily the case: not all policy mistakes and shocks lead to a crisis). These shocks (and other similar events) tend to destabilise the economic system. In the EMT interpretation, financial markets, being a reflection of the under-lying economic activity and expectations of various economic agents, merely manifest them in currency crashes and debt defaults. As Schwartz (1986) argues, 'A real financial crisis occurs only when insti-tutions do not exist, where authorities are unschooled in the practices that preclude such a development, and when the public sector has reason to doubt the dependability of preventive arrangements.' This, in a very schematic way, is the standard, orthodox explanation of financial crisis offered by classical and neoclassical economic theory. In this vision, the crises of the past decade were essentially, a series of isolated shocks, unrelated to each other, and were managed accord-ingly by an intervention of monetary authorities.

Why, say, did the dotcom crisis happen in 2001? Or rather, why were the dotcom stock values allowed to grow beyond proportion and for such long time? Already in 1996 Alan Greenspan warned about irrational exuberance of the markets. Others, like Martin Wolf of the *Financial Times* and the *Economist* had been warning about the unsustainability of the boom for a long while. The EMT has an interesting answer to this question: the crisis was not a crisis at all. Rather, it was a timely and totally expected correction of stock market prices down to their underlying, long-term values. The 1995–2000 'new economy' financial euphoria saw the emergence of new ideas, concepts and industries. This new economy was not only quantitatively, but more crucially, qualitatively different.

> The physical embodiment of these symbols increasingly becomes secondary to the economic process. If the industrial marketplace was characterised by the exchange of things, the (new) economy is characterised by access to concepts, carried inside physical forms. (This) new era prizes intangible forms of power bound up in bundles of information and intellectual assets (Rifkin 2000: 47).

Since these changes have brought brand new, qualitatively different products into the market, it was unclear what the exact market value of these previously unknown products would be. When the bulk of economy's assets were physical and its markets were relatively stable, valuation was more straightforward. Now, a growing proportion of a firm's assets – brand, ideas, and human capital – are intangible and often hard to identify, let alone value. They are also less robust than a physical asset such as a factory (*The Economist* 16 May 2002: 18). Financial markets, excited about the prospects of a better economic future, probed the new products, over-inflating their prices in the process; once the long-term effects of the IT revolution had fed through into the rest of the economic system, the market self-corrected itself, cleansing the system of some 'excess fat'. The crisis of the dotcom economy was therefore not a crisis at all, but a healthy and foreseeable correction by the market as it learned to handle a new type of an economy.

Indeed, there is evidence that in the wake of the dotcom crash and attendant corporate scandals, the US corporate sector had no choice but to eliminate the remains of the bubble. Already in 2000, the ratio of net worth to disposable income fell from 6.2 to about 4.8, which is close to its long-run average. Since its peak in April 2000, the world's market capitalisation had dropped by $11,3000 billion (35%) in 2002, and at its low point that year, a cyclically adjusted price-earning (p/e) ratio had fallen to 17 (from 40 at the peak), the average during the pre-bubble years of 1990–1995 (*The Economist*, 17 October 2002). In the following year, world financial markets, although subdued under the influence of bad news and shocks, have stabilised. Internet and IT industries found their firm place, and peace, in today's capitalism: indeed, it is difficult to imagine life without easyjet, internet banking or Google.

Similarly, according to mainstream financial theory, the Russian crisis occurred in 1998 because of the Yeltsin's governments' stupidity and ineptness, coupled in a very unfortunate timing, with the contagion effect of the Asian financial crisis. The August 1998 crisis in Russia was dramatic and painful, yet according to orthodox finance, the Russian default was not necessary. Instead, a substantial, orderly devaluation of the rouble back to its real market value would have done the job; while naturally, lesser corruption and more foresight on behalf of the young reformers in Russia would have provided foreign investors with more reassurance and thus kept their money in the Russian market. In any case, the August 1998 crisis is considered a constructive event in the new Russian economic history: it has exposed many mistakes of the naïve reformers of the 1990s, and has prompted the country to start building a strong financial system. Similar explanatory 'templates' could be applied to East Asian, Mexican, Turkish crises. In all such explanations, we find a lot of analytical place for human mistake and external influences, yet we learn little about the role of finance in the crisis. It is not surprising. Founded on the EMT of finance, financial orthodoxy – although increasingly tricky to identify in itself – simply does not have a developed theory of financial crisis.

Why EMT is not a theory of crisis

The EMT position has been heavily criticised lately. Some of the criticisms derive from heterodox research in finance; some are driven by an ideological critique of the depoliticised nature of economics and finance generally (Altvater 1997; Kirshner 2003; K. Singh 2000; Grabel 1999; Granville 1999). It is not the intention of this chapter to provide yet another critical account of the economic orthodoxy, but rather to identify why mainstream theories of financial crisis have gone out of fashion. What can possibly be wrong with such reading of financial instability?

Notwithstanding the merits of orthodox explanations of the crises mentioned above, the EMT does not offer a theory of crisis *per se*. The reason for the lack of such theory can be explained at least in two ways. First, there is an historical explanation. Modern EMT has its roots in the classical economic thought of the 18th and 19th centuries, which generally assumes markets to function smoothly, not in a crisis-ridden manner. It would be quite naïve to expect a tradition that is more than 200 years old to offer an up-to-date understanding of the mechanics of financial instability and crisis. Second and correspondingly, at the level of methodology, the EMT does not differentiate between the nature of finance and other commodities: to financial orthodoxy, markets in finance are similar to markets in tradable goods. Financial markets and financial intermediation exist simply to smooth out and speed up the exchange process in the wider economic system: finance is thus a 'veil over real economy';[2] it does not, in itself, influence the trajectory of the economic cycle, but merely facilitates it:

---

2   The expression derives from Say's law.

In the complete absence of financial instruments, therefore, no unit would be able to indulge its needs and preferences for an intertemporal pattern of spending that differed from the time profile of its income. Under such arrangement, resources would be allocated inefficiently (Bryant 1987: 7).

In the orthodox model, money is added as an afterthought, as fiat or 'dropped by helicopter' money, necessary to facilitate transactions and hence reduce the costs entailed in barter exchange. According to EMT, it makes absolutely no difference how positions in physical capital are taken – whether they are financed out of savings, earnings, sales of equity or debt. Thus, EMT ignores the role of financial institutions and mechanisms of financing, assuming that the principles of the operation of a modern financialised economy are analogous to a naturalised, barter economy[3] (Binswanger 1999; Papadimitriou and Wray 1999).

Conceived in the 1960s, the EMT revolutionised the field of finance. Academic finance in general, and securities analysis in particular, was created on the basis of the EMT and its applications (Shleifer 2000: 1; Malkiel 1987). In a classical formulation, Fama (1970) defined an efficient financial market as one in which security prices always fully reflect the available information. If this information presents knowledge of the 'true' behaviour of the economy, then financial assets embody the true value of their real counterparts (Griffith-Jones 1998: 13). If financial assets were persistently mispriced relative to their fundamental values, rational investors could exploit the mistakes and make easy money – so the mispricing would get corrected. When ill-informed investors move prices away from their true values, informed investors will arbitrage them back to the right level, so there is no chance that a financial bubble can develop.[4] The efficiency of markets has become an article of faith.

---

3 An Papadimitriou and Wray (1999) stress, since the orthodox model of finance assumes no uncertainty (markets are thought to work on full information), liquidity has no analytical value in the EMT theory of finance. As we shall see later in this book, such an abstraction from the problem of liquidity is one of the key reasons the EMT has been unable to conceptualise problems of credit expansion, financial innovation and speculation and thus, provide a coherent understanding of financial crisis today.

Especially for those, as we will see in Chapter 8, who know how to use arbitrage pricing.

The major problem with EMT and its followings, as Shleifer (2000: 2) explains, is that theoretically, it rests on three fundamental, yet progressively shaky, assumptions. First, financial investors are rational and fully-informed, and hence it is assumed that they value securities rationally. Second, although some of investors do behave irrationally, their 'out-of line' trades are random and therefore cancel each other out without affecting the general price level at the market. Third, although investors can sometimes be irrational in similar ways, they are met in the market by rational arbitragers who eliminate their influence on prices.[5] Thus, the essence of the EMT is epitomised in the following remark:

> the ultimate social functions of [financial markets are] spreading risks, guiding the investment of scarce capital, and processing and disseminating the information processed by diverse traders ... prices will always reflect fundamental values... The logic of efficient markets is compelling (Summers and Summers 1989: 166, in Davidson 2001: 15).

In micro-level analyses of finance, various models of asset pricing and portfolio selection developed the EMT further; while at the level of macroeconomic theory, EMT was supported by the ideas of monetarism. A key precondition for investor confidence in the economy, and of a stable growth, is low inflation. Keeping prices low has been the ruling principle of economic theory and policy since the high- and even hyperinflationary 1970s and 1980s. As the quantitative theory of money holds $(MV=PQ)$, price level is a direct function of the money supply in the economy; therefore the key to low inflation rates is a tight control by the central banks over the money supply. As long as there is no (nominal) money creation in excess of the growth rate of the economy and as long as the

---

4 Peter Garber defined bubble as a high price 'at odds with any reasonable economic explanation' (2000).

5 Arbitrage – simultaneous buying and selling of the same security (or very similar securities) in different markets in order to equalise the price.

income velocity of money does not change, there should be a stable price level; inflation is considered to be a purely monetary phenomenon (Binswanger 1999). Accordingly, the rules and conduct of prudent monetary regulation prevent financial crises from occurring.

These perceptions have long underpinned the so-called 'first generation' crisis models in economics. Their foundations lay in the belief that market disturbances, financial crises among them, are typically the result of a deviation from a normal operation of a free competitive market, disrupted by government intervention or some external shock. The dominant strain in economic theory in the 20th century – the mathematical general equilibrium theory – is used to support the 'invisible hand' conjecture of Adam Smith as a guide to policy (Minsky 1991a). In 'first-generation' models, financial crises were seen as the inevitable outcome of ongoing fiscal imbalances coupled with fixed exchange rates (Velasco 1999). 'First-generation' models typically viewed crises as a result of fundamental inconsistencies in domestic policies, such as a persistent money-financed fiscal deficit and a commitment to a pegged exchange rate. When official reserves fall to a critically low level and are perceived by the market to be insufficient, there will be a sudden speculative attack on the currency.

A drawback of such models, as economists themselves note, is that they represent policy in an essentially one-dimensional and mechanical manner – the government automatically monetised budget deficit while the central bank accommodated the pressures on the exchange rate by selling reserves without due regard to other developments in the economy (Aziz *et al.* 2000: 8–9). Moreover, analogies between commodity and financial markets are fallacious, and the differences are not confined to the nature of goods and services transacted in these markets. In commodity markets, one good is exchanged for another but in financial markets a real good is exchanged for a future promise. Financial markets are markets in information, and information by its nature is asymmetric and incomplete. Money and credit instruments not only are at the very core of every single transaction in a market economy, but are also peculiarly susceptible to swings of confidence. Prices of financial assets are subject to frequent and sharp changes, and these fluctuations are especially pervasive in the international sphere (Singh

2000: 44; Eichengreen 2002: 4; Eatwell and Taylor 2000: 12; Toporowski 1999). Moreover, since many contemporary crises seem to
lack the crucial fiscal disequilibria, the 'first-generation' models of
crisis have fallen out of fashion (Velasco 1999).

A major flaw of the EMT approach, therefore, is that despite its
econometric sophistication, its framework is too narrow to capture
the multiplicity of effects of the innovations in the financial sector.
Implicitly, it assumes that financial innovations drive the economic
system towards efficiency, correctly signalling the conditions of the
underlying real fundamentals (Binswanger 1999). EMT seems to be
correct in a longer-term historical perspective: financial markets
have been turbulent throughout the post-Bretton Woods period, yet
the world has escaped a recurrence of the Great Depression of the
1930s. At the same time, EMT is unable to offer an adequate and
systematic explanation for the long chain of crises in the post-1973
world. While some of the EMT observations about governmental
misconducts and external shocks are true, they are insufficient in
explaining crisis tendencies and dynamics within the financial
system.

Mutation of the orthodoxy

The globalisation of the economy, the growing interconnectedness
of trade and financial linkages between different countries, herd
behaviour and the expanding variety of financial institutions and
practices, have prompted some revisions of orthodox financial
models. Gradually, the new theoretical insights into the nature of
financial markets, and evidence of recurring bubbles and financial
panics challenged the basic assumptions of the EMT, and the field of
behavioural finance has emerged as an alternative view of financial
markets (Shleifer 2000: 2). Moreover, for many emerging markets,
private financing now plays a far greater role than in the past, relative to official financing. As the global economy becomes tightly
interconnected through trade and financial channels, external
financing difficulties and exchange rate pressures are more strongly
linked with distress in the financial and corporate sectors (IMF
2002a, b). Gradually, economists started to take these processes into
consideration, developing the so-called 'second-generation' models
of financial crises. The change in perspectives acknowledged the role

of financial intermediation and a possibility of a market failure, which often is the result of the self-fulfilling expectations of market participants.

'Second-generation' crisis models (Obstfeld 1986, 1994; Obstfeld and Taylor 2004) exploit the trade-offs among alternative policies and the tensions in the government's objective to generate mutually conflicting incentives both to abandon a currency peg and to defend it. As such analyses demonstrate, typically, prior to a crisis the economy is overheated, with expansionary monetary policy, strong domestic credit growth, an overvalued currency, and in many cases, high inflation. The economy is also increasingly vulnerable financially, with rising liabilities of the banking system not backed up by foreign exchange reserves and falling asset prices. In this environment, some event, such as an increase in foreign interest rates or a deterioration in the terms of trade, can easily aggravate vulnerability of the economy, leading to crisis (Aziz *et al.* 2000: 5).

Second-generation models of financial crisis also pay greater attention to speculative dynamics within finance itself, emphasising the herd-like behaviour of financiers in the face of a shock or a piece of bad news. What distinguishes revisionist views on crises is that in second-generation models a currency collapse may occur even if the government is pursuing prudent monetary policy, because in essence, the crisis is generated by self-fulfiling speculation (Rivera-Batiz and Rivera-Batiz 1994: 601–2). This self-fulfiling component generates multiple equilibria in international asset markets, rendering the timing of crises indeterminate. By extension, the combination of self-fulfiling attacks and multiple equilibria signifies that good macroeconomic fundamentals are an important but not a sufficient condition for avoiding currency crises (Griffith-Jones and Kimmis 1999: 72). As the Asian 1997–1998 crashes proved, crises occur even in economies with sound macroeconomic fundamentals.

According to an IMF study (2002b), most contemporary financial crises 'have their origins in an unsustainable economic and financial imbalance – a large current account deficit, a large fiscal deficit, or some mismatch between the assets and liabilities of financial or non-financial companies'. These imbalances, in turn, are often associated with unsustainably high asset prices (usually corporate or real estate) or an overvalued currency.

Accordingly, crises can be categorised according to the sector in which they originate; the nature of the imbalances; and whether the imbalances relate to borrower's short-term financing needs or longer-term capacity to repay. In reality, financial crisis today is likely to be the result of a number of sources of instability, but let us briefly review the scenarios individually.

Currency crises

A foreign exchange, or currency crisis, occurs when a speculative attack on a country's currency results in a devaluation or sharp depreciation of the currency, forcing the central bank to defend the currency by selling large amounts of reserves, or by significantly raising interest rates (IMF 2002b). A currency crisis was initially understood by Krugman as a balance-of-payments (BoP) crisis, defined as a sharp change in the official foreign exchange reserves, caused by the expectations of the future exchange rate (Krugman 1979; Krugman and Obstfeld 1997: 498). Krugman later termed it a 'canonical' currency crisis, which results from a 'fundamental inconsistency between domestic policies – typically the persistence of a money-financed budget deficits – and the attempt to maintain a fixed exchange rate' (Krugman 1979: 3; 2000).

Essentially, the currency crisis model describes how fears of market participants of an imminent change in the currency value lead to a BoP crisis. A crisis of this type can occur even without capital flows, creditors, lenders and banks. The only necessary precondition for currency collapse is that the central bank is attempting to maintain the exchange rate at an unsustainable level. Hence currency crises can be the outcome of purely speculative disturbances that are based not on the current macroeconomic policies of domestic authorities but on *anticipations* of future policies. These speculative outbursts may be based on bad experiences with previous administrations. They may be linked to a lack of private sector credibility about a government's resolve to stick with prudent economic policies. Whatever the reason, the impact of the expectations is self-fulfilment: anticipation of a BoP crisis does eventually result in one (Obstfeld 1986; Rivera-Batiz and Rivera-Batiz 1994: 601).

The ability of the central bank to defend against a downward pressure on the currency is limited by foreign exchange reserves, which usually are sufficient to sustain several months of import financing or several days of financing of capital outflows at most (Popov 2001: 132). The immediate impact of an expected devaluation is to make domestic assets relatively unattractive at their initial interest rates. Hence, investors shift to other currencies *en masse*, causing large capital outflows and a corresponding loss of international reserves. The outflows stop only when domestic interest rates rise by an amount sufficient to compensate investors for their anticipated losses from holding domestic currency (Rivera-Batiz and Rivera-Batiz 1994: 601).

Once a brisk devaluation or revaluation occurs, there is a shift in relative prices and terms of trade, which may provoke a supply-side recession. Changes in relative prices of assets may cause disruptions in the repayment of credits (Popov 2001: 132). The external imbalance can lead to crisis *via* several channels. Falling reserves imply that the trade deficit cannot be maintained indefinitely. At some point it becomes rational to expect the devaluation to occur; a currency attack follows and the economically untenable fiscal expansion is rapidly erased (Eatwell and Taylor 2000: 141–2). When the profit from liquidating a 'distortion' created by state intervention becomes too large, investors choose their moment to punish the government for interfering in the market. Such sentiments underlie BoP crisis models and assert that monetary expansion can provoke a flight from the local currency, when the economy is subject to a foreign exchange constraint (Taylor 1998: 666). If the household and business sectors do not alter their savings levels, foreign savings or the external current account deficit will have to rise. This diagnosis lies at the heart of traditional IMF structural adjustment programmes (SAPs) that have thrown many countries into recession.

These scenarios of currency collapses have been applied to many developing countries. For instance, as Krugman and Obstfeld (1997) explain, the Mexican 1982 crisis was caused both by domestic factors and external shocks. In the mid-1970s, Mexico turned to be a major oil exporter, so much so that by the mid-1980s the share of oil exports was 60% of the country's export earnings. The oil industry is state-owned in Mexico, and thus the government received extra resources to finance subsidies, public expenditure and social programmes. Government expenditure, however, was higher than export earnings, and the deficit was partly covered by monetary emission, partly by foreign earnings. The monetary injections led to fast growing inflation and increased real exchange rate of the peso. In early 1982, the economic slowdown got worse in the USA and this resulted in declining American demand for Mexican exports. Mexico too, was suffering from a major economic downturn. In response, the Mexican government devalued the peso in February 1982. Devaluation, however, failed to reassure foreign commercial banks in the government's policy credibility. By the summer 1982, the traditional sources of foreign borrowing were exhausted, and Mexico was left with an unsustainable debt burden. By mid-August 1982 the government, completely depleted of foreign exchange reserves, turned to the international creditors for a multilateral loan package (Krugman and Obstfeld 1997: 697–8).

In some orthodox interpretations, the Russian 1998 financial crisis followed a similar currency crisis pattern, since the rouble was overvalued since 1995. Export growth slowed, while imports continued to rise, so that current account shrank and turned negative in the first half of 1998. In view of the possible devaluation, capital outflow escalated, thus depleting the foreign exchange reserves of the Russian central bank. The IMF emergency loans advanced to the country in the summer were used up in about four weeks and the government had to devalue the rouble on 17 August 1998 (Popov 2001: 132). As we will see in Chapter 7, this interpretation, although it does illuminate the dynamics of foreign trade and currency value, does not take into account Russia's internal processes of credit creation; neither does it offer an explanation for the domestic causes of financial fragility that was at the centre of the crisis of 1998.

Banking crises

A banking crisis occurs when actual or potential bank runs induce banks to suspend the internal convertibility of their liabilities, or force the government to intervene to prevent this by providing banks with large-scale financial support. While banking crises were relatively rare in the 1950s and 1960s, they have become increasingly common since the financial deregulation reforms of the 1970s. In the economies of emerging markets, they often occur in tandem with currency crises (IMF 2002b). For an excellent review of banking crises and policy responses see Goodhart and Illing (2002).

Debt crises

A debt crisis occurs either when borrowers default or when lenders believe default is likely to take place and therefore withhold new

loans and try to liquidate existing ones. Debt crises can be associated with either commercial (private) or public (government)
debt. A perceived risk that the public sector will cease to honour its
repayment obligations is likely to lead to a sharp fall in private
capital inflows and a foreign exchange crisis (IMF 2002b). Meanwhile countries with trade surpluses and strong currencies often
face substantial capital inflows as a result of expectations that the
currency will be revalued. To avoid having an explosion in the
domestic money supply, monetary authorities sterilise the effects
of BoP surplus on monetary base through open market operations.[6]
Yet if these operations involve the sale of government debt, the
accumulation of public debt may in fact generate fears of higher
debt-service payments. The high debt service may then lead to
expectations of budget deficits and future monetary expansion
(Rivera-Batiz and Rivera-Batiz 1994: 602). As a result of self-fulfiling
expectations, capital inflows turn into capital outflows, losses
of reserves, and a crisis of international liquidity (Chang and
Velasco 1998).

If the debts are denominated in foreign currency – like Mexican
Tesobonos in 1994 – the outflow of capital leads to a depletion of
reserves, triggering a devaluation. If the obligations are denominated in domestic currency, investors, fearing inflationary financing
of public deficits (leading to inflation and devaluation), switch to
foreign exchange. The Mexican peso in 1994 and many other Latin
American currencies in the early 1980s were undermined by this
mechanism. Once investors realise that the advantages of the depreciation of the debt denominated in domestic currency are greater
than the costs associated with devaluation, they attack the currency
and a crisis breaks out (Popov 2001: 133).

---

6   Sterilisation is the process of controlling the money supply by the gov-
    ernment in order to prevent a currency value from changing. If the cur-
    rency is at risk of depreciation, for instance, the government sells its
    reserves of foreign currency and buys its own currency from the markets.
    Conversely, if the government wishes to prevent the currency from
    appreciating, sterilisation involves reducing the money supply. Open-
    market operations can include buying and selling of foreign exchange
    reserves, as well as of government securities (bonds).

Private sector debt crises

This type of crisis occurs due to an overaccumulation of private debt. In a model, developing country governments self-insure by accumulating international reserves to back up poorly regulated financial markets. National players feel justified in offering high returns to foreign investors, setting up a spread. Outsiders acquire domestic liabilities until the moment when the stock of insured claims exceeds the government's reserves. A speculative attack follows (Eatwell and Taylor 2000: 143). This, many economists argue, is what happened in East Asia in 1997.

For example, Krugman has suggested that the currency crises in East Asia in 1997–1998 'were only part of a broader financial crisis', which had very little to do with currencies or even monetary issues *per se*. Nor, he believed, did the Asian crises have much to do with the traditional fiscal issues, but rather were related to issues 'normally neglected in the currency crisis analysis': the role of financial intermediaries, the associated moral hazard, and the prices of real assets such as capital and land. Thus the Asian crisis was not brought on by fiscal deficits, as in first-generation models, nor by macroeconomic temptation, as in second-generation models. The crisis was really the culmination of a bubble in, and subsequent collapse of asset values, with the currency crises more a symptom than a cause of the underlying problems (Krugman 1998, in Popov 2001: 133).

The models of private sector crises often are based on the assumption that it is the private sector, alert and astute, that through its financial functions, 'chastises' an inept and often hesitant government. By creating moral hazard, the government in this model encourages reckless investment behaviour. All a sensible private sector operator can be expected to do is to make money out of such misguided public action (Eatwell and Taylor 2000: 143). Yet in East Asia, the assumption that the costs of risky private sector borrowing would be internalised proved to be wrong. The Asian 'tigers' boasted nearly perfect fundamentals – high savings rates, strong growth, low inflation, balanced or even surplus budgets and low government debt. It was the excessive borrowing of the private sector (banks in Thailand, industrial companies in Indonesia and *chaebols* in Korea) that caused the mistrust of investors and resulted in the outflow of capital (Popov 2001: 133–4; Corsetti *et al.* 1999).

The distinctions between types of crises outlined above are not clear-cut, however, because the elements which are at the centre of financial vulnerability increasingly overlap. Imbalances in one sector are often mirrored in vulnerabilities in others; liquidity problems can easily lead to insolvency. Moreover, once a crisis erupts in one sector, it can quickly feed into others, through both balance sheet interlinkages and vulnerability to falling asset prices (IMF 2002b). For example, Jan Toporowski (1999) distinguishes between the following factors that can be regarded as the proximate or initial causes of financial crisis:

- A speculative attack on the exchange rate.
- A 'financial panic' – a bank run or its international analogue.
- The collapse of an asset price bubble.
- A crisis induced by moral hazard (implicit or explicit guarantees of bailout).
- The recognition of a 'debt overhang', followed by a disorderly workout.

Therefore, in contrast to earlier formulations of the efficient market theory of finance, revisionist readings of financial instability do recognise that global capital markets are characterised by information asymmetries that in turn, lead to overshooting, sharp corrections and financial crises. Even in the age of advanced technologies and instantaneous communications, information remains costly to obtain and evaluate. Data relevant to prognosis of government's policy commitments tend to be based on opinion and speculation as much as hard evidence. This encourages 'herd-like' behaviour of international investors that can precipitate sharp market moves and, in extreme cases, financial crises. As this book will show in the following chapters, distress originating in one market segment can easily cascade through the financial system, because of the widespread use of leverage and because information asymmetries prevent financial intermediaries from raising liquidity in a crisis (Eichengreen 1999; Shiller 2000).

While most of the models sketched out above are rich in technical language and hence can be quite alienating to non-economists, they convey one general message about today's financial system: finance has become complex, diverse and fragile. The transformations within the global financial system not only entail threats of economic instability, currency crises and unemployment. Financial crisis has assumed many guises, involving currency crashes, bank runs, and over-indebtedness at various levels, bewildering governments, experts and analysts whose task it is to make sense of economic developments and try and prevent financial crises in the future. It is clear that problems of such scale cannot be addressed simply through technical analysis and econometric modelling. A deeper, more nuanced and perhaps, even intuitive, insight into finance, is necessary. With this objective in mind, one turns to Keynesian financial theory that for many years has been a source of alternative visions of finance and financial volatility.

3
Keynesian and Heterodox Theories of Financial Crises[1]

The scholarship of John Maynard Keynes marks a revolutionary turn in the 20th century development of economic theory. His macroeconomics of effective demand became an alternative to micro-level economics of the individual and his preferences, and facilitated a policy reform that helped the USA and Western Europe recover from the Great Depression. A major part of Keynes' political economy was his vision of finance and investment. Being aware of the in-built volatility and speculative drive of financial markets, Keynes believed in strong, pro-active governmental policy of regulation and control over financial markets, investment flows, and international monetary affairs. His design for the Bretton Woods regime of international economic cooperation included a world central bank (ICU – International Clearing Union) and a global neutral currency (*bancor*). These institutional mechanisms were supposed to alleviate current account imbalances, and promote global distribution of savings and investment in accordance with the flows of trade and services. Although Keynes' vision of the Bretton Woods system was never implemented due to the

---

1 There exist quite different versions of the 'Keynesian' tradition in current macroeconomics. They range from more mainstream-oriented new Keynesians to post-Keynesians, who reject the basic assumptions of monetarism and neoclassical economic theory. But they would probably all agree on the fact that money (and financial structures) matter too much to be assumed neutral given the actual functioning of capitalism. Moreover, the difference between financial and real transactions is much more emphasised in Keynesian framework than in the neoclassical perspective (Binswanger 1999: 7).

opposition of the US side, his conceptual insights into the nature of finance, speculation and monetary and fiscal policies continue to shape alternative approaches to finance and financial crises to this day.

Money, finance and speculation

Ironically, although Keynes has pioneered heterodox research in the psychology of financial markets, it is hard to find a comprehensive formulation of financial crisis theory in Keynes' own works. He produced a revolution in general economic theory, offering a new vision of the economic system and policy – a theory of macro-economic demand economics. Yet it would probably be fair to say that it was Keynes' followers such as Hyman Minsky, Michael Kalecki, Charles Kindleberger, Paul Davidson and many others, rather than the man himself, who have developed what is now called (post)-Keynesian theory of financial fragility and crisis. Before we take a look at the work of these scholars though, let us briefly review the foundations of Keynesian political economy.

Keynes' *General Theory* is a portrait of a monetary economy with sophisticated financial institutions. In such an economy, money is not just a vehicle that makes 'the double coincidence of wants' unnecessary for trading to take place. Instead, money is a special type of bond that emerges as positions in capital assets are financed. Consequently, in an economy with a sophisticated financial system, the 'financing veil' encompasses many more financial instruments than any narrow money concept includes (Minsky 1982a: 61, 62). In this instance, Keynes pointed out that the price of existing assets, both real and financial, as well as the cash payment constraints imposed by the liability structures of the holders of capital assets, may lead to an inappropriate amount or type of investment. 'Speculation, the activities identified with Wall Street, make business cycles, including the occasional deep depression cycles, rather than equilibrium seeking and sustaining behaviour, the normal result of economic processes' (1936, in Minsky 1991a, 1975).

In the Keynesian view, the monetary mechanism is tied to credit and therefore, to the financing of enterprises in the real economy. This close focus on the interaction between the financial and the production systems sharply contrasts with the Smithian theory, where some asymmetry in the perceptions of an assumed exogenous shock in the monetary system transforms an equilibrium seeking system into a cycle generating system. The centrality of money, credit and the pricing mechanism of capital assets is what distinguishes the Keynesian from the classical financial theory (Minsky 1991a).

A basic premise of Keynes's theory of finance – also known as the theory of liquidity preference (LPT) – is that contrary to classical economics which holds that savings determine investment, in reality, the opposite is true: investment determines savings. In this context, the primary function of financial markets is to provide liquidity for asset holders. Accordingly, Davidson notes, when bullish sentiment about the uncertain future dominates financial markets, rising market prices encourage savers to provide the funding for new investment projects that (i) far exceed their current incomes and (ii) induce exuberant expectations of future returns. The result is an investment boom. If some time in the future doubts suddenly arise concerning the reliability of these euphoric expectations, then bearish sentiment will come to the fore and the investment boom will turn into a bust (Davidson 2001: 21, 23).

In a normally functioning capitalist economy, in which money is mainly debts to banks, money is constantly being created and destroyed. In contrast, if money is viewed as a 'veil' that masks the ultimate ownership of wealth, then the major concern of monetary and financial theory becomes the expected profits that induce debt creation and the realised profits that lead to the validation of debt. Thus, the transition from abstract economics to an economic analysis of advanced financialised capitalism depends upon defining money as a product of financial interrelations. The neoclassical synthesis – which ignores the 'financing veil' aspects of money and persists in viewing it only as a 'bartering veil' – cannot explain why instability is a normal functioning occurrence in a capitalist economy. Hence, Minsky concludes, neoclassical economic theory is a *defective instrument to be used in formulation of policies that aim at controlling instability* (1982a: 72–3).

According to the Keynesian tradition, profit expectations can easily become overly optimistic or pessimistic, hence the economy is prone to volatility and speculative bubbles. There might be times when financial activities increase instability or grow at the expense of real economy, as they offer higher returns or are considered to be less risky. There also might be negative correlations between financial activities and growth: in certain instances the financial sector may be allowed to divert resources from the industrial sector, leading to a fall in real output. The overall impact of financial activities on economic growth depends on the particular institutional circumstances (Binswanger 1999).

As was illustrated in the previous chapter, conventional economic wisdom, when it does recognise a possibility of financial crises and recessions, usually rationalises their appearance as a necessary disciplinary device. Keynes, on the contrary, believed that a liquidity crunch is not a necessary purgative device for restoring economic health. Instead, he argued that liquidation processes and crucially, the resulting unemployment involves a 'public scandal of wasted resources' (Keynes 1936: 381). Accordingly, his principle of effective demand indicates (i) the need for central controls over the exchange rates and (ii) international agreements that place the major responsibility for resolving international payments imbalances on the creditor nations (Davidson 2001: 30–1). And although Keynes' idea of the ICU and a world currency was rejected in 1944, some of these principles of demand management lay at the heart of the Bretton Woods system of fixed exchange rates, the period now often referred to as the 'golden age' of financial stability and economic growth.

In the age of liberalised and globalised financial markets, Keynes' work continues to exercise tremendous influence on critical research in finance. Following Keynes, heterodox scholars attempt to advance conceptual understanding of the role of money and finance in the macroeconomic stability. Here, the greatest challenge is to capture the nature of financial institutions and markets as generators of credit at the global level (Strange 1997, 1998). The myriad of Keynes' sympathisers and followers stretch far beyond the academic boundaries of economics. Political science, sociology, human geography and international relations have developed their own original approaches to the understanding of finance, placing it in the wider political system, social climate and international context. Of all these social science disciplines, students of International Political Economy (IPE) have been at the forefront of critical and socially-aware research in finance.

International political economy and the 'disjuncture paradigm'

Keynesian notions of speculation, self-fulfilling prophecies and financial irrationality have informed an IPE school of thought that explains financial fragility through the gap that apparently exists between a bloated financial sphere, and the real economy of production, services and trade. We shall call this tradition the 'disjuncture paradigm' of financial crisis. The 'disjuncture paradigm' and related accounts of financial volatility lead us into an almost intuitive, yet attractive, vision of finance as an economic bubble thriving on top of the world economy. This bubble is oversized and overblown, it is filled with numerical digits representing some value. For example, while the global foreign exchange markets are trading approximately two trillion US dollars worth of transactions daily, only a small portion of that money can be attributed to the needs of the real economy. Similarly, at present, the combined outstanding value of financial derivatives is nearing 200 trillion US dollars, what is approximately five times the estimated GDP size of the entire planet. Since 1980, the global stock of financial assets (shares, bonds, banks deposits and cash) has increased more than twice as fast as the GDP of rich economies, from $12 trillion in 1980 to almost $80 trillion today. In the US corporate sector in the second half of the 1990s, the values of the price-to-earnings ratios, which are well over 40, were far outside the historical range (Shiller 2000: 12–13).

These sums seem incredible indeed, yet they bear little relation to the underlying economic values and thus when pricked, collide with the real economy, producing crashes and crises. As various explanations of heightened volatility of finance contend, capitalism has always been about making money with money, and throughout its history, there has always been a delicate balance of power between the financial sector, real economy, and the state. But the breakdown of the Bretton Woods regime in 1973[2] unleashed a shift towards the empowerment of finance *vis-à-vis* the traditional (national) economy, and the state. Much of the flux, instability, and gyrating can be directly attributed to this enhanced capacity to switch capital flows around in ways that seem almost oblivious of the constraints of time and space that normally pin down material activities of production and consumption (Harvey 1990: 164; K. Singh 2000; Bello *et al.* 2000; Grahl and Teague 2000).

Coupled with the rise of the highly sophisticated systems of financial coordination on a global scale, this shift had led to

---

2   Or what also is often called the era of 'Fordism-Keynesianism'.

an explosive growth of new financial instruments and markets. Through options, swaps and futures, money is traded for more money. It seems that the elusive world of finance is becoming increasingly fictitious, being progressively detached from the real economic process to which it once referred (Hart 2001: 73–118; Harvey 1990: 145, 168; 1999; Arrighi 1994: 3; Lash and Urry 1994: 285–92; Boyer 2000). The overblown financial market bears little correlation to the stagnating economies of manufacturing, trade and even services sectors. In this process of financial ascendance, not only financial markets dominate production and trade, but within the financial sector itself, the most abstract and obscure of 'dematerialised' financial markets – those concerned with the pure trading of complex financial instruments and therefore most detached from 'productive' investment – predominate (Cerny 1994: 226). This growing gulf, or disjuncture, observers maintain, is what defines the inherent fragility of today's finance.

Back in 1986 Peter Drucker identified three fundamental characteristics of the post-Bretton Woods era. First, he argued that the primary-products economy had become 'uncoupled' from the industrial economy. Second, in the industrial economy itself, production had become 'uncoupled' from employment. Third, he noted that capital movements, rather than trade, had become the driving force of the world economy. While the two had not quite become uncoupled, he admitted, the link between them has become loose and worse, unpredictable. The most significant transformation for Drucker was the changed relationship between the symbolic economy of capital movements, exchange rates and credit flows, and the real economy of the flow of goods and services:

> ... in the world economy of today, the 'real' economy of goods and services and the 'symbol' economy of money, credit and capital are no longer bound tightly to each other; they are, indeed, moving further and further apart (Drucker 1986: 783).

The rise of the financial sphere as the flywheel of the world economy, Drucker noted, is both the most visible and the least understood change of modern capitalism. With financial revolution progressing further, Drucker's ideas received sympathy of many other observers. Most of the analyses pointing to the unprecedented position of the financial sphere in post-1973 capitalism tend to associate it with the emergence of a qualitatively new system of economic organisation and production, a new 'knowledge' economy of information, internet technologies, brand capitalism and post-modern consumption (Castells 1993, 1996, 2000). For example, Rifkin (2000) argues, in the increasingly weightless global economy, the money used to negotiate market transactions and other financial arrangements is dematerialising into electronic bits capable to travel at the speed of light in the form of pure information.[3] In a new era, where holding property, in all forms, becomes less important than securing short-term access to commercial opportunities, savings also become less important to hold on to. The dematerialisation of money has been compounded with the decline in savings and the rise in personal and corporate debt. He calls the new economy an 'era of borrowed existence', since the boom in individual consumption and corporate profits is mainly explained by the growing reliance on borrowed funds (Rifkin 2000: 37, 40–1, 47).

There is indeed evidence to the thesis that the tensions between the globalising financial markets and the requirements of production and trade are intensifying. First, far from drawing its dynamism from lending to industry, the remarkable growth of the financial system during the last two decades has been mostly associated with speculation in foreign currencies, stock market securities, real estate, leveraged buyouts and the like (Fine *et al.* 1999: 71–3). Thriving on speculation, global financial markets divert funds from long-term productive investments. Second, financial institutions maintain a regime of higher real interest rates, which restricts the access of productive industries and enterprises to credit. Third, financial capital brings uncertainty and volatility in interest and exchange rates. This volatility is extremely harmful to various sectors of the real economy, particularly trade. Lastly, it undermines efforts by governments to support full employment and reduce inequality. Altogether, many critics conclude, liberalised and internationalised finance, in relative autonomy from industrial accumulation, tends

---

3   Rifkin notes that today, less than 10% of US money supply is in the form of currency. If all the coins and bills currently circulating were added up, it would amount to less than $400 billion. Much of that is no longer circulating in the US but rather in other countries.

to create bubbles of fictitious prosperity. When these burst, the entire economy is thrown into turmoil (Fine *et al.* 1999: 72–3; K. Singh 2000: 13; Webber 2001).

These and similar pessimistic theories of the financial evolution have been rather popular among (post)-Keynesian economists since the 1980s, when financial markets started to rely on speculative practices in connection with mergers and acquisitions, leveraged buyouts and junk bond issues. As Kurtzman (1993) for instance, writes, with the removal of gold as an anchor to the world financial system, the size of finance had been enlarged by several orders of magnitude. The global economy as a whole has been moved 'onto the new standard: the interest rate standard...From that point onwards, all investors have one simple goal: to earn more money than the cost of money' (1993: 93–4). Typically in this and other similar accounts, global finance is likened to a vast casino, the ultimate effects of which is to subdue, exploit and 'crowd out' the traditional economy of labour, trade and production (see Binswagner 1999 for a good summary).

These hypotheses tend to establish a negative correlation between the ascendance of the financial sector and real economic growth as a fundamental source of financial fragility. As Magdoff has noted recently, 'with profits ... more difficult to make in the 'real' economy (where something is actually made or a service delivered) ... another of capital's responses to stagnation has been the expansion of the financial system, along with many new gimmicks designed to appropriate surplus value from the rest of the economy' (2006: 14). Interestingly, this negative correlation is not supposed to hold under all economic circumstances. Rather, it applies to periods in capitalist evolution when the financial sector grows at the cost of the real economy. The positive correlation between the two spheres is not denied under 'normal' economic conditions, which characterised the world economy of the 1950s and 1960s. Yet according to most heterodox critics, it has been critically undermined by the negative repercussions of the breakdown of the Bretton Woods regime. Today, rather than investing in the sluggish real economy, it is much more attractive for firms to channel capital into the financial sector (Ben-Ami 2001: 4). In such a system, the art (and not science, as the economics profession would have it) of valuing assets becomes harder because of the changes in the nature of the economy, creating even greater scope for bubbles and crises to form.

In the 'disjuncture' framework, financial crisis occurs period-
ically, when the bubble of fictitious financial value collides with
the constraints of the 'old' underlying economy. In this interpretation, the dotcom bubble crashed because the capitalisation of
the new companies has far outreached the value of the 'old'
economy-manufacturing giants (Brenner 2000: 24). A powerful
combination of financial and virtual technologies has created a
colossal pool of funds that were necessary for the new economy's
advance. Since the value of the new dotcom services was restricted
by the purchasing power of the 'old' economy, the value of
'new economy's' companies was calculated not according to the
existing balance of costs and profits, but out of a potential, *virtual*
profit. Since income flows were calculated exponentially through
financial/marketing manoeuvrings, the sustainability of this new
mode of profitmaking was extremely fragile. And under the
influence of external shocks to the market stability, the bubble
was pricked, unleashing a financial crisis.

At a glance, this reading of a financial crisis does not differ too
much from a standard economic understanding of speculative
bubbles: both perspectives recognise the over-stretched profit
expectations in the market, some degree of irrationality of financial
investors, and the decisive impact of an external shock. However,
there is a marked difference between the two schools of thought: if
mainstream finance contends that bubbles happen occasionally,
signalling a transition to a new type of economic organisation, the
disjuncture paradigm sees the problem as *a structural gap* between
the perpetually overblown speculative financial markets, and the
real economy that is starved for long-term, 'greenfield' money. In
this latter vision, crisis is an inherent element of capitalist economy. Crucially, as many critics argue, the dominance of finance
over the real economy is not accidental: it thrives due to powerful
social constellation of class interests and groups of capital (e.g.,
Harmes 1998; Soederberg 2002b; van der Pijl 1998).

While the conflict and contradictions between the financial and
real economic spheres are apparent in the capitalist system, and
while there can be little doubt about the role of multinational giants
in the allocation of resources and other significant matters as well,
there is an added consideration that critics stress. Big corporate
capital and the occupants of corporate boardrooms are themselves

increasingly constrained and controlled by financial capital as it operates through the global network of financial markets. In Sweezy's words, real power rests not so much with corporate board-rooms as with the global financial markets. The giant corporations are also major players in these markets, adding to their importance. It looks 'as though Adam Smith's invisible hand is staging a come-back in a new form and with increased muscle' (Sweezy 1994: 10). Although the return of finance to hegemony was accomplished in close connection with the internationalisation of capital and the globalisation of markets, Dumenil and Levy (2001: 579) insist that it is finance, and not the internationalisation of markets, that dictates the form and contents of the new stage of financial capitalism.

The errors of the disjuncture thesis

Explanations of financial fragility centred on the elements of a bubble economy are attractive. They illustrate lucidly an increas-ingly apparent lack of solid foundations of the expansion of financial markets, tracing the sources of financial fragility to its 'detachment' from the rest of the economic system. It seems that when the two spheres were in closer unity – supposedly, during the Bretton Woods period – crises were rare and financial fragility did not endanger the overall macroeconomic, much less global, stability. As one observer noted at the time,

> it is a fact that financial crises have become rarer and less acute and indeed have almost disappeared since the early 1930s, ... in sharp contrast to the decennial recurrence in the preceding century. Financial crises are a childhood disease of capitalism, not an affliction of an old age (Goldsmith 1982).

Today in contrast, when financial trading is increasingly detached from 'real' economic processes, fragility and crisis have become the curse of finance-driven globalisation. Much more worryingly, much of this fragility is hidden in offshore financial centres, complex pyramids of credits, and intricate financial portfolios of the many layers of financial institutions.

Attractive as this picture might appear, there is a fundamental problem with any disjuncture-centred explanation for financial fragility. The juxtaposition of the financial sphere and the rest of the economy tends to view the two spheres as more or less fixed, rigid entities. Such understandings do not pay due attention either to the ongoing transformations within the so-called 'real' economy itself, or to the extraordinary flexibility and fluidity of finance, and consequently, to the changes in the interrelationship between 'financial' and 'non-financial' economies. This rigidity of the outlook gives rise to at least three further doubts concerning the validity of a structural understanding of fragile finance.

First of all, although it is true that crisis has become both more common and intense during the last few decades, it is unclear why the 'normal face' of capitalism should be attributed to the Bretton Woods era. Granted, the 25 years after the Second World War were the period of growth, full employment and economic recovery, both in Europe and in the USA. Yet there could be other plausible explanations to the economic resurgence of the Bretton Woods era. First, considering the magnitude of the disruption left by the war, the speed of the post-1945 recovery is not surprising: the lower the starting point, the faster the subsequent economic growth tends to be.

Second, while internationally, the Bretton Woods era was the age of financial stability and relative economic balance, the governments' ability to control and regulate capital flows and financial expansion could principally have been accounted for by the sheer easiness of the task. International flows of capital were not active, they consisted of large-scale coordinated intergovernmental financial transfers, which by their very nature, were easy to monitor and regulate. Once financial markets began to expand into the private realm in the 1960s, seeking more profit-able niches, the stability of the Bretton Woods order was shaken irreversibly. Today's capitalism is fundamentally different: it is tightly interconnected through trade, capital and IT linkages, it is flexible, privatised, and approximately 80% of all international financial transactions take place within the offshore financial markets, largely out of reach of financial regulators (Palan 2003).

In line with the globalisation of markets, the traditional functions of finance and investment, easy to identify in the Bretton Woods era, are also undergoing major changes. There are several such tendencies. The first concerns the distinction between equity (share) and bond (debt obligations) financing. Traditionally, equity financing was considered more risky and volatile than government obligations. Today, in contrast, reliance on leveraged financing is becoming so widespread that the functional difference between debt and equity is eroding. For example, at the time of writing, the volume of cash coming into the secretive private-equity firms is ballooning (over $300 billion worth of buyouts were done in first half of 2006). In the UK these secretive institutions, operating mainly through leveraged buyouts, now own several 'real' economy companies, such as Focus DIY, Boots and National Car Park (NCP). They are also expanding their investments into the emerging markets: more than $22 billion was raised for these markets in 2006, up from $3.4 billion in 2003. The fastest growing markets were Africa and the Middle East.[4] Therefore, today both debt and equity serve the same purpose in the same way: lending themselves to arbitrage operators. In the era of the dominance of speculative capital, that is the primary function of markets; it supersedes other technical and legal differences. The bond markets' volatility is in part due to this blurring of the lines separating the markets. Worse, contrary to what finance textbooks wrote back in the 1980s, the two markets – equity and debt – are now becoming more synchronised (Saber 1999: 130).

Additionally, there has also been a marked convergence of financial strategies. Corporations are choosing more similar debt vs. equity financing strategies. As arbitragers and other participants compare returns and risks on a more global spectrum of financial assets, the best common strategies are chosen (Allen 1999: 17). Big firms increasingly use similar internal risk-management systems. These are sensitive to movements in the markets, and lead their users to respond in similar ways, so the few big firms that dominate the markets increasingly behave as 'herds', reducing diversity of opinion and liquidity (*Economist* 16 May 2002: 10).

The distinction between 'direct' and 'portfolio' capital flows is also becoming increasingly meaningless. The popular perception is that direct investment creates new, long-term productive capacity; in contrast to 'portfolio' investment, which is merely a short-term, speculative shuffling of commercial paper or computer bits. But as Nitzan (2001) argues, this notion has become obsolete. Foreign investment –

---

4   Figures from *The Economist*.

whether portfolio or direct – is merely an alteration of ownership titles. In fact, both are paper transactions whose only difference is definitional: investments worth more than 10% of the target company's equity are commonly classified as direct; whereas those worth less are considered portfolio. Conceptually, both direct and portfolio investments occur on the liabilities side of the balance sheet, whereas the creation of capacity affects the asset side. There is no, therefore, one-to-one correspondence between their underlying components. In this way, the proceeds from a public offering sold to portfolio investors can end up financing a new factory, while direct investment may be used to buy government bonds (Nitzan 2001).

With the implications of these profound changes in mind, it seems that not only a return to the economic organisation of the 1950s and 1960s is unlikely to resolve the problem of financial fragility; it is plainly, unattainable. Many students of IPE tend to view financial speculation and asset bubbles in very negative terms, regarding both as destructive tendencies of the economy. Yet both speculation and even short-term credit have not only been normal, healthy elements of the commercial exchange throughout capitalism's evolution, but also before the existence of modern money forms (Braudel 1982; de Goede 2005). A certain amount of short-term credit is considered a healthy component of sustainable economic growth. It facilitates foreign trade, providing working capital for seasonal enterprises; it helps to regulate imbalances between revenue and expenditure (*Monthly Review* 2002).

Investor euphorias and bubbles tend to coincide with periods of innovation that in the long-run, make society better off (Eatwell 2004: 44).[5] The Dutch tulip mania of 1636 and the financial boom in the USA in late 19th century were followed by a deep financial crisis. Both bubbles, however, left long-run legacies for the economies concerned. Holland became a horticultural centre for the world economy; while the USA has acquired a vast network of railroads, power and communication lines that helped it become a

---

5 Eatwell argues that if bubbles did not exist, rational individual actions may have led to socially irrational outcome; the bubble, by inducing irrational acts in individuals may shift the economy towards a more socially rational position.

world technological leader and a hegemon already by 1914 (Wood 1999; Golub 2004). In such a view, rather than being a symptom of a profound structural disjuncture, the dotcom bubble was more of an example of 'messy Schumpeterian creative destruction' (*The Economist*, 16 May 2002: 18). The 'new economy' boom of 1995–2000 represented a fast-forwarding of experimentation, facilitating and probing new technologies that later became embedded in the economic system and society.

More fundamentally, the concept of the 'real' economy, against which the 'financial' economy has so often been contrasted, relies on a juxtaposition of material and symbolic dimensions of economic activity that are inseparable even in principle. As Dodd argues, ideas, expectations and symbolic associations play an integral role *within,* rather than simply being a *reflection on,* real economic activity, on the way in which individuals use and handle money, on the way in which money works in a society, on the way it is administered by governments, and on the consequences its operation has across societies (Dodd 1994: 157; also de Goede 2005).

Therefore it appears that finance has become fragile not simply because of a vast structural shift to worldwide speculation in fictitious values and disregard of 'real' economic needs. True, there have been phases in capitalist history when 'finance capital' (however defined) seemed to occupy the position of paramount importance, only to lose it in the speculative crashes that followed. In this vision, there is hardly anything fundamentally novel about the current conjuncture of global capitalist dynamics. Yet at the same time, critics note that in the current phase, it is not only a concentration of power in financial institutions that is astounding, but the explosion in new financial instruments, practices and markets, paralleled with the rise of highly sophisticated systems of financial coordination on a global scale. It is the hazards of the endogenous financial expansions that typically contain crisis tendencies in the capitalist system. In what follows, we will attempt to address this problem more closely.

4
Hyman Minsky and Fragile Finance

All three major schools of thought on financial crisis reviewed in Chapters 2 and 3 would probably concur, despite their disagreements and normative differences, on the following. Finance itself, and its relation to the economic system, has become incredibly complex and difficult to read. Market-friendly approaches, such as EMT and other versions of neoclassical synthesis agree that instability may be a by-product of such complexity. They do not agree, however, that the recent spate of financial crises is a symptom of a structural fragility. Rather, they contend that the financial revolution has facilitated the progress of capitalism towards a new stage of development. In contrast, 'structuralist' accounts maintain that the 'financialisation' of capitalism is proceeding through a recurrence of crises and under the clout of endemic financial fragility.

Analysing these disconcerting tendencies through historical lens, one unavoidably looks back at previous 'new economy' eras and financial implosions that paralleled them; in particular, at the Wall Street crash of October 1929 and the ensuing Great Depression of the 1930s. Many lives and fortunes were lost in the stock market crash of 1929; its aftermath was long and painful, engulfing the US and the international economy in a mire of deflation and depression. With memories of the 'Great Crash' still lingering in the economic literature and popular culture, little wonder that fear of a new great depression exercises the minds of many economists ever since. Among those who contemplated a recurrence of financial crisis, the work of Hyman Minsky in particular stands out. It is to his scholarship that we turn now.

The financial instability hypothesis

Hyman Minsky is perhaps the most prolific and original theorist of financial instability. Yet, within the discipline of international political economy at least, his name remains inexplicably overshadowed by the likes of Keynes and Kindleberger. The wave of the recent crises has sparked, however, renewed interest in Minsky's scholarly legacy: his followers in the so-called post-Keynesian economics and political economy provide some of the most insightful and original ideas about finance, financial regulation and crisis management (Arestis and Sawyer 2001; Arestis *et al.* 2001; Toporowski 1999, 2001; Portes 1998; Dymski 2003; Davidson 1992, 2001, 2004; Gray and Gray 1994; Bellofiore and Ferris 2001; Bartholomew and Phillips 2000).

Susan Strange once described Minsky as a 'loner', a highly original economist whose analytical framework and normative standpoint did not only stand in stark contrast to the ideas of his contemporaries, but were also developed in isolation from the big 'intellectual armies' of economic theory (1998: 77–8, 96). Minsky himself identified his work as a variant of Keynesian economics, or more accurately, as financial Keynesianism. Although he is widely considered to be a theorist rather than an economic historian, his vision of financial instability is founded, in effect, on an original interpretation of economic and financial evolution of American capitalism. Minsky's major conceptual foundation is predicated on the assumption that neither the economic activity nor the actions of governments are able to 'fix' finance and credit. Instead, credit and finance tend to expand, often uncontrollably, being driven by a perpetual quest for financial innovation. Hence, he concluded, in an advanced financialised economy, instability is ever-present: 'as long as an economy is capitalist, it will be financially unstable' (Minsky 1982b: 36).

In its emphasis on the instability of the credit system, Minsky's vision of finance is a descendant of an academic current set out by a host of economists including J.S. Mill, Irving Fisher and John Maynard Keynes. Like Fisher, Minsky attaches great importance to the role of debt structures in causing financial difficulties, and especially debt contracted to leverage the acquisition of speculative assets for subsequent resale. His thinking also drew on Keynes' probability theory (Kindleberger 1996: 12; Rima 2002). Like Keynes, Minsky believed that for a given financial system at any point in time, monetary means of payment may be expanded not only within the existing system of banks, but also by the formation of new banks, the spread of new credit instruments, and the expansion of personal credit outside of banks. Following Fisher, Minsky analysed the process of debt deflation, but he changed the emphasis so that debt accumulation, especially debt contracted to leverage the acquisition of speculative assets for subsequent resale, was the focal element of his model (Isenberg 1994: 224; Kindlerbeger 1996; Rima 2002).

Minsky's financial instability hypothesis (FIH) stresses the importance of time and uncertainty. One of its biggest theorems is that a capitalist economy with sophisticated financial institutions is flexible: its behaviour at any time depends upon institutional relations, the structure of financial linkages and the history of the economy (Minsky 1982a: 92). FIH is also pessimistic: it holds that financial capitalism is fundamentally flawed because each success at crisis containment leads to further risk taking. This fundamental flaw, in turn, results from the necessity of complex financial arrangements that exist in an economy in which capital assets are expansive (Papadimitriou and Wray 1999).

Alongside the process of financial innovation, the other most critical, and intimately related, element in Minsky's model, is the debt structure of the economy. The monetary system, he writes, is at the centre of the debt creation and repayment mechanism. Money is created as banks lend to business; and money is destroyed as borrowers fulfil their payment commitments to banks. Money is created in response to the view about prospective profits, and money is destroyed as profits are realised. Monetary changes are therefore the *result, not the cause* (as monetarists believe), of the behaviour of the economy, and the monetary system is stable only as long as profit flows enable businesses that borrow from banks to fulfil their commitments (Minsky 1982a: xx).

Analysing the Great Depression of the 1930s, Minsky criticised the neoclassical synthesis for its inability to recognise that a serious economic depression can occur as a result of *internal* operations of the economy. For orthodox economists, a depression can only be the outcome of policy errors or of non-essential institutional flaws.

One popular monetarist explanation for the Great Depression, for instance, holds that it was the result of the Federal Reserve policy errors (Friedman and Shwartz 1963), while Keynesians hold that it was the outcome of an exogenously determined decline in investment opportunities or a preceding decline in consumption activity. In both variants of the neoclassical synthesis, Minsky continues, the financial structure is represented by 'money'. Monetarists use money as a variable that explains prices; Keynesians use money as a variable that affects aggregate nominal demand. Yet in both accounts money is an outside factor; the amount of money in existence is not determined by internal processes of the economy (1982a: 16–17).

Minsky, in contrast, developed his framework assuming that for a given financial system at any point in time, monetary means of payment may be expanded not only within the existing system of banks, but also by the formation of new banks, the spread of new credit instruments, and the expansion of personal credit outside of financial institutions. Therefore, crucial questions of policy turn on how to control all these avenues of endogenous credit expansion (Kindleberger 1996: 12; Minsky 1986). As he explains, in the advanced financial capitalism, cash flows are a legacy of past contracts in which 'money today' was exchanged for 'money in the future'. Business debt is thus an essential characteristic of a capitalist economy. The validation of business debt requires that prices and outputs be such that almost all firms earn large enough surpluses over labour and material costs, either to fulfil the gross payments required by debt or to induce refinancing. Refinancing takes place only if gross profits are expected to be large enough to either validate the new debt or induce further refinancing (Minsky 1982a: 61–3).

Like other analysts of the psychology of investments, Minsky saw the preconditions for financial crisis develop during an investment boom. The main emphasis of his theoretical structure lies in the explanation of the endogenous processes by which these conditions are put in place. He calls this *a theory of systemic fragility*. Financial fragility is an indispensable attribute of the financial system; systemic financial fragility means that the development of a fragile financial structure results from the normal functioning of the economy (Wolfson 1994: 16–17). What defines the overall fragility (or robustness) of a financial system is the sum-total of existing financing mechanisms. Conceptually, Minsky identified three possible forms of investment financing. The method of classification depends upon the relationship between the cash receipts due to normal operations and the cash payment liabilities due to debt (Wolfson 1994).

First, there is *hedge financing*. For a hedge unit, conservatively estimated expected gross income exceeds the cash payments on debts from contracts for every period in the future. Second, there is *speculative finance*. A unit speculates when for some periods the cash payment commitments on debts exceed the expected gross capital income. The speculation is that refinancing will be available when needed.[1] Third, and most importantly for the question of whether fragility turns into a crisis, there is *Ponzi finance*.[2] Ponzi units are speculative units, the special feature of which is that for some if not all near term periods *cash payment commitments to pay interest are not covered by the income portion* of the expected excess of receipts over current labour and material costs. In other words, these units must borrow in order to pay the interest on their outstanding debt: their outstanding debt grows even if no new income yielding assets are acquired (Minsky 1982a: 25–8).

The overall stability of an economy depends upon the mixture of hedge, speculative, and Ponzi finance. Over a period of good years, the weight of short-term debt in the business financial structure usually grows, and the weight of cash in portfolios declines. Thus there is a shift in the proportion of units with different financial structures – and the weight of speculative and Ponzi finance increases during a period of optimism (Minsky 1982a: 33). Financial crisis occurs if units need or desire more cash than is available from their usual sources and they must resort to other ways of raising cash, such as liquidating positions. To the extent that businesses are funded by financial assets, every position in the financial market that is liquidated cuts off businesses in the real sector from invest-

---

1   Minsky restricts the term 'speculative' to a liability structure in which the income portion of gross profits exceeds the income portion of payment commitments.

2   The name comes from Carlo (Charles) Ponzi.

ment channels. Thus financial instability may cause serious declines in production and employment (Bezemer 2001: 14).

With these general assumptions, Minsky identified both systemic and idiosyncratic preconditions for financial crises. The systemic preconditions include heavy indebtedness of the economy and a large element of either Ponzi or speculative finance (which in time can become Ponzi). At the same time, he did observe that the extent to which indebtedness rises before a crisis changes through time. The fragility of the system does not solely depend on the payment commitments on debts relative to cash receipts. Each period of increased indebtedness is unique, and the most pertinent cause of changes for Minsky is financial innovation. Thus, newly emerging financial institutions and practices influence the overall stability of the economy. For example, in his interpretation, the Mexican collapse in 1982 was the outcome of private indebtedness of enterprises in the booming north of Mexico and some portfolio diversification by the Mexicans who took advantage of the support to the peso that came from oil revenues (Minsky 1991a: 23).

To Minsky, new technologies, instruments and practices of financial trading is what differentiates different episodes of financial instability and crises. Minsky understood that the Great Depression was unique but that episodes of financial fragility are not. Dynamic capitalist systems always (although unpredictably) generate profit opportunities that, if coupled with easy availability of finance, can set the stage for increasing the ratio of debt financing to the value of an investment. It is the collapse of the ratio between the cash payment liabilities of firms and the market values of the assets supporting them that signifies that a crash follows financial fragility. Whether a situation of financial fragility in fact manifests itself depends on the specifics of the institutional changes of the economy's recent past (Rima 2002: 408; Minsky 1982a: 36–7).

In Minsky's critique, the speculative bubble phase is an irrational, euphoric stage that precipitates financial crisis. Financial traumas are thus an inevitable feature of the deregulated capitalist system: the seeds of crisis are planted in the beginning of the euphoric phase and speculative bubbles are merely the catalysts of inevitable financial crises. The policy implications of such theory are profound: supporting Keynes, Minsky argued that conventional monetary policy alone cannot ameliorate crisis.

During phases of crisis and deflation, endogenous market processes by themselves are inefficient; capitalist economies need a robust financial structure and strong policies to guide the evolution of finance. Unregulated financial decisionmaking propels unsustainable asset price rises and the central bank must be prepared to act as a lender-of-last-resort and to 'float off' untenable debt structures when financial crises emerge (Baddeley and McCombie 2001: 226–7).

In sum, Minsky's FIH emphasises the way in which investment demand is generated by the combination of the valuation of the stock of assets, the financing available from internal funds and financial markets, and the supply price of investment output. Thereby it shows how a collapse of asset values, caused chiefly by economic agents engaged in speculative and Ponzi operations, leads to a collapse of investment. Such a collapse brings a shortfall in the profit flows on capital assets, which in turn makes the fulfilment of business financial commitments difficult if not impossible. Financial structures and interrelations make the development of those long-term expectations that lead to a collapse of investment an endogenous phenomenon in the particular circumstances that arise in the aftermath of a sustained expansion (Minsky 1982a: 102).

The centrality of various forms of debt in the process of capitalist evolution, and their place in the organisation of financial portfolios, is the reason why Minsky's theory of financial fragility proves so attractive to today's economists. Since the late 1970s, levels of indebtedness have been growing at all major tiers of the global economy: private corporations engaged in the largely unregulated process of credit expansion; governments too, became big borrowers (Skene 1992: 38). In the 1980s, the government of the world's largest economy – the USA – became a *de facto* Ponzi unit, borrowing in order to pay interest on outstanding debt. On the international front, the stimulation of the Reagan deficits shifted the position of US from a net creditor to the world's biggest debtor. Thus the USA as a country also become a Ponzi unit, borrowing in international capital markets to pay the interest as well as the principal on its international debt (Mehrling 1999: 148). According to Minsky's theory of financial fragility, such debt-laden economic expansion was bound to collapse in a crash that would match the scale of the 1929 crash in the USA. But 'it' did not happen again, and to his surprise, the system continued to function.

Minsky concluded that he had underestimated the flexibility of the capitalist system. As Mehrling writes,

> The apparent stability of profit flows, even in the face of great stress, supported the value of a growing structure of financial assets. The accumulation of those assets into large pension and insurance institutions began the process of shifting the centre of the system from industry to finance. Money market mutual funds created alternatives to bank deposits, while securitisation of bank assets created alternatives to bank lending. Traditional financial institutions continued to issue commercial paper, but the capacity to hold it increasingly lay elsewhere, with the managers of money (Mehrling 1999: 148–9).

At the same time, the ascendance of speculative finance made the economy vulnerable to the unpredictable effects of financial speculation. Mergers and acquisitions (M&As), leveraged buyouts followed by the sell-off of assets, increase profits and speculative fevers, often reducing the productive capacity of the traditional sectors of production (Cox and Sinclair 1996: 181–2). Wielding their newfound financial strength in the market for corporate control, the managers of money came to dominate the managers of industry (Mehrling 1999; Nitzan 1998, 2001).

What does Minsky's model suggest about recent financial history? A lot, his followers and sympathisers contend. As Doug Henwood argues, the economic slump of the early 1990s in the USA originated in a Ponzi financial structure going sour, yet the authorities moved in to contain the crisis. Specifically, between 1989 and 1994, the Fed drove interest rates down. At the same time, the US government bailed out savings and loans industry through the Resolution Trust Corp., spending $200 billion in public funds. These moves, Henwood continues, did prevent the collapse of the American financial system, but unlike in the 1930s, the debts were not written off. With low interest rates, they were easier to service. 'For non-financial corporations, total indebtedness in 1995 was nearly 11 times after-tax profits – an improvement from over 22 times level of 1986, but still twice the levels of the 1950s and 1960s. For households, the figures show no such improvement: in 1995, consumer debts were equal to 91% of after-tax incomes, the highest level since 1945, and well above 1980s levels, which were themselves well above 1970s levels... In Minsky's language, the business sector seems to have settled back from Ponzi to speculative financing mode, but households continue to explore fresh Ponzi territory, with no signs of temperance' (Henwood 1997: 223; also Stiglitz 2004).

Over the last ten years, consumers in major Anglo-Saxon economies have been running progressively bigger debts, effectively using credit cards and mortgages to compensate for the fall of real wages (Montgomerie 2006). In this regard, Minsky has warned that an economy with private debts is especially vulnerable to changes in the pace of investment, for investment determines both aggregate demand and the viability of debt structures. The instability of such an economy follows from the subjective nature of expectations about the future of investment, as well as subjective determination by bankers and their business clients of the appropriate liability structure for the financing of positions in different types of capital assets. In the financial economy of today, uncertainty is a major determinant of the path of income and employment (Minsky 1982a: 64–5).

It would be naïve, of course, to argue that Minsky's analytical framework is a panacea to the many dilemmas that global financial markets entail. One problem with many revisionist crisis theories is that they view international finance in isolation from the processes of economic transformation more generally. Minsky himself, while recognising the importance of the 'interrelation between the financial and real aspects of an enterprise economy' admits that a necessary comprehensive examination of these issues lies beyond the limits of his theoretical model (1982a: 4). Yet the central elements of the alternative crisis theories – financial speculation, booms and investment bubbles, and debt deflation processes – are significant precisely because ultimately they are counterpoised to the underlying economic activity that may not match financiers' expectations. Moreover, it is through feedbacks on the economy – monetary, trade, industrial and social sectors – that financial crises are felt most painfully.

Minskyan financial fragility in the international context

Minsky's scholarship has attracted considerable interest among heterodox economists and some political economists. Although his original model analysed a closed economic system, it was later advanced to the realm of international finance. Notably by Charles Kindleberger, who developed the so-called called Minsky-Kindleberger hypothesis when examining a series of international financial crises (1988). Key elements that frame the vision are speculation, financial innovation, and indebtedness.

Charles Kindleberger and 'manias, panics and crashes'

Kindleberger noted that in terms of intellectual affiliation, his view on financial instability and crises combines rational expectations and the psychological model (1988: 4–5). Drawing both on theoretical analyses and on historical evidence, Kindleberger charts a pattern of a financial cycle. It unfolds in five stages: displacement, followed by euphoria (overtrading) and possibly distress, possibly further revulsion (a crash and/or panic) leading again, unless alleviated by a lender of last resort (LLR) to deep discredit, serious trouble for the banking system, and economic depression (1988: 18). Displacement is typically some significant event that greatly improves the perceived and real economic outlook. 'There is nothing so disturbing to one's well-being and judgement as to see a friend get rich', he notes (1996: 13). As firms and households see others making profits from speculative purchases and resale, they tend to follow: 'monkey see, monkey do'. For example, the growth of the Eurocurrency market in 1970–1971, before the OPEC price rise, stimulated multinational banks to embark on lending programmes to the Third World that became excessive.

Indeed, the recognition that the world financial system was in distress came shortly after the oil price shock in 1979. Yet some financial institutions, notably Citicorp, refused to recognise that lending to developing countries had been excessive up until August 1982. Mexico had expanded oil production rapidly since 1973, largely on borrowed money, and as oil exports levelled off, it continued to borrow in order to maintain its debt service. In the crisis that ensued, the IMF was called in, organising more commercial loans under rigid conditions of macroeconomic austerity. Similar arrangements had to be made in Brazil in 1983, in Argentina in 1984 and in a number of less severe cases (Kindleberger 1988: 61–2).

For Kindleberger, just as for Minsky, a key type of displacement originates in financial innovation. Innovations in various credit instruments, such as swaps (currency and interest rate), do not reduce risk (as EMT would claim); rather, they merely shift it. Critically, a market participant that reduces one risk may thereby be moved to take on more risk, thus increasing the risk for the system as a whole (1988: 36). According to Kindleberger, as early as 1986 a BIS report (1986: 201) recognised that underpriced new financial products take the market demand beyond the prudential risk limits. Where the spread of innovations is drawn out, the last institutions to adopt the new techniques are under temptation to carry them too far in an effort to displace the first who have established positions with the best customers. In the case of Third world syndicated bank loans, for instance, the regional banks that were drawn in at the end may not have had the stamina to stay the course when it transpired 'that the approved therapy is to hang on, shovelling good money after bad, and lend more' (Kindleberger 1988: 35). Yet as history reveals, financial innovation and risk-management tools continued to transform the markets during the 1980s and the 1990s, driving much of the financial system further and further away from the gaze and expertise of regulatory bodies, to the brink of financial crisis.

Another type of displacement is the deregulation of the financial market. In the late 1980s and 1990s, such a 'displacement' could occur when a country was perceived to have become 'a successful reformer'. New opportunities for profits are seized, and overdone, 'in ways so closely resembling irrationality as to constitute a mania'. However, once the excessive character of the upswing is revealed, the financial system may experience 'distress', in the course of which the rush to reverse the previous process may be so precipitous as to resemble 'panic' (Kindleberger 1996: 13, 44). This, as we will see in the following chapters, is precisely what aggravated the crises of the 1990s in the emerging markets.

In times of boom, Kindleberger sees speculation develop in two stages: in the first, sober stage of investment, households and firms respond to a 'displacement' in a limited and rational way. In the second stage, however, capital gains play a dominating role. When the number of agents engaging in these speculative practices increases, bringing in segments of the population that are normally aloof from such ventures, speculation for profit leads away from normal, rational behaviour to what has been described as 'manias' or 'bubbles.' The word 'mania' emphasises the irrationality; 'bubble' is any deviation from fundamentals[3] (Kindleberger 1996: 13–14). The author links these two stages to two groups of 'speculators', the insiders and outsiders. The insiders destabilise the situation by driving the price up and up, selling out at the top to the outsiders. The outsiders buy at the top, and sell out at the bottom when the insiders are driving the market down. For example, such a distinction seems very relevant for developments in Mexico leading to the December 1994 crisis, as initially it was mainly Mexicans (insiders) who invested on a large-scale, by returning capital that had previously fled. However, since mid-1992, these local investors – fearing a large devaluation – started to pull out, selling paper to more bullish investors (who were mainly foreigners) who still had confidence (Griffith-Jones 1998: 8).

A study of the adverse consequences of financial liberalisation and international speculation was advanced by Taylor (1998).[4] Analysing financial crises that affected Turkey in the late 1970s, the Southern Cone in 1980–1981, Mexico and many others in 1982, South Africa in 1985, and East Asia in 1997–1998, Taylor notes that these boom and bust episodes were not caused by excessive fiscal expansion or the creation of wholesale moral hazards by market-distorting state interventions. Rather, they pivoted around governments' withdrawal from regulating the real economy, the financial sector, and especially the international capital market. This premeditated laxity created strong incentives for destabilising private sector financial behaviour, on the part of both domestic and external players. Feedbacks of their actions to the macroeconomic level upset the system (1998: 663).

---

3 Kindleberger defines a bubble as an upward price movement over an extended range that then implodes. An extended negative bubble is defined as a crash.

4 Following Neftci-Frenkel framework, Taylor outlined a number of essential elements that can trigger a financial crisis: a fixed or predetermined nominal exchange rate; few barriers to external capital inflows or outflows; historical factors and current circumstances that generate capital movements which push the domestic financial system in the direction of being long on local assets and short on foreign holdings; regulation of the system is lax and probably pro-cyclical; macroeconomic repercussions *via* the BoP and the financial system's flows of funds and balance sheets set off systemic instability (1998).

A more plausible perspective on these crises, Taylor suggests, is that the public and private sectors generate positive financial feedbacks first at the micro, and then at the macroeconomic levels, ultimately destabilising the system. A financial cycle begins in financial markets that generate capital inflows. They spill over to the macroeconomy *via* the financial system and the BoP as the upswing gains momentum. At the peak, before a downswing, the economy-wide consequences can be overwhelming (1998: 669). As Taylor observes, the crises of the 1980s and 1990s in Latin America in East Asia are most adequately explained by private agents' (both domestic and foreign) acting to make high short-term profits when policy and history provide the preconditions and the public sector acquiesces. Ultimately, it was mutual feedbacks between the financial sectors and the real side of the economy that led to a crisis. Yet at the same, he notes, the ability to regulate each of the five components of the financial instability lies, to a greater or lesser degree, in the hands of national policymakers (1998: 670).

Advancing Minsky's framework beyond the boundaries of a closed economy, Kindleberger focussed on the international dimensions and character of financial crises; he even suggested that his model of financial crisis probably applies best to the foreign exchange markets. In an ideal world of economic theory, he claims, a gain of specie for one country would be matched by a corresponding loss for another, and the resulting expansion in the first case would be offset by the contraction in the second. In the real world, however, while the boom in the first country may gain speed from the increase in reserves, it may also rise in the second country despite the loss of reserves, as investors respond to rising prices and profits abroad by joining in speculative chase. In other words, the potential contraction from the shrinkage on the monetary side may be overwhelmed by an increase in speculative interest and the rise in demand. For both countries, the credit system is stretched tighter (Kindleberger 1996: 14).

In order to ensure stability in such a fragile system of international finance, there has to be a general stabiliser, namely, a lender of last resort. Markets, Kindleberger writes (1996: 3), generally work, but occasionally they break down. When they do, they require government intervention to provide stability for the public good. As he continues, while better monetary polices would moderate manias and panics in most cases, and probably eliminate some, even optimal policies would leave a residual problem of considerable dimensions. Even if there were exactly the right amount of liquidity in the system over the long-run, there would be still crises, and therefore a need for additional liquidity, to be provided by a lender of last resort. In this regard, Kindleberger was highly sceptical of the existing institutional arrangements for an international LLR. As he argued, in a crisis, when it is fast action that is needed, the IMF cannot fulfil its LLR function adequately: the Fund takes time to reach decisions, and moreover, it cannot create money; instead, it only advances monies made available to it by member states. In addition, 'the amounts made available are fixed at any one time, and can be raised only slowly by a series of legislative acts in the member countries; with the total time taken governed by the slowest to approve' (1988: 62). While the international dimensions of a LLR function are undergoing changes, with commercial and national central banks assuming some of the functions, Kindleberger noted that there is 'no meeting of minds' on the issue of a global LLR, nor is there strong leadership (p. 67). As a result, the world economy remains in danger of a severe recession, if not depression, and distress persists...

Historically, emerging markets have been the most vulnerable constituents of the global economy, being particularly susceptible to speculative attacks and financial crises. These economies typically have less mature and thus more fragile financial markets and banking systems; lacking a strong domestic investment base, they depend on attracting foreign capital. At the same time, the monitoring and regulatory capacity of national governments in the developing economies tend to be weaker for a variety of reasons; crucially, emerging markets depend on the amount of foreign exchange reserves as a basis for their currency regimes and investment credibility (see Armijo 2001; Altvater 1997; Soederberg 2005). It is notable in this regard that Minsky's vision of financial fragility, originally developed for a closed capitalist economy with sophisticated financial linkages, had been extended to explain crises and instability in an economy that opens itself up to global financial markets (Arestis 2001; Arestis and Glickman 2002; Arestis and Sawyer 2001; Wolfson 1994, 2000, 2002; Davidson 2001; Dymski 2003; Bartholomew and Phillips 2000; also Pettis 2003).

According to Arestis and Glickman (2002: 243), the primary impact of openness in an emerging economy is to import the drive towards financial innovation, as foreign investors seek out investment opportunities and local households, firms and banks begin to look abroad for finance. Sooner or later, the economy falls into a state of internationalised financial fragility. It then becomes prone (i) to crisis that is domestic in origin but impacts on its external situation, (ii) to crisis that is external in origin but impacts on the domestic situation and (iii) to crisis-intensifying interactions between (i) and (ii).

A type (i) crisis would have its origins in classic Minskyan factors such as the advent of rising costs on the domestic capital goods industries. The result will be present-value reversal and a decline in asset prices, which means that speculatively financed units will find refinancing difficult to attract and service. 'As they default in growing numbers and commercial failure spreads, a flight towards liquidity breaks out. Some investors will seek to diversify the now larger liquid element in their portfolios by shifting into other currencies. Others will act in anticipation of behaviour of this kind. The domestic currency will be sold heavily, triggering an exchange rate crisis. Even units that are hedged in the sense that their asset and liability maturities are matched will now become vulnerable to the fact that they are speculatively financed: their debts are denominated in foreign currency whereas their cash inflows are not. The potential of contagion will have a global reach' (Arestis and Glickman 2002: 243). This scenario, the authors suggest, can explain the contagion of the Thai currency in the summer of 1997 throughout East Asia.

The authors analyse the possibility of type (ii) crisis on the basis that, once an economy is open to global financial markets, its government can be regarded as a financing unit in relation to external value of its currency. So long as reserves are substantial in relation to debts, the country remains in the equivalent of a hedge-financed position: the payments necessary to maintain the external value of its currency can be met. However, as endogenous processes drive the foreign liabilities up, the country's debt-to-reserves ratio rises and doubts arise as to whether the authorities will be able to protect the exchange rate. The state will then become, in effect, a speculative- and, ultimately, a Ponzi-financing unit in relation to the wider world (Arestis and Glickman 2002: 244). As we shall see later in Chapter 7 of this book, this mechanism was at work at the time of the Russian 1998 default, when the government was responsible for the construction of a large Ponzi-type pyramid of debt in order to finance the chronic budget deficit.

5
Dilemmas and Paradoxes of Fragile Finance

Finance then, is neither a cloud that daunts over the real economy, nor a well-anchored structure that parallels the progress of the economy in a predictable and straightforward way. The conclusion we draw from a Minskyan reading of financial capitalism suggests that finance is highly complex, flexible and capable of mutation. It is in the inner transformations of the financial system, typically in a link with the rest of the economic system, where fragility and crisis arise. Moreover, it appears that the obscurity and complexity of today's finance, although a problem for regulators in itself, conceals several important paradoxes of the privatised financial system. These paradoxes centre on the ever-present capacity of financial markets to expand through the process of financial innovation.

Destabilising stability

First, one problem of the post-Bretton Woods decentralised global credit system is that traditional monetary tools and regulatory practices developed by states no longer seem sufficient. With the growing depth of financial and secondary markets, money has effectively become an 'information product'. When new investments no longer require the stock of accumulated capital but thrive on the availability of credit, the lending process cannot be stopped. But when almost all economies are open to the world market and the system allows debts to be incurred in any currency, private debts are easily translated into public ones. Often, the collapse of share prices for private debtors mutates into the collapse of the national currency, for which the government is ultimately responsible (Strange 1997: 80; Smithin and Wolf 1999: 212; Germain 1997; Altvater 1997; Surin 1998). Second, the daunting challenges for governmental policy today are compounded not only by the fact that financial risk has been privatised, and capital controls lifted. Fundamentally, they reflect one of the most perplexing paradoxes of financial capitalism, which was clearly evidenced by the implosions of the late 1990s–early 2000s. Namely, that due to the very nature of finance, where, according to Keynes, investment is largely about predicting how others will behave, *stability is destabilising*.

Financial history is rich with examples of 'new eras of prosperity' and benign endorsement of 'new era' prophecies by prominent public figures and the media (Wood 1999). In 1925 the USA for instance, there were claims that 'there is nothing now to be foreseen which can prevent the USA from enjoying an era of business prosperity which is entirely without equal in the pages of trade history' (Sutliff 1925, cited in Shiller 2000: 104). In a 1928 article, John Moody proclaimed that 'a new age is taking form throughout the entire civilised world; civilisation is taking on new aspects. We are only now beginning to realise, perhaps, that this modern, mechanistic civilisation in which we live is now in the process of perfecting itself' (Shiller 2000: 105). It was within less than a year that such optimism was crashed, together with the fortunes of financial investors. Fast forward to 1997 (70 years later), and we find Jeffery Sachs evaluating the success of East Asian industrialisation, incidentally, just a couple of weeks before the Thai baht collapsed:

> ...Taiwan, Hong Kong, Singapore, Malaysia, Thailand, and Indonesia all created profitable conditions for labour-intensive manufacturing exports, through realistic exchange rates, moderate tariffs, duty-free access for exporters to capital and intermediate goods, attention to infrastructure such as ports and telecoms and so on...The already fast-growing East Asian economies should continue to catch up with the richer economies, though supercharged growth should gradually taper off as they succeed in narrowing the gap... (Sachs 1997).

The major danger of 'new era' thinking, Robert Shiller (2000: 103) warns, is that it concentrates on the effects of events currently prominent in the news. Little attention is paid to 'what-ifs', even if they have substantial probability. The 'what-ifs', however, have a dangerous ability to prick the bubble even among the strongest of optimisms; the stability and euphoria that seemed so solid just a day ago can turn into a bust and crisis practically overnight. And the reason may lie not in the tone, or the message, of the 'what ifs' itself; but rather, in the process of the complex interaction between choices and strategies of individual investors, and the effects of their actions on the financial and economic system as a whole.

The problem is that in the age of liberalised markets, periods of economic optimism tend to invite excessive risk taking by financial operators. For example, the policy of low interest rates supports the markets' calm and thus contributes to a build-up of investments. While some of these investments may generate sound profits, others are driven by pure speculation. As the period of optimism continues, more and more speculative investments are being made, committing the existing equity bases to a growing pyramid of liabilities and risks. As a result, individual financial structures become overstretched; and thus, increasingly fragile and prone to failure. Once expectations about the future are shaken by an external shock, bad news or even a rumour, distress cascades through the system, provoking a crisis. In other words, the inner mechanics of a financial crisis are rooted in the dichotomy between individual choices and aggregate outcomes: perceptions of individual financiers about the resilience of their portfolios and stability of market segments often translate into adverse dynamics at a system level. While every individual agent may perceive her portfolio to be safe and liquid, the system itself is not: the aggregate outcome of individual perceptions is a progressively fragile state of the financial system itself (Keynes 1936; Minsky 1977, 1982a, 1986, 1991a; Mehrling 2001; Savona 2002).

The illusions of liquidity

In large part, as this book contends, such dichotomy centres on one tricky and relatively trivial notion: *liquidity*. Trivial, because 'liquidity' is one of those dry technical terms describing the state of the financial market, used in the commentary and business news almost on an hourly basis. Tricky, because only a select few, if anybody, seem to know what it really is. So what is the problem with liquidity? Economic theory offers many answers to this question (Cohen and Shin 2003; Fernandez 1999; Grossman and Miller 1988; O'Hara 2004). Despite their methodological differences, existing analyses tend to agree that the difficulty of understanding what liquidity is lies primarily in its duality: liquidity is both a quality[1] and a quantity.[2] This implies that 'liquidity' means different things to different people in different contexts. Moreover, the conceptualisation of liquidity and its behaviour is obscured by the fact that the nature of liquidity has changed over time. As one official of the Bank of England has put it recently, 'liquidity clearly ain't what it used to be. But it is much less clear what such a statement means, still less whether that is a "good" or a "bad" thing' (Smout 2001). During good times, the two sides of liquidity – quantity and quality – are easily conflated, often entrapping investors into a false sense of security and optimism. Problem is, such false perceptions can become self-fulfilling in their own right: beliefs in liquidity can help disguise a systemic problem for a while. Often, until it is too late.

The emergence of new forms of financial intermediation and a variety of financial products in the wake of the breakdown of the Bretton Woods have led many analysts to assume that issues of the adequacy of international liquidity have become obsolete in the regime of deregulated and privatised credit. In particular, the low inflationary period of the past two decades, underpinned by the regime of flexible exchange rates in the main capitalist economies and growth of private international credit markets have led many commentators to conclude that 'the concept of international liquidity has lost its strategic significance for the conduct of macroeconomic policy' (in Horne and Nahm 2000).

---

1 Of an investment portfolio or a market.
2 Of credit available to economic agents, or, as measured by monetary aggregates, to the economic system generally. Global liquidity is conventionally measured by the amount of international reserves held by national central banks.

In contrast to most mainstream interpretations of the post-1973 financial revolution, a Minskyan reading of the privatised and deregulated system of international credit suggests that the expansion of financial markets, both geographically and in absolute terms, *disguises systemic fragility of modern capital structures and their progressively illiquid character.* To Minsky, the most glaring inadequacy of mainstream finance theory is that it ignores the issue of liquidity scarcity (Mehrling 2001: 154–6). This abstraction, as we will see later in this book, has caused many pains and problems across the financial markets in the 1990s.

As a consequence of the expansion of secondary markets, the global economy is bound together by a complex, hierarchical structure of financial assets of varying degrees of liquidity. By expanding, hedging and diversifying their portfolios, financial dealers and bankers play a critical role in 'knitting together' the various layers of that structure into a unified system. Yet the systemic effect of private financial innovation in liberalised markets, first identified by Keynes as 'the paradox of liquidity', remains one of the most perplexing tendencies in today's finance. While every individual trader may feel liquid and safe, the system as a whole is not; as a consequence, it is inherently prone to distress and failure (Mehrling 2001: 154–5; Savona 2002: 181).

According to Warburton (2000: 93), one of the biggest crimes of financial terminology today is the abuse of the word 'liquidity' to describe the increased availability of capital funds that is the result of a massive wave of private financial innovation. 'Ease and anonymity of trading, or *fluidity* or *velocity* of the market, he writes, are genuinely important market characteristics, but in a Ponzi-type capitalism it is very confusing to describe them as liquidity'. Minsky believed that in a system where contractual liabilities are denoted solely in terms of money, one can define the concept of being liquid as possession of the ability to meet one's contractual obligations as they come due. Hence strictly defined, 'the ultimately liquid assets of the economy consist of those assets whose nominal value is independent of the functioning of the economy' (Minsky 1982a: 9). Securities, and especially modern secondary vehicles of speculation, are traded in the market day by day; their value changes throughout their life. For these reasons, securities and the funds used to invest in them cannot be described as liquid assets: these instruments cannot be easily reconstructed in terms of their ingredients (Warburton 2000; Stiglitz and Bhattacharya 1999).

Minsky's FIH provides a helpful framework that reveals the paradox of liquidity associated with the emergence of new financial techniques and products. The availability of new finance tends to raise confidence and profits, increasing the volume of debt-financed investment (Wolfson 1994: 17). Yet as Minsky warned,

> Every institutional innovation which results in both new ways to finance business and new substitutes for cash decreases the liquidity of the economy. That is, even though the amount of money does not change, the liquidity of the community decreases when government debt is replaced by private debts in the portfolios of commercial banks. Also, when nonfinancial corporations replace cash with government bonds and then government bonds with debts of bond houses, liquidity decreases. Such a pyramiding of liquid assets implies that the risks to the economy increase, for insolvency or even temporary illiquidity of a key nonbank organization can have a chain reaction and affect the solvency or illiquidity of many organizations (Minsky 1986: 173).

Particularly in an environment where interest rates on short-term interest rates are lower than the level of long-term interest rates, 'one can make on the carry[3] by financing positions...in long-term financial assets by short-term, presumably liquid, debts' (Minsky 1986: 211). Yet despite the expanding chain of financial disintermediation, the functioning of securities and derivatives

---

3 The term 'carry trade' describes a transaction where you borrow and pay interest in order to buy something else that has higher interest. In currency markets, carry trade is a strategy where an investor borrows in a foreign country with lower interest rates than their home country and invests the funds in their domestic market, usually in fixed-income securities. More recently, given the low level of interest rates in most capitalist economies, 'carry trades' involve transactions in which loans are raised with the central bank on favourable terms and used to purchase high-yielding securities like bonds. This type of raising liquidity has become an attractive way for banks to make a profit on maturity spreads (Heise *et al.* 2005: 25).

markets relies fundamentally on the availability of cash liquidity. In the end, banks have to accept these substitutes for money proper; and the very stability of the financial system rests on the stability of the banking system. To Minsky and his followers therefore, every institutional innovation that leads to both new ways to finance business and new substitutes for cash assets, *decreases* the volume of the liquidity available to redeem the debts incurred. This Keynesian vision of the liquidity paradox implies that while throughout the boom period, the distinction between near-moneys and money fades away; it comes to the fore again when distress and crisis erupt. As distress cascades through the system, liquidity providers turn into liquidity demanders (Bellofiore and Ferris 2001: 7; Bookstaber 2000).

The danger inherent in the process of credit (or for Minsky, debt) expansion, is that in the process of financial expansion the financial system contrary to appearances, becomes *progressively illiquid*. Once the system comes under stress, the newly opened credit lines would not be closed in time, and investor herding will quickly translate individual illiquidity into a systemic crisis. In times of distress, the combination of falling asset prices and the erosion of creditworthiness pushes financiers to liquidate their positions. While this process may be rational at the micro-level, it adds to macro pressures on asset prices which in turn trigger the initial evaporation of market liquidity for one or more classes of assets. The evaporation of asset liquidity aggravates both market and credit risk and begins to question balance sheet liquidity for some institutions. Since many companies use broadly similar analytical tools to model their price fluctuations and exposure to external shocks, the risk of precipitous price changes in the face of 'crowded trades' rises significantly. In these circumstances, the escalation of credit concerns exacerbates the defensive behaviour of investors, all of which acts to reinforce adverse market dynamics at the systemic level. As risks unfold through the system, a financial crisis ensues (CRMPG, 27 July 2005).

Liquidity presents an increasingly complex dilemma confronting financiers, policymakers and academics. Liquidity is the single factor in the global financial markets that links up all categories of players in a complex chain of assets and liabilities. Liquidity is a key criterion for individual financiers in their daily trading; liquidity is a major concern for financial regulators striving for the stability of markets. In times of distress, liquidity provision becomes an intensely political issue, often being the single factor that can determine the fate of a company or even a country. Liquidity is also intimately related to the process of financial innovation and credit creation.

According to Claudio Borio, financial developments of the late 1990s across the global financial system have shown that perceptions and theories of the behaviour of liquidity and consequently, the products of financial innovation affect the systemic balance and precipitate crises of confidence and valuation. During the investment booms of the late 1990s, markets have created trillions of dollars' worth of new financial claims, with a belief that many of these financial assets are safe, profitable and liquid. Yet in late 2000, the same financial trading strategies that only a year ago proved consistently profitable, suddenly turned sour, generating huge financial losses. The turmoil accelerated the departure of market players who had been contributing to a perception of systemic liquidity by taking the other side of trade-ins amidst the period of optimism (Borio 2000: 41). Thus along with the internationalisation of the market, the widespread use of leverage and financial speculation, systemic illiquidity has become a major factor in today's crisis dynamics.

More and more economists recognise that changes in underlying liquidity are a much more important factor in causing investment booms and busts than other aspects of the business cycle – such as overproduction, underconsumption, and overcapacity (Pettis 2001: 39). The reduction in liquidity levels is typically followed by falls in economic activity in the industrial and commercial sectors; and this holds true both for the case of highly leveraged financial firms and for entire national economic systems, particularly in the developing world (Kindleberger 1993; Minsky 1986; Toporowski 1993; Pettis 1996, 2001).

The dilemma of liquidity, both at methodological and practical levels, and the increasingly prominent role of illiquid capital structures in precipitating large-scale financial crises, seems to be one of most potent lessons of the crises of the late 1990s. The collapse of economies has highlighted progressive illiquidity and Ponzi-type finance as key factors in the crisis-prone nature of global financial structures. Mainstream finance theory has yet to analyse the role of endogenous credit developments and financial innovation in the analyses of financial crisis. But to heterodox economists, the crises in East Asia, Russia, Brazil and Argentina, as well as the scandals in the US corporate sector, served as stark reminders that financial innovation in general, and derivatives in particular, are accentuating the Keynesian paradox of liquidity, now operating at an international level (see Savona 2002).

The ability of financial institutions to take on greater risks and thus build up large volumes of credit, accumulating massive debts in a pyramid-like fashion can help sustain an investor euphoria and thus suggest that the recipient country is a successful reformer (Pettis 2001). Yet in itself, this process is a major factor contributing to the progressive illiquidity and fragility of today's financial structures. A political consequence of this liquidity paradox is that the central banks, when confronted with a danger of a systemic crisis brought on by excessive speculation, have to act as lenders of last resort, accommodating the market's need for a monetary base (Savona 2002: 181; Griesgraber and Gunter 1996).

With the enormous expansion of the financial services industry and the widespread use of leverage, deteriorating liquidity positions of individual economic entities – companies or countries – easily translate into large-scale defaults. During the booming investment years, asset price inflation enhances the availability of credit in the economy; inevitably, given the run-up in asset prices, part of the credit expansion is diverted into speculation. As credit expands, the quality of credit declines. After several good years, the generation of excess liquidity is reversed. In the context of an advanced economy, investment boom ends as investors try to redeem their illiquid assets, which often leads to corporate bankruptcies. In the case of an emerging market, this process is intensified by sudden capital outflows from the country. The country loses creditworthiness and consequently, the access to international capital markets. Often, a fall in the value of currency enhances expectations of a further liquidity crunch and a chain of insolvencies. This self-fulfiling process leads to defaults and bankruptcies, as the total volume of outstanding obligations becomes less likely to be repaid. As assets are sold, their values tumble. Such outflows lead to deflation, recession or even depression (Toporowski 2001: 126; Pettis 2001: 43–4; Puplava 2002; Bird and Rajan 2002).

Therefore, one of the most important, yet puzzling, lessons from the past decade of crises is the recognition that the fluidity, or velocity of financial circulation – the key products of financial deregulation and liberalisation of credit – are not synonymous with liquidity, and hence stability, of the system as such. On the one hand, the ongoing process of financial innovation ensures that the whole matter of liquidity has to do with not with proximity to cash, but with the question of facility in the exchanging of future for present purchasing power. Hence notions of absolute liquidity and 'cash' are in fact, anachronisms, which bar the way to a true understanding of the credit system (Smith 1935: 640). Their meaning and function are mostly defined by legal norms, and depend crucially on the existing investor conventions, confidence in the system, as well as specific economic conditions. Indeed, in today's financial markets funding liquidity implies command not only over cash and deposits, but also over other instruments that can be used to meet margin calls and effectively, settle transactions (Borio 2000).[4]

On the other hand however, the interaction between cash and market liquidity remains critical for the overall robustness of financial markets. The mechanisms that lead to the disappearance of cash liquidity under stress can be similar to those that lead to the evaporation of market liquidity. The dislocations generated by the evaporation of liquidity in systemically important markets in 1998–1999 are a clear illustration of the heightened significance of systemic liquidity for financial stability (Borio 2000: 38–9; 2004; Pettis 2001, 2003). Crises of illiquidity are commonplace in a capitalist economy; they can be dealt with quite efficiently by a timely restructuring of debts or a credit injection. By itself illiquidity is not necessary for corporate bankruptcies or currency crashes to occur; moreover, lack of liquidity under stress is usually a symptom of problems that originate elsewhere (Borio 2000: 45). However, in the regime of financial ascendance worldwide and the overwhelming reliance on debt finance – from households to corporations to national governments – illiquidity is often sufficient to trigger a crisis (Velasco 1999; IMF 2002b; Pettis 2003). Indeed, where liquidity is *perceived* to be adequate, confidence can be maintained and the self-fulfilment of

---

4   Most commonly government securities.

expectations may imply that liquidity *is* adequate. But together, illiq-uidity, leveraging and self-fulfiling expectations tend to bring the system to the brink of a systemic crisis (Bird and Rajan 2002: 365).

One implication of this reading of the systemic effects of financial innovation in the deregulated environment, is that in the run-up to a period of financial strains, markets may appear 'artificially liquid' (Borio 2000, 2004). Contrary to the beliefs of mainstream finance theory, market liquidity is only partly associated with market arrangements; ultimately, it rests on the way financiers perceive and respond to risks and returns. The success of leveraged trading generates high profits, adds to market-making capacity and lulls investors into a false sense of security. As a consequence, Borio argues, liquidity may be perceived as highest precisely when it is most vulnerable. 'The *illusion of permanent market liquidity* is probably the most insidious threat to liquidity itself. Markets are *expected* to be liquid, loans are *known* not to be' (Borio 2000: 45, emphasis in the original; Borio 2004).

A new type of crisis

At a conceptual level, insights into the nature of liquidity have led to significant shifts in the understanding of financial crisis itself. The elements of risk, speculation, asymmetric shocks and inter-dependencies between markets ensure that the dynamics of financial crisis deviate from the theoretical assumptions of the EMT. Traditionally understood in orthodox economics as a product of balance of payment imbalances or a result of an adverse shock to an economy, crisis is now viewed as a much more complex phenom-enon. Indeed, Frederick Mishkin acknowledged that in today-type crises, it is no longer mere government misconduct that triggers a crash or a crisis, and the potential outflow of capital is not phased over time. Instead, the disruptions occur all at once, as investors rush for the exit when the crisis strikes. In this process, 'current account measures do not have predictive power for financial crises; while illiquidity and problems in the banking sectors do' (Mishkin 1999: 13).

Liquidity difficulties and the innate financial fragility are increas-ingly being recognised as crucial components of a present-day financial crisis. As a result, these two elements have received central attention in the 'third-generation' crisis models currently being researched by heterodox critics (Chang and Velasco 1998, 1999; Detragiache 1996; Goldfrain and Valdes 1997). Typically such models focus on financial institutions that issue demandable debt as a liability, placing themselves in a potentially illiquid position. In an open economy, the ability of governments to rescue the banks under speculative attack is severely limited by the availability of international reserves. With capital mobility, printing unbacked money can only cause the exchange rate to crash, as both standard theory and the recent experience of emerging markets suggest. As Velasco explains, domestic bank runs often interact with panics by foreign creditors. The nature of this interaction depends, in particular, on the structure of international debt and how strongly banks can commit to repay their international obligations. Real exchange rate depreciation may both cause bank runs and multiply their deleterious real effects. The logic is circular: if bank runs cause the real exchange rate to depreciate, then producers of non-tradable goods may go bankrupt. If these firms had borrowed from local banks, the banks' liquidation value would have declined, and a run would have been even more likely (Velasco 1999). In a Minskyan framework, financial fragility today increasingly centres on the problems of speculation, illiquidity and debt.

In this instance, Fratianni and Pattison (2002: 147–8) have distinguished two types of liquidity crisis. Type 1 illiquidity is essentially an institutional development: it stems from gridlocks in the infrastructure of payment, clearing, and settlement mechanisms that, in turn, reduce liquidity in international and systemically important domestic financial markets. This type of illiquidity leads to the failure of solvent institutions because of their inability to settle or hedge transactions. Type 2 illiquidity is a broader macroeconomic phenomenon: it relates to the lack of (international) liquidity of individual countries, which usually manifests itself in inadequate levels of foreign reserves.

Importantly, both types of illiquidity interact in the world financial markets. As both Asian and Russian crises showed, macroeconomic illiquidity increasingly entails international ramifications through its impact on domestic and global markets and settlement mechanisms. In the regime of liberalised and inter-dependent financial markets, the risks that an external shock can force both the borrower's revenue and its debt servicing expense to reverse sharply are very large (Fratianni and Pattison 2002: 147–8). Shortening the duration of financial contracts in order to raise liquidity breeds fragility and leads to a liquidity crisis, causing sharp increases in interest rates and compressing asset values (Sheng 2003). A liquidity crunch thus transforms into a solvency crisis. The process is self-reinforcing and continues until the initially small shock either forces the borrower into bankruptcy or is resolved by a lender of last resort.

Pettis argues (2001: xviii) that this mechanism is applicable not only to explaining crises of corporate borrowers in advanced capitalism, but is also relevant for a broader macroeconomic picture of a sovereign borrower in the case of an emerging market. Indeed, Russia's default on its debt in August 1998 became a direct trigger of a major financial debacle in the USA – the collapse of the Long Term Capital Management Fund (LTCM), discussed in greater detail in Chapter 8 of this book. In the chapters that follow, this book delves into the workings of the financial crises of the late 1990s and early 2000s. As argued here, the central role of speculation, debt and progressive illiquidity of financial structures in precipitating the crises implies that sovereign borrowers, much like individual institutions, can be subjected to liquidity runs and Minskyan dynamics of systemic financial fragility.

6[1]
The East Asian Crisis: A Minskyan View

There is no shortage of explanations for the series of crises that engulfed East Asia in 1997–1998. While there is no easy way to group up the various interpretations of what is now widely referred to as the 'Asian financial crisis (AFC)', three theories stand out. To many mainstream economists, the crisis represented a typical 'twin' financial crash, a dangerous cocktail of information asymmetries, financial market failures and, crucially, inept government interference in the workings of the markets. The Asian model of state *dirigisme* has proved deficient, prone to inherent cronyism and corruption. In essence therefore, the Asian financial crisis of 1997–1998 was a crisis, as a World Bank report concludes, of crony capitalism:

> [t]he interaction of these institutional weaknesses with international capital markets imperfections, and the use of inconsistent macroeconomic policies to manage surging capital inflows generated crucial vulnerabilities that laid the groundwork for the subsequent financial crises – and ensured that their consequences would be severe (World Bank 1998/99: 57).

On the opposite side of the analytical spectrum, heterodox economists trace the causes of the 1997/8 Asian collapse to unpredictable and unstable behaviour of the international financial markets. In these interpretations, the crisis contagion, regionally

---

1   I am indebted to Virot Ali for his research help and expertise on East Asia.

and internationally, is the result of the speculative attacks on the region's currencies and herd-like behaviour of foreign investors, most notably banks and hedge funds (Radelet and Sachs 1998; King 2001).

Finally, according to many radical critics, the crisis was rooted in the inner dynamics of the capitalist system itself: both in the East Asian national structures of accumulation, and in the trans-formations in the global market (Tabb 1998). In these interpreta-tions, the crisis was caused by a growing discrepancy between the East Asian principles of export-led growth and the changing com-petitive edge of the world market. The latter had been increasingly oriented towards the production of advanced, high-tech products and services, while Asian 'tigers' produced 'mass-market, banal, interchangeable goods' (Godement 1999: 8, 24; Johnson 1998). The emergence of China as a competitive power, the export of the Japanese property and stock market bubbles, the US–Japan deal to lower the value of the yen, the regional credit crunch – all weak-ened the structural coherence within and between the production and finance in the East Asian economies. The disjuncture was accentuated when the export-oriented sector, overproduced from within, failed to secure cheap and exchange-risk-free credits from without (Tabb 1998: 32; Sum 1999). Here, institutionalist accounts of the crises also point to the asymmetrical presence of the 'developmental state' across the region and the difficulties the political regimes had encountered when faced with the unfetter-ing forces of global capital. As a consequence of domestic liberal-isation policies, structurally weak economies have emerged across the region, and these have been distorted by speculative activities focussed on stock, but particularly property markets (Henderson 1999: 361–2).

What are we to make of such a plethora of views of one of the most devastating crises of finance in recent years? Considering all the factors at play – local, national, global, financial and non-financial – it is hardly surprising that the crisis cannot be traced back to one cause. There was, nonetheless, one identifiable chain of processes which, through various institutional channels, has set out the precondition for a devastating financial malaise. Namely, it was the cocktail of financial liberalisation, widened channels of investment and consequently, progressive illiquidity and over-indebtedness, that became the epicentre of the financial crises of 1997–1998.

In what follows, this part of the book offers a Minskyan reading of the crises in East Asia 1997–1998.

The rise of financial fragility in East Asia

Practically all of the problems facing the East Asian economies in 1997–1998 can be traced to the difficulties they have experienced in introducing liberal reforms of the financial sector throughout the 1980s–1990s (Arestis and Glickman 2002: 246). In East Asia the liberalisation process began in the late 1970s–mid-1980s, but was completed only in early to mid-1990s.[2] The reform included the deregulation of interest rates and the easing of reserve requirements on banks. In Korea, for example, lending interest rates were liberalised between 1991 and 1993, and marginal reserve requirements, which had been as high as 30% around 1990, were reduced to 7% in 1996. In addition, new policies promoted competition and entry of financial institutions: licenses for bank branches were relaxed in Indonesia and Malaysia in 1988–1989; restrictions on activities of foreign banks were eased in Korea and Thailand in 1991 and 1993, respectively (Chang and Velasco 1998: 28).

In all five economies of the region most affected by the crisis, South Korea, Indonesia, the Philippines, Malaysia and Thailand, the stability of currency pegs under favourable economic conditions and in the absence of the dollar appreciation ensured that foreign investments would be repaid at no exchange rate risk. The image of 'miracle Asia' shared by international investors contributed to over-estimation of the credibility of currency regimes. Both the IMF and government agencies encouraged financial deregulation further, and the presence of these optimistic lenders of last resort raised the spectre of moral-hazard whereby 'even if

---

2 As a measure of the degree of market deregulation, the authors contrast the share of assets owned by state-owned banks in the year prior to when liberalisation reforms were introduced, and the most recent year for which the information was available to them (Arestis and Glickman 2002: 246–7).

something goes wrong the agencies involved have an interest in bailing me out' (Allen 1999: 138).

During the 1990s across the region, expectations of future growth became plainly extravagant; capital was cheap, encouraging over-borrowing. Local currency and credit supplies expanded: supported by currency pegs and confident convertibility into the hard currencies, the spiral of investment soared perilously. Foreign lenders and domestic borrowers, free of governmental supervision and regulation, eagerly stretched out risky credit lines, exploiting international arbitrage opportunities and investing in the booming Asian asset and property markets (Arestis and Glickman 2002: 246; Chang and Velasco 1998; Grabel 2000). Eventually, capital inflows put upward pressure on the currency pegs. Yet the attention of the monetary authorities and financiers was focussed on the chances of preventing appreciation of the nominal exchange rate. As Robert Wade noted, nobody was thinking depreciation; and nobody was hedging against a currency sell off (Wade 1998: 697).

In a Minskyan analysis of the crises, it is important to note that lower reserve requirements allow the banking industry to maintain a lower degree of liquidity. In an emerging economy, this directly exacerbates the problem of international illiquidity and raises the possibility of financial runs. Likewise, the fostering of competition in the financial industry may deliver institutions that, while 'leaner and meaner, are less liquid'. Increased competition typically forces banks to offer more attractive terms (that is, higher interest rates) to depositors. Yet it also implies that the short-term liabilities of the banking system, in this case the face value of demand deposits, must increase, impairing international liquidity (Chang and Velasco 1998: 29; Wolfson 2000; Velasco 1999; Dymski 2003).

Across the East Asian region, much of the incoming finance was squandered on speculative property investment or the overexpansion of industrial capacity. At the same time, a fatal combination of pegged exchange rates and an over-hasty opening of economies to short-term foreign capital inflows, caused a surge of indebtedness to foreign banks. The resulting financial bubbles were inflated further by inadequate bank regulation and close, sometimes corrupt, relationship between banks, firms and governments, which encouraged borrowers and lenders to believe that governments would bail them out if need be (*The Economist*, 5 March 1998). The worsened international economic environment also contributed to the 1997–1998 crises. By mid-1997 the restrictive US dollar monetary policies and the imbalance between the dollar and Asian currencies had become critical (Allen 1999: 138–9; Sum 1999).

Since much of the Asian economic miracle was based on the high-savings-high investment model, a question naturally arises: Why did the East Asian economies, so highly praised for their levels of savings, have had to rely so heavily on external credit supply? In terms of macroeconomics, interest rates differentials are part of the explanation for Thailand and South Korea (Hirst and Thompson 1999: 143). Another, and perhaps a more salient factor, is the autonomous tendencies generated by domestic financial liberalisation. Since it was becoming more and more difficult to service past credit without accessing new loans, deregulated markets provided East Asian economies with a source of 'easy finance' when they found themselves over-stretched domestically. Foreign credit was also a way to fund risky activities, since the 'original' investors were getting increasingly suspicious (Chandrasekhar and Ghosh 1998).

As we have seen earlier in the book, the inability to service debts without accessing new loans is a central factor leading to the spread of Minskyan Ponzi finance schemes. In East Asia, the development of Ponzi debt pyramids was made worse because most incoming borrowings were foreign investments. The attraction of short-term capital in the form of trade credits was a relatively inexpensive source of international finance. But, as Stiglitz argues, when savings rates are already high, and when the funds are mis-allocated, the additional capital flows only exacerbate the fragility of the economy (Stiglitz 1998).

The opening of the East Asian financial markets invited short-term financial flows into the region, and with it, the associated dangers of a sudden reversal of capital flows had increased. Between 1996 and 1997, the inflow of capital was in order of $109 billion, or approximately 11% of the pre-crisis aggregate GDP of the five most affected countries. In 1996, Indonesia was the world's most popular destination of private foreign capital flow ($17.6 billion), Malaysia the fourth ($16 billion) and Thailand the sixth largest ($13 billion). Combined, net inflow of long-term debt, FDI and equity purchases, soared to more than $110 billion in 1996. Most of the funds were directed towards speculative activities, primarily the property sector. Banks and their clients, both at home and abroad were zealously seeking quick profits quickly as the wave of optimism unleashed by liberalisation gathered strength (Arestis and Glickman 2002: 248; Velasco 1999). The magnitude of net capital inflows combined with lack of foreign exchange reserves, meant that short-term foreign debts could easily translate into a full blown liquidity crisis. The combination of domestic liberalisation, the expansion of world capital markets and the spiral of financial innovation suggest that, while FDI and equity investment did not directly cause the Asian crisis, they added to the underlying weaknesses of some of the affected economies, as well as to the transmission of economic shocks which precipitated the crisis in Malaysia, Thailand, Korea, Indonesia and the Philippines (Bird and Milne 1999: 431; Bisigano 1999; Woodward 2001: 197).

By 1997, many institutional players began abandoning the region, 'but what converted a nervous departure into a catastrophic stampede was the speculative activity of the hedge funds and other arbitrageurs'. The previously optimistic market sentiments faded fast as concerns over the 'health' of the Thai political-economic system became serious, triggering the first attack on the Thai baht. The most spectacular assault occurred on 10 May 1997, when in one day hedge funds are said to have bet $10 billion against the baht (Bello *et al.* 2000: 15).

The Thai government tried in vain to defend the currency, but foreign exchange reserves were insufficient to counter the attacks, and on 2 July 1997 the baht was floated and immediately began to fall in value. The devaluation meant that that all the 'cheap' foreign currency debt suddenly became much costlier to service, since almost all of it was unhedged. Inevitably, too, the property bubble burst, leaving banks with a pyramid of bad debts. As concerns about the ability of firms to repay their borrowings grew, foreign capital dried up, foreign exchange reserves dwindled and the Thai government was forced to approach the IMF. By 1998, the subsequent wave of competitive devaluations throughout the region, imperfect market information and investor expectations, trade, financial and real linkages between the Asian economies have contributed to the contagious spread of the crisis.

The Thai crisis

The causes of Thai financial crisis have been discussed extensively (Siamwalla and Sopchokchai 1998; Hewison 2000; Lauridsen 1998), yet it is helpful to summarise the major views on the crisis preconditions. From the mid-1980s, the rapid growth of export-oriented industrialisation aided by the large FDI inflows (Phongpaijit and Baker 1995)[3] unleashed structural problems that in turn, undermined export competitiveness. First, the supply of some factors of production, particularly skilled labour and infrastructure, had been exhausted, which led to supply constraints and rising costs. Second, capital inflows eventually contributed to a Thai version of 'Dutch Disease' – over-inflating prices of non-tradable goods (especially property) relative to tradable goods, causing a misallocation of resources and real appreciation of the currency. This in turn, harmed the country's export niches (Warr 2005: 21–3).[4]

By the early 1990s, these difficulties caused a slowdown in the Thai economy, but the slowdown was disguised by financial liberalisation, deregulation and the introduction of capital account convertibility in 1991–1993. These liberalisation measures invited a further massive inflow of capital. Gross domestic investment rose above 40% of GDP, more than the economy could absorb. In the absence of any effective policies to govern these inflows, a large portion of the new investments consisted of short-term debt (portfolio holdings and bank loans), which, as the events of the summer of 1997 showed, was particularly vulnerable to swings in market sentiment.

In the context of decreasing export competitiveness and the structural distortion of tradable/non-tradable prices, the financial inflows

---

3   After the Plaza Accord of 1985 and the rise of the currencies of Japan and other East Asian Countries, East Asian capital migrated to Southeast Asia on a large scale. Capital of Japanese firms in Thailand rose from 2,836 million baht in 1986 to 38,755 million baht in 1991 (Phongpaijit and Baker 1995: 155).

4   Peter Warr estimates that the real exchange rate appreciated by 30% between 1988–1997. In Peter Warr, 'Boom, Bust and Beyond' in *Thailand Beyond Crisis*, Peter Warr (ed.), London: Routledge Curzon, 2005, pp. 21–3.

generated a sharp rise in domestic consumption, a similarly sharp decline in the current account balance, an asset price bubble and excessive investment in property and many domestically-oriented industries (steel, automobiles, petrochemicals, services). Thai policymakers failed to control those factors (either by de-pegging the baht from the dollar and thus sterilising the inflows, or by using fiscal and other measures to manipulate resource allocation). In fact, they compounded the crisis by their attempts to sustain the existing policy regimes. In an attempt to retain the currency peg, the government in effect, emptied the foreign exchange vaults, creating the Financial Institutions Development Fund (FIDF) as a stopgap fund,[5] which only allowed the financial industry to accumulate massive bad debts. Each group of factors had played a role in the lead-up to the crisis of 1997, affecting the financial markets, the labour sector, agriculture, industry and governmental regulation. What interests us in the discussion of financial fragility, is the state of the country's capital market and the financial system under the effects of financial liberalisation.

Until the early 1990s, there were two main sources of credit in Thailand: domestic commercial banks and foreign direct investments. The Thai government set out incentives to attract foreign investment into priority sectors, yet the strategy was relatively lax and a large part of financing took place outside the incentive framework. Foreign investment was driven more by investors' perceptions of Thailand and less by specific Thai government incentive schemes.[6] The Thai government, in turn, played a relatively minor

---

5 The Financial Institutions Development Fund (FIDF) was set up as a result of the financial crises in 1979 and in 1983 to rehabilitate ailing financial institutions. In the crisis of 1996–1997, the role of FIDF was expanded. By the time of the float, the FIDF had paid out 700 billion baht to assist ailing financial institutions. In Nukul Prachuabmoh, *Facts About the Economic Crisis* [In Thai], Bangkok: Ministry of Finance, 1998.

6 Here, it is notable that after 1975 the USA, previously the largest foreign investor in Thailand, regarded Thailand as unsafe and unpromising. Apart from oil companies and a few consumer goods vendors, very little Western investment flowed into Thailand until the mid-1990s. By contrast, Japan identifies Thailand as a site for offshore manufacture and cultivated its knowledge of and relations with Thailand over the long term. From 1973 onwards Japan was Thailand's largest source of FDI.

role in the allocation of domestic credit, but provided a protection for a cartel of Thai commercial banks. These banks emerged between the 1940s and 1960s, when Western banks had little interest in the country. From the 1950s onwards, having secured government protection against foreign competition, they amassed capital from the high saving propensities of the largely rural population. The banks prospered by spotting the sectors with high potential and directing finance to these sectors by investing in subsidiary companies, or supporting groups of associates (Akira 1989: 154–72). Five major banks became such a large factor in the whole economy that their decisions on credit allocation were critical not only for their own profits but to overall direction of the economy. These banks became the centres of sprawling business conglomerates. The government did not favour these corporate groups overtly, but the governmental machinery was susceptible to their great influences. Since the government encouraged foreign investors to enter into joint ventures with domestic partners, FDI also became part of the process of formation of financial-industrial conglomerates.

The mid-1980s was a watershed for the Thai economy. The oil crisis of the late 1970s led to a balance of payment crisis, devaluation and a banking shakeout in 1984–1986. Among several important institutional transformations that emerged out of the ensuing crisis in the Thai political economy,[7] financial liberalisation became the central factor to shape the international dimension of the country's political economy for most of the 1980s and 1990s.

Financial liberalisation and credit expansion in Thailand

In 1990, restrictions on convertibility were removed, and over the following three years, the Thai financial system was liberalised. In 1993, an offshore banking facility (BIBF) was set up to enable foreign banks to lend into the Thai market. In addition, rules and supervision arrangements in stock market were reformed to increase

---

7 The rise of technocratic governance, financial deregulation, a distancing of conglomerates from the policymaking process, and the emergence of new business groups. These economic changes ran in parallel with the expansion of democratic politics.

the attractiveness for foreign investors. The liberalisation of the capital account was one of the crucial measures to exacerbate the financial fragility of the country. Not only did it open the unprepared Thai financial market to sudden movements of capital within the economy; the dominant position of banks as credit providers had declined due to the ensuing proliferation of domestic credit institutions, as well as the newly available direct access of overseas financial markets to domestic borrowers. At the same time, there was an increase in the inflows from non-Japanese sources in East Asia and from the West. Over the following years, the dominant form of capital inflows changed from FDI to bank loans and portfolio investments. Capital was no longer scarce: between 1988 and 1990, net private inflows quadrupled and then maintained that new level until the final bubbly surge in 1995–1996.[8]

As a result of such explosion of new credit instruments and institutions, foreign debt accumulated rapidly. Between 1988 and 1996, the private sector's foreign debt increased almost ten times, from $7.8 billion to $73.7 billion. Unsurprisingly however, the opportunities for profitable investment did not expand in this rate. Much of the investment was poorly planned and was redundant, resulting in the falling rates of return, growing over-capacity in certain sectors and self-feeding bubbles in finance and real estate. By 1996, Thailand's total foreign debt amounted to $90.5 billion (half of the GDP), of which 81% was held by private sector.[9]

By 1994–1995, the financial fragility that had been breeding at the juncture of structural weaknesses of the export-led economy and overheating financial markets became tangible. First, challenged by the increased competition from countries such as China, Indonesia and Vietnam, export growth had slowed down, putting strains on the current account. Second, macroeconomic control of the economy had been weakening. Trying to maintain the currency peg in the context of capital account openness, the government had

---

8   Board of Investment, *A Guide to the Board of Investment*, Bangkok: The Office of the Board of Investment, 2000.

9   For further detail see, Phatra Research Institute, *The Way Out of Economic Crisis*.

effectively lost control over the tools of macroeconomic management. Previously, the government had reacted against overheating
by raising interest rates and restricting liquidity. After the financial
market was deregulated, policymakers attempted to continue
with the same policy line (Tivakul 1995). However, high interest
rates attracted capital inflows, particularly short-term funds, while
encouraging Thai firms to borrow at better rates offshore. Furthermore, although the property sector had been overpriced since 1994,
new foreign capital was still flowing in, inflating asset values
further.

Despite these unfolding problems, up until July 1997, the government did little to address the warning signs of crisis. From 1994,
the Bank of Thailand imposed some penalties on short-term
loan inflows, what brought the ratio of short-term debt down
from half to third of the total. The central bank also restricted
bank lending to the property market, but failed to extend any
similar restriction to financial companies. Key figures in the central
bank ruled out any more drastic policy change (Wibulsawasdi 1996).
Instead, the main direction of the policy was to silence the
bad news which extended ineffective bailouts, first the stock market,
then the finance companies (FIDF), and then the property sector
(PLMO).[10] Politically, the central bank's policy to defend the
baht was supported by financial institutions and other firms which
feared the impact of currency depreciation on their over-leveraged
balance sheets.

The political pressure of over-leveraged companies on the
central bank allowed the collapsing financial firms to muddle
through by borrowing more from the FIDF, in order to cover the
gap in their accounts caused by falling repayments on the one
side, and increasing withdrawals of foreign loans on the other.
The Fund tried to withstand the attacks of increasingly nervous
hedge funds and other currency speculators by injecting foreign
exchange into the market. As a result, by the end of June 1997,
the vaults of the central bank had been depleted, and the baht,

---

10   The Property Loan Management Office (PLMO) was established to
     take over viable property projects from bankrupt developers but the
     organisation never got off the ground.

doomed to collapse, was finally floated on July 2, 1997. Over the next 12 months, the currency bottomed to just under half of its pre-float value. Many over-indebted firms facing liquidity strains and ultimately, bankruptcy, stopped operating. With banks restricting credit further, most of the loans could not be serviced or repaid. This led to layoffs, stagnation in sales and debt deflation. As a result, the Thai economy tipped into downward spiral centred on debt deflation, which continued unabated for 18 months (Nidhiprabha 1998).

The crisis brought devastation for the Thai economy, and, to the shock of many, became the trigger of a massive contagion of financial fragility that had engulfed not only the neighbouring economies (Malaysia, Indonesia, Philippines, and South Korea) but also the far-way markets like Russia and Brazil. The domino effect of the Thai devaluation and the collapse of other Asian currencies and the financial markets led many to perceive the crisis as a reflection of the region's common problems, such as crony capitalism, over-valued currencies and inadequate implementation of financial reforms. In what follows, this chapter reviews the trajectory of the financial crisis in South Korea, in an attempt to illustrate how financial fragility and crisis was played out in a different institutional context.

The South Korean crisis

In its immediate aftermath, the financial crisis in South Korea was attributed to the country's crony capitalism and the failure of state-led development. Indeed, for four decades before the crisis, the Korean government had managed economic growth by allocating capital among big conglomerates (*chaebols*) and small and medium-size companies (Hunter *et al.* 1999: 127–33). The government controlled the allocation of finance by managing both the country's commercial banks and state-owned special banks. Since Korean bond and equity markets were relatively underdeveloped, it was the banking system that carried out most of financial intermediation. This nexus between the Korean government, *chaebols* and the banking industry resulted in inadequate financial supervision and regulation, and inefficient use of capital (Borensztein and Wha 1999).

The merchant banks, some of which were owned by chaebols, were regulated even more loosely than the commercial banks.[11] As a result of the chaebols' rapid expansion and weak financial supervision, the debt/equity ratio of the 30 major *chaebols* reached 500%.[12] In January 1997, Korea's second largest steelmaker, Hanbo Iron and Steel, was unable to honour its promissory notes, and was forced into bankruptcy. The collapse of other mid-size chaebols, such as Kia Motors, Jinro, and Haitai, followed in early 1997.

The weaknesses of the Korean financial and corporate sector had become obvious. On top of these difficulties, the speculative attack on the Thai baht exposed the merchant banks' liquidity problems. Since the early 1997, Korean merchant banks were experiencing problems over their short-term dollar loans. This problem of debt rollovers, although common throughout the region, was more profound in Korea than in any other East Asian economy. Korea's ratio of short-term foreign borrowing to foreign exchange reserves was 285%, far above the ratios of other Asian countries. For example, Thailand had a 135% ratio, and the Philippines 105% (Takatoshi 1999). One of the consequences of the Korean governmental policy to encourage domestic banks and corporations to borrow in foreign currencies for industrial development, were severe maturity and currency mismatches: The external borrowings, denominated in foreign currencies,[13] were mostly short term, while domestic loans were designated for long-term projects.

---

11   Korea's merchant banks specialise in short-term corporate lending and have different regulations and structures than commercial banks. Korean chaebols typically financed their capital expenditures by borrowing from commercial banks. However, they often financed their working capital by issuing promissory notes. When suppliers needed paying, they turned to merchant banks, which discounted the note and gave them funds. In the run up to the crisis, the merchant banks generated easy profits with their aggressive investments in Southeast Asia, Russia, and other emerging markets. These risky investments turned into a $3 billion loss by late 1997.

12   The debt/equity ratio in Taiwan is about 120%, and the norm for industrial countries is below 200%.

13   The maturity mismatches by Korean merchant banks were riskier than the mismatch of other deposit institutions because the number of depositors (foreign lenders) was smaller than in other types of deposit institutions, such as commercial banks.

As the crisis was unfolding in Thailand, Korean merchant banks' difficulties spread to commercial banks. The panic started. The Japanese banks, suffering from their lending to Southeast Asia and their growing share of non-performing domestic loans, were major players in a massive withdrawal of loans.[14] Japanese loans to Korea dropped from $21.9 billion at the end of 1996 to $8.8 billion by the end of 1997. In response, the Korean government announced on August 25, 1997, that it was committed to providing financial support to commercial and merchant banks and would ensure repayment of all Korean financial institutions' foreign debt. The markets, however, did not react to the promise. The inability to roll over short-term loans triggered runs in the Korean currency markets. The won began to fall, and by late November, lost 25% of its pre-crisis value.[15]

Interventions in the currency markets left less than $6 billion in Korea's foreign exchange reserves. On December 4, 1997, the IMF approved a $58.4 billion standby arrangement to support foreign exchange reserves. This rescue plan included a range of structural reforms in the financial and corporate sectors to address what the IMF believed to be the causes of the crisis. President-elect Dae-jung Kim approved the IMF package, and monetary policy was tightened. As a result, the overnight call rate shot up to 25% (Ha and Kim 2003: 60). The turbulence in the currency market quickly crushed the banking sector. By early 1998, most Korean commercial banks and other financial institutions were in technical default due to the severe depreciation and high interest rates. Damage to the economy was substantial: in the third quarter of 1998 real GDP shrank 8.1%, compared with the previous year.[16] In summary, the short-term debt rescheduling, the IMF bailout, and the collapse of import demand following a tight monetary policy stabilised the currency market, mainly by severely contracting domestic economic activity.

---

14   Japan's response supports the premise that Korea's liquidity problem was triggered by the contagion from Southeast Asian countries rather than by intrinsic problems within its economic structure.
15   The Bank of Korea. http://www.bok.or.kr/eng/index.jsp
16   Statistics, Korea. http://www.worldbank.org

Crisis contagion

What caused the contagion of the Thai crisis in 1997? The spread of volatility from Thailand across the region shows that the financial panic was at least as crucial in transmitting turbulence through the markets as were the structural linkages in real economies and trade (Lo 2001: 104). Moreover, according to most observers, financial channels amplified the impact of the crisis (Wade 1998: 703). By December 1996, the Asian-5 stock markets were already down from their peaks (Shiller 2000: 130). Hence the collapse of speculative bubbles in these countries preceded the crisis and was part of the ambience that produced the collapse. At the same time, the responsibility for the Asian crashes should not be confined to the international financial speculators. Although hedge funds launched the initial attack on the Thai baht in July 1997, the heaviest sellers of currencies soon after were local firms forced to repay dollar loans (and foreign banks unwilling to roll over), desperately trying to hedge their foreign exchange liabilities for fear that the currency might fall (*The Economist*, 5 March 1998). Also, King (2001) found that it was the Japanese commercial banks who triggered the crisis by reducing their exposure to the region. The nature and directions of capital flight following the Asian crisis also highlighted the role played by banks, rather than hedge funds, as the chief propagators of the crisis (Wincoop and Yi 2000).

Events in East Asia ignited a slow-burning fuse in the global credit system. Policymakers at various levels of the global economy scurried to find ways out, while the people of East Asia suffered from the extraordinary devastation (Warburton 2000: 263; Wolfson 2000: 370).

The crisis and its aftermath destroyed wealth on a massive scale and shot up absolute poverty. Poverty levels increased dramatically across the region, with Indonesia suffering the biggest increase. If prior to the crisis approximately one-fifth of the population of Indonesia were unable to fulfil their minimal needs, after the crisis this rose to 30–35% of the total population. With growth slowdown in 2000–2001, reductions in poverty levels came slower than anticipated. In the banking system alone, corporate loans equivalent to around half of one year's GDP went bad – a destruction of savings on a scale typically associated with a full-scale war (*The Economist*,

6 February 2003: 4). Across East Asia, because of the introduction of SAPs, social services have been shrunk; fees were introduced for previously publicly provided goods such as education and healthcare. In addition, subsidies for food, transport and other services were cut (Crotty and Dymski 2001: 90–1; Young 2002).

The turmoil in East Asia came as an enormous shock to the global economy, pulling Russia, Brazil and other emerging markets into a chain of financial crises. The 'tigers' had been performing exceptionally well for decades. Few whistleblowers aside (Young 1994, 1995), nobody foresaw such a massive outbreak. It is true that contrary to popular wisdom, the East Asian 'tigers' have been in trouble before. South Korea saw its GDP fall by 3% in 1980s; Indonesia and the Philippines suffered financial crises in 1983, Thailand in 1984, and Malaysia and Singapore in 1985. Taiwan had a banking crisis in 1989. Each time the future looked grim, but these countries eventually bounced back. In 1997, however, the 'tigers' have all caught a chill at the same time. Financial and trade linkages with each other magnified the region's problems. In addition, thanks to international capital liberalisation these economies now had much higher levels of foreign debt than a decade ago (Krugman 2000; *The Economist*, 5 March 1998).

This time around, in the context of deregulated and privatised credit, the financial collapse has been greatly aggravated by the availability of innovative trading techniques. Modern communications technology has made transmission of the current play of preferences much more rapid and widespread than in the past. The inability of derivative contracts to allow important players to hedge against the risks worsened the Asian crisis and its consequences (Dodd 2002; Kregel 1998a, b; 2001). Due to the self-fulfiling transmission mechanism of the financial system, the 'punishment' for the East Asian economies turned out to be much larger than the crime: the post-crisis currency devaluations were far greater than warranted by all calculation of fundamentals (Eatwell and Taylor 2000: 85; Toporowski 2001).

Therefore, three key elements associated with changes in the global financial sphere have contributed to the crisis: The liberalisation of domestic financial markets and the capital account; the inappropriate use of capital inflows for speculative investment; problems with resolving excessive corporate indebtedness.

Notably, as the book will show in the next chapter, similar problems brought about by economic liberalisation, financial speculation and excessive debt structures have also been at the epicentre of the Russian financial crisis of August 1998. Yet before we proceed to the analysis of the Russian case, it is instructive to take a closer look at the problem that lies at the epicentre of financial fragility, and which the Asian crisis has brought into light: namely, the issue of systemic illiquidity in a crisis.

Illiquidity and Minskyan debt deflation in East Asia[17]

The volume of the short-term foreign currency funding and the underdeveloped nature of the capital and money markets made the East Asian economies particularly vulnerable to an international liquidity squeeze. Many investments made by the East Asian conglomerates went into sectors with substantial global, regional and domestic overcapacities (Bevacqua 1998). These included real estate (Thailand, Malaysia, Indonesia); automobiles (Korea and Indonesia); steel (Korea), and semi-conductors (Korea and Malaysia). The value of the collateral on bank loans depended heavily on increase in asset prices. According to many Minskyan scholars, this was fragility in the making, with property companies and banks being vulnerable to a downturn in prices, a rise in interest rates or currency depreciation (Arestis and Glickman 2002: 248). Therefore, East Asia had been in the midst of a Minskyan cycle of systemic financial fragility, at the centre of which were short-term unhedged financing projects with long gestation lags, directed into sectors with overcapacities. Due to a mismatch in the term structures of their assets and foreign liabilities, the region's economies were vulnerable to an international liquidity crisis (Prakash 2001: 124; Kregel 1998b, 2001).

The combination of high interest rates and falling currencies put enormous pressure on domestic borrowers whose loans were denominated in dollars or yen. The number of speculative and Ponzi units rose. Borrowers trying to repay their dollar- or

---

17 This section relies, among other sources, on Woodward (2001) and Chang and Velasco (1998).

yen-denominated debts sold domestic currencies to obtain the necessary hard currency. But the very process of selling led to even more downward pressure on the currency values, increasing the burden on borrowers. Thus an interactive debt-deflation spiral got underway, in which the borrowers' actions to repay debt reduced the value of their currency and thus increased the burden of their debt, which led to further selling, etc. (Wolfson 2000; Kregel 1998b, 2001).

This chain of events fuelled the crisis in the ostensibly stable Asian 'tigers.' According to Chang and Velasco, although macroeconomic performance varied across the Asian-5, what the crisis-hit countries had in common was a striking situation of international illiquidity. This was evidenced by sharply rising ratios of hard currency short-term liabilities to liquid assets. As such, they were extremely vulnerable to a reversal of capital inflows, which unfolded in the second half of 1997. Bankruptcies and financial panic fed on itself, causing foreign creditors to call in loans and depositors to withdraw funds from banks; this exacerbated the illiquidity of domestic financial institutions and forced yet another round of costly asset liquidation and price deflation (Chang and Velasco 1998: 4; Wolfson 2002; Kregel 1998b).

'Financial systems that are internationally illiquid effectively live at the mercy of exogenous economic conditions and of the moods of depositors and creditors'. Acute illiquidity left East Asia vulnerable to a sharp reversal in the direction of capital flows. Net international inflows of capital to the Asian-5 fell dramatically to –$12 billion in 1997, from $93 billion in 1996. This fall in inflows is largely attributed to the behaviour of foreign banks, whose positions in the Asian-5 dropped by $21.3 billion in 1997 after increasing by $55.5 billion in 1996 (Chang and Velasco 1998: 37). In 1997 net capital outflow reached more than $100 billion – equivalent to 10% of the GDP of these countries (Wade 1998: 697). As investors fled the Asian financial markets and as exchange rates fell, the pressure on domestic borrowers to repay debts in hard currency intensified. As falling exchange rates increased the real value of debt repayment in hard currency, more borrowers were unable to meet debt payment commitments, and more loans were defaulted. Thus an interactive process developed that ultimately spiralled downward and intensified the crisis, a process akin to domestic debt-deflation (Wolfson 2002). As a direct consequence of the depleted liquidity channels, barter trade grew across the region:

> With national and corporate coffers from South Korea to Indonesia depleted of foreign exchange, companies are being offered everything from tea to textiles instead of cash. Southeast Asian leaders are calling for regional trading programs that avoid the mighty US dollar, or any other currency for that matter. Because credit is unavailable to many Asian companies, their trading partners and bankers are chasing ways to keep commerce flowing (WSJ 1998, in Saber 1999: 229).

Seen in this light of the Minskyan cycle of financial fragility, the Asian crisis is a story of unsustainable bubbles in asset prices, illiquidity and debt. Relatively cheap and ostensibly plentiful finance led to a surge of essentially speculative investment, mainly in the property market, as it exceeded profitable opportunities for productive investment. This speculative investment pushed asset prices up to unsustainable levels, and the acceptance by banks of property at inflated prices as collateral for their loans made the whole financial system vulnerable to the inevitable bursting of the bubble. According to Woodward, the oversupply of capital was, to a great extent, a result of large capital inflows on top of the region's unusually high savings rates. The result was very high investment as a proportion of GDP: 42% in China, 41% in Thailand and Malaysia, 38% in Korea and 32% in Indonesia in 1996. The average for the East Asia and Pacific region as a whole was 39% (Woodward 2001: 187–8).

The problem of corporate indebtedness was exacerbated by the fact that East Asian businesses are typically more leveraged than the Anglo-American ones: debt-equity ratios of 3:1 are common versus 1:1.5 in Anglo-American firms (Prakash 2001: 122). The ratio increased between mid-1994 and mid-1997 in every case except for Indonesia. At the end of 1996 the levels of short-term debt to reserves were substantially over 1 in Korea, Indonesia, and Thailand. This dynamics reflects a progressively fragile financial structure, in the sense that international reserves would not have been sufficient to repay the shorter debt had foreign banks decided not to roll it over. While the level of the short-term debt to reserves ratio was below one in Malaysia and the Philippines, it doubled between mid-1994 and mid-1997 (Chang and Velasco 1998: 25). The evidence, the authors argue, strongly indicates that the short-term external liabilities of the financial system were growing faster than its liquid international assets. This trend deteriorated international liquidity position of the Asian-5 to the point where a loss of confidence from foreign creditors could bring the financial system to a crisis.

One of the many lessons of the Asian crisis is that moderately weak (or even stable) fundamentals and small changes in exogenous circumstances can cause large swings in asset prices and economic activity. The magnifying mechanism lies in the financial system: its collapse causes costly asset liquidation and an unnecessarily large credit crunch (Chang and Velasco 1998: 2–3). Furthermore, the costs of the crisis are socialised: those who are innocent typically suffer together with those who have made the wrong investment decisions. Many private corporations, which would otherwise be profitable, are made insolvent because the devalued domestic currency has increased their debts to unsustainable levels, and previously surplus government budgets have to endure cuts in public expenditures to help pay off the foreign debt largely accumulated by the private sector (Liew 1998: 304; Eatwell and Taylor 2000; Taylor 1998).

Therefore, contrary to the assumptions of the traditional finance theory, and more in line with a Minskyan vision of international finance, events in East Asia in 1997–1998 have demonstrated that the crisis was the result of endogenous processes generated by private economic agents. Moreover, a Minskyan emphasis on illiquidity and indebtedness in the attempts to understand the dynamics of financial fragility highlights the fact that financial factors are at least as important as non-financial ones in determining what the range of fundamentals is in which self-fulfiling crashes can occur (Chang and Velasco 1998: 38–9). While the behaviour of real macroeconomic fundamentals was quite varied across Asia, progressive illiquidity was a common feature to all of the ones that eventually found themselves in a crisis. As the next chapter of this book shows, systemic illiquidity and the persistence of government debt were also acute in the next victim of the 1990s wave of fragile finance, Russia, where, as this book argues, the Minskyan dynamics of crisis constituted the epicentre of the 1998 default and economic collapse.

7
Ponzi Capitalism Russian-style

There is, of course, little doubt that post-Soviet Russia was even more remote from the capitalism of Minsky's time than East Asian 'tigers.' Large, structurally disrupted, ungoverned and saturated with corruption, the 1990s Russia had neither an established system of property rights, nor a functioning system of financial intermediation. The only segment of the economy where the cosmetic progress of 'transition' reforms was somehow notable was the financial market. It was the design of the Russian financial market, and its key players, that became the centre of a giant Ponzi pyramid that ultimately brought the era of the Yeltsin 'marketeering' of the 1990s to the end.

At the same time, it is difficult, if not impossible, to discuss the crisis that engulfed the Russian economy in 1998 as a mere financial crash in isolation from other aspects of the transition to capitalism. The malaise of August 1998 was triggered, in part, by endless political miscalculations, combined with economic disruptions and what can only be described as social catastrophe. The complexity and diversity of the causes of the crisis notwithstanding, in the eyes of many, August 1998 encapsulated the very essence of what the Russian road to capitalism of the 1990s was all about, and became a painful, and extremely costly, symbol of the era of 'primary accumulation' in Russia. Or of what can also be described as Russia's Ponzi capitalism in the age of financial globalisation. August 1998 became a watershed in the new Russia's history of capitalism, separating a period characterised by disembedded *laissez-faire* reforms of the Boris Yeltsin era, from the new reconfiguration of the Russian political economy under Vladimir Putin. Why did Russia experience such a severe crisis, and what can explain its timing?

Russian *laissez-faire*

Not unlike the experience of other emerging markets during the 1990s, Russia's 'transition' from communism to capitalism was based on three distinct and yet related, principles. First was the adoption of 'the market', domestically as well as internationally. Here, financial deregulation and privatisation became the two central drivers of the Russian transition towards a market economy (Aslund 2002: 77–8). Second was the aim to overcome the dependence of most economic, social and political institutions on centralised state command, provision and ideological guidance. Third was the creation of a new middle class – property owners and entrepreneurs – who would have recognised the material benefits of marketisation and thus would constitute the social base of neoliberal reforms (Gustafson 1999: 12; Aslund 2002: 405). The concurrent implementation of all three levels of *laissez-faire* reforms in an incredibly short time frame was a severe challenge to the Russian elites, while for ordinary Russians, the reforms of the early 1990s became a nightmare. The challenge of transformation also posed great difficulties to international economic institutions and foreign governments involved in the Russian reform. Despite the enthusiasm of Russia's young reformers and their Western advisers, the process met with countless difficulties, and, unsurprisingly, was ridden with mistakes and failures. One of the most glaring, and according to many observers, unforgivable of such miscalculations, was the government's fixation on the ubiquity of *the market* in the early 1990s.

An anecdote from that time captures the absurdity of the obsession of Yeltsin and his governments with a speedy 'transition' to capitalism. During a trip through Moscow on one sunny day, Yeltsin suddenly ordered his cortege to stop, and stepped out of his car to a sidewalk in one of the central avenues of Moscow. The sidewalk was busy with private traders, mostly 'babushkas' selling newspapers, beer and cigarettes. Yeltsin confronted a 10-year-old boy selling beer. Instead of inquiring why the boy was not at school, Yeltsin uttered: 'well-done son, you have entered the market!'

One of the greatest puzzles of the 1990s transformations, and specifically, behind the 1998 crisis, is that Russia's twisted and deeply disjointed socio-economic system had long been on a brink of a disaster. Yet despite the many signs of failure no one seemed able to time the crisis accurately. Cynthia Freeland explains the failure to predict the crisis by the very gradual, yet unstoppable, nature of the decline. 'The Russian financial demon was slow and cunning; consuming the country with a salami strategy sufficiently delicate that the government didn't realise what was happening until it was too late' (2000: 284). Partly, the crisis had been brewing for such a long time because all three stages of marketisation (mentioned above) had brought a measure of ostensible success. Sadly, none of the declared achievements in the conversion of the Russian economy from communism to capitalism was genuine. Economic and financial liberalisation were one-sided, aggravating the economic fragility and in fact, accelerating the social disintegration in the country. Despite the prominent rise of new owners of capital, there emerged no substitute for the welfare functions of the state which remained at the centre of the political-economic machine. While a new middle class had risen in Moscow, St. Petersburg and other large cities, much of the new wealth was illusionary, originating mainly in financial speculation.

Since the early 1990s, the Russian government had come to the view that the price mechanism of the free market would, in and by itself, be capable of mending the distortions of command economy and central planning. To achieve those aims, in January 1992, just weeks after Russian became a sovereign state again, the Gaidar government deregulated practically overnight the majority of prices of consumer goods, strictly controlled by the state for almost seven decades. Later during that year, foreign trade and financial markets were also freed from state control. This sequence of liberalisation reforms at such rapid pace would turn out to be a crucial policy mistake, since other segments of the economic system, such as domestic prices for raw materials, the rigid industrial complex inherited from the command economy, as well as the labour market, had been neglected.

The command economy relied on centralised, large-scale, vertical redistribution of resources. Abandoning this huge complex of rigid inter-enterprise links in the new market environment, leaving it far behind the changes in the financial sphere and foreign trade was a fundamental error of Russia's reformers and foreign advisors. The loss of production integrity and technological links, the prioritisation of export-oriented activities and operations in the financial markets contributed to the loss of the country's economic autonomy. The result was rapid decline in domestic production. By 1998, Russia imported over 50% of food products and up to 80% of domestic appliances. The disappearance of internal foundations of a stable economic growth aggravated the country's dependence on external economic factors and hence, made it particularly vulnerable to external shocks (Glaziev 1998: 246–9; Robinson 1999).

At the same time, like in many other cases of the implementation of SAPs in the emerging markets, financial deregulation in Russia was pushed through at the expense of institutional and structural balance (e.g. Bezemer 2001). Within weeks, the deregulation of prices resulted in hyperinflation. By late 1992, annual rate of inflation rates reached 2500%. Meanwhile, the liberalisation of trade and prices deepened the gulf between the non-financial economy and the financial sector. With no concrete improvements in the productivity in the manufacturing or services, nor in the efficiency of regulation and control, the deregulation of prices and finance contributed to the spread of financial fragility and speculation. While investment in new production and services remained in its embryonic stages, speculation on price differentials between wholesale and retail trade, investing in new financial services and in particular, short-term speculation on currency rates have become the principal business activities for the initial years of reform.

In 1992 for example, the domestic price of oil, still controlled by the state, stood at only 1% of the open-market world price; domestic prices of other commodities were approximately 10% of their world levels. Having identified a window of opportunity, managers of state companies bought oil, metals, and other commodities from the very state enterprises they controlled, acquired export licenses and quotas from corrupt officials, arranged political protection for themselves, and sold these commodities abroad at world prices (see Stiglitz 2002; Solnik 1998). According to Solnik (1998), two key groups of people drove this process of 'stealing the state'. Later they became Russia's most powerful businessmen and billionaires with global reach, the infamous oligarchs. The first group, particularly prominent in banking, included young men who set up commercial banks with the help of *Komsomol*[1] assets in the late 1980s. In the chaotic and opaque economic and political climate of 1986–1987, local *Komsomol* agents rushed to appropriate Party assets over which their committee could assert control. In the last years of the USSR, these Komsomol-related acquisitions became the first private businesses and cooperatives, making profits mostly on trade and small-scale production. After the collapse of the USSR, the cooperatives were converted into bigger firms and banks, thus becoming the first vehicle for the accumulation of capitals in Russia (e.g., Freeland 2000; Klebnikov 2000; Hoffman 2002).

The second large group of the first generation of new Russian capitalists were industrial managers of previously state companies who led the nomenklatura privatisation and asset striping. This group, sometimes known as 'red directors', secured control over state-owned assets that they managed at the expense of central state administrators (Solnik 1998: 124, 251). Thus, the Russian mass privatisation and deregulation of 1992–1994 in practice turned out to be a device for transforming political authority of the former nomenklatura into an economic power in the new privatised economy. The hyperinflationary conditions of the time reinforced this process, crowding small entrepreneurs and the ordinary public out of the market. For, as Bedirhanoglu notes, although 'mass privatisation enabled the workers and managers to become major stakeholders in about 70% of the privatised enterprises, given their inherited ability to control the labour collective, the managers became *de facto* owners of the enterprises without any formal responsibility' (Bedirhanoglu 2004: 24–5, Gray 1998).

Meanwhile the liberalisation of foreign trade and domestic retail markets encouraged a flood of cheap imports into the Russian markets. Still struggling with the legacy of planning and command, domestic producers were inefficient, and could not compete with imported goods. The Soviet-style inter-enterprise links had been broken down; the disruption in industrial networks was compounded by rapidly rising prices for inputs and supplies. While industrial producers struggled to survive, consumers could not

---

1 The young wing of the Communist party.

afford to buy final goods at market prices, since increases in real wages lagged drastically behind price inflation. The spiral of deteriorating conditions contributed further to the crisis in the industrial sector. The combination of apparent wealth accruing to the new groups of oligarchs and their cronies who were busy 'stealing the state,' and the rapid decline in real domestic production was only aggravated by the 'shock therapy' proposed by luminaries such as Jeffery Sachs, Balcerowicz, Gaidar and Chubais. Already in 1992, in the wake of first deregulation measures, Russia's GDP contracted by about 15% from its 1989 level.[2] The overall recession of the Russian economy and the contraction of output continued for eight years and were one of the deepest among all transition economies in Eastern Europe (Kolodko 2001).

Structurally, the reforms of the 1990s had split the Russian economy into two disjointed parts. One on one hand, there appeared to be a booming financial market, bringing huge profits, fast returns and, with the pegged rouble, a seemingly exchange rate risk-free environment. On the other hand, there was the rigid industrial complex, characterised by low profitability, acute illiquidity, uncertainty regarding ownership rights, shrinking demand and generally unfavourable market environment (Ershov 2000: 222). While employment in the banking and financial sector increased by 80% during the 1990s, employment in industry, in contrast, fell by 40%, construction by 44% and science by 54%. Total employment fell by over 20% (Clarke 2003). The imbalances between the two sectors – financial and the non-financial – were not a new phenomenon, and have been present since as early as the 1970s, when growing export incomes spurred the disassociation of the currency circuit from the domestic industry. Structural deficiencies are also inherent in the institutional structure of the post-command economy. But the 'shock without therapy' packages authorised by the IMF and advisors like Jeffrey Sachs made Russia's fate even worse.

Some analysts refer to the first half of the 1990s as a necessarily painful, but unavoidable, phase of Russia's 'primitive accumulation'

---

2 It was only in 1999 that the country's GDP reached a 1.5% increase over its 1989 level.

of capital, often likening this process, for example, to the formation of American capitalism in the late 19th century (Novodvorskaja 2000). The formation of American capitalism was similarly uneven, chaotic and poorly regulated by the state (Josephson 1934 [1962]). Yet having survived the black Friday of 1869 and the panic of crises of 1873–1874, by 1914 the USA had emerged as one of the world's military, political and industrial superpowers (Golub 2004). Could it be then, that the 1990s chaos in Russia was a necessary and unavoidable, 'moulding' period for the country's long-term trajectory of capitalist evolution?

This question will undoubtedly occupy economic historians and political economists for years to come. What interests us in the context of this book is the role that finance and financial liberalisation have played in the process of capitalist restructuring in Russia during the 1990s. While debates about Russia's idiosyncrasies abide (e.g., Gustafson 1999; Lane 2000; Reddaway and Glinski 2001), there is little doubt that finance and financial globalisation have played a leading role in setting the path for Russia's political-economic developments during the 1990s. The *laissez-faire* reforms of 1991–1992 brought many previously alien concepts, products and activities to the Russian life. One of the most noteworthy among the outcomes of these changes was a brand new sphere of the economy, unknown in the Soviet economy but central to capitalism: the financial sector.

During 1991–1992, capital requirements for a banking license were ridiculously low, while monitoring and supervision were at best, formal. As a result, in the early 1990s, the number of listed Russian banks went from fewer than 10 to over 2500. Like many other attributes of Russia's perilous journey into capitalism, these banks were often cosmetic, if not outright fraudulent, institutions. While Moscow and a few other big cities became besieged by expensive advertising campaigns of foreign banks and investment firms, most of the new banks were no more than money-changing boutiques, or former Soviet state banks with a new name, often with old Communist bureaucrats still in charge (Gustafson 1999). As this chapter details below, in the peculiar neoliberalism-driven context of the 1990s, financial liberalisation has given rise to a Ponzi-type system of finance in Russia. And Ponzi schemes, however grandiose and wide-reaching they can be, are bound to collapse.

Speculation, Ponzi finance and debt

Since Russia did not have an efficient network of either institutional control or property rights, the newly formed commercial banks could hardly lend to business enterprises. They tried to survive by establishing exclusive, long-term relations with the business sector and the politicians (Mennicken 2000: 46; Ledeneva 1998). The large Moscow banks, such as Oneximbank, SBS-Agro, Alfa Bank, Most Bank, were dominated by controlling stakes in large industrial enterprises. After Yeltsin issued a decree 'On measures governing holding companies activities'[3] in 1992, key banks were incorporated in the so-called Financial-Industrial Groups (FIGs) (Sakwa 2000: 200; Slavic Research Centre 1999).

In light of the new measures, ten holding companies including Gazprom, Russian United Energy System, YuKOS were authorised to conduct business. Gazprom developed into a FIG by establishing its own private banks such as Gazprombank and acquiring a share of the Imperial Bank (Slavic Research Centre 1999). As the financial system expanded, the well-connected banks capitalised on political support, with profitable assignments to manage the balances of state authorities, or to finance certain expenditures (Perotti 2002: 367). The capitalisation of individual banks was low, and the banking system was highly centralised. On the one hand, the high degree of centralisation of the banking system can make regulation and control easier. On the other hand, however, highly centralised banking systems contribute to the concentration of risk, making the whole system fragile and particularly susceptible to crisis. Given the lack of a coherent system of monitoring and control in Russia, the highly centralised banking structure became an easy channel of transmission of financial risk, contagion and thus, crisis. A few large banks controlled a sizeable portion of the economy through their widespread political connections and media holdings. As of July 1997, 20 largest banks controlled 57.8% of the total assets in the banking system. The 220 largest banks controlled 86.5% of total assets (Dubinin 1997).

Throughout the 1990s, around 80% of the Russian banks conducted business with dangerously low funding capital, creating

---

3　On November 16, 1992.

serious systemic risk. On the eve of the 1998 crisis for example, the overall volume of banking capital of all the Russian banks put together was around $10 billion, which was lower than a capital base of a single large American bank (Ershov 2000). Given the low capitalisation, combined with a large proportion of bad loans and low deposits, the banks were increasingly vulnerable to a shock or market distress. Russian regulators, legislators and prosecutors failed to keep pace with changes in the financial system, or have acted in ways that did not fairly balance the different interests involved. Legal loopholes, outdated laws, slow and contradictory decisions by the regulatory authorities have had little positive impact (Perotti 2002). Despite the ostensible boom in the financial sector, the Russian banking system was not able to provide reliable and timely clearing services and failed to become a serious channel of financial intermediation. In 1998, for instance, the Russian public still held an estimated $40 to $60 billion at home 'under the mattresses' and in jars, showing little confidence in the financial system. Only $2 to $3 billion were placed in the hands of the official banking system (Shmelev 1998).

During the first half of the 1990s, many new banks, especially the so-called 'pocket banks' of big FIGs, simply performed clearing functions, capital flight and whitewashing services for enterprises or shadowy organisations, gaining most of the profits by speculating on the rouble. Exploiting the high rates of inflation, banks could hold on to transfer payments for clients while earning on the float. The hyperinflationary climate also attracted many non-banking institutions which emerged under the names of 'investment funds' and 'financial companies', quickly developing into pure Ponzi pyramids. As Radaev (2000) details, new 'hedge' and 'investment' funds launched to attack on the unprepared Russian public, luring people into buying the 'shares' in their 'funds' on the promise of buying for 15 roubles today and selling them for 20 roubles tomorrow. The 'funds' were mere fronts for money-changing boutiques, there was nothing real behind their 'shares', yet the promise of easy and quick gains attracted thousands of Russians. The most infamous of such pyramids was the MMM fund, which collapsed scandalously in 1994, ripping its 'shareholders' of millions of roubles.

To make things worse, Russia became a member of the IMF in February 1992. After that date, the reform measures implemented by the government were conducted in close consultation with the IMF staff, and crucially, in accordance with the signals given by the IMF to other international forums, namely the World Bank, London and Paris Clubs, international credit rating agencies and private investors (Bedirhanoglu 2004: 23). The IMF advice to Russia can be summed up in two terms: monetary discipline and fiscal austerity. Both components of the IMF strategy exacerbated the structural problems in the Russian economy in the medium term and ultimately, precipitated the financial crisis of August 1998. Throughout the 1990s, the attention of the IMF and the World Bank was focussed on macroeconomic indicators. Although the Bank provided technical assistance on ways of targeting 'safety nets', little practical efforts were made to reform social expenditures apart from general fiscal austerity. For example, having registered a dramatic increase in poverty levels in Russia, the Commonwealth of Independent States (CIS) [formerly the USSR], Central and Southern Europe and the Baltics (CSB), the World Bank commented:

> ...positive developments largely explain the rise in inequality in CSB: rising returns on education, decompressing wages, and emerging returns to risk-taking and entrepreneurship. These forces are welcome despite the increase in inequality, because they signal that the market is now rewarding skills and effort, as in more mature market economies (World Bank 2002a: xiv).

The monetarist drive of the IMF programmes appeared to have helped Russia to stabilise its economy, the rouble and in particular, to tame the high inflation in 1992–1994. Much of the IFIs' guidance, technical advice and financial assistance proved, however, counterproductive and politically biased. As Aslund has observed, Western decision not to support Russian reforms in early 1992 doomed the whole of the CIS to hyperinflation, delayed stabilisation and perverted later reforms (Aslund 2002: 406–11). Joseph Stiglitz (2002) charges the Bretton Woods institutions with pushing Russia to privatise far too rapidly, to open up external trade and capital accounts, and thus effectively, with creating the chaotic environment conducive to 'asset stripping' and kleptocracy in Russia. Despite its concerns about the situation, the IMF did not push hard for higher social expenditures or a reform of the social safety net.

As one official later admitted, 'in general, the IMF felt that it could not, against a background of weak revenues, insist on achieving both a satisfactory overall fiscal balance and the protection of social expenditures' (Smee 2004). At the same time, the Fund's demands on Russia to maintain the schedule of debt repayments severely constrained the resources of the national budget available for social and welfare needs. In 1997 for instance, Russia spent only 52 billion roubles on education, health and social policy combined, while 118 billion roubles were directed to external and domestic debt repayments. In 1999, these figures stood at 88 and 288 billion roubles, respectively (IMF 2004b: Table 15). Altogether, between 1992 and 1999, the IMF disbursed $22.1 billion in loans to Russia. Notably, the most substantial amounts of money came in at most uncertain times of the Yeltsin presidency: the presidential campaign of 1995–1996 ($5.5 and $3.8 billion); and in the summer of 1998 ($6.2 billion), when the country was on the brink of a financial disaster (Smee 2004: 19).

In accordance with the IMF 'stabilisation packages' of the early 1990s, the Russian central bank was forced to cut back on monetary emission and raise interest rates. Following the radical monetary tightening of 1993–1995, the money supply shrank to as low as 15% of Russia's GDP (Commander and Mummsen 2000: 116). Although the main aim of monetary restriction was to tame hyperinflation, the unexpected side-effect of the policy became a profound, and largely uncontrollable, spread of the arrears throughout the country (e.g. Gaddy and Ickes 1998, 1999). From mid-1993, the system of Russian finance was locked in a vicious circle: the federal government experiencing a severe short-fall of incoming tax revenues, was running a growing deficit. As a result, regional administrations and budget enterprises, dependent on budget transfers, did not receive federal transfers and subsidies. To compound the problem, often when transfers did reach the regional administration, the money was diverted into the financial market, thus leaving regional enterprises without cash for months. In the words of David Woodruff,

> many Russian firms found that they had run up debts to suppliers that they were unable to repay... They started to rely on barter and various kinds of IOUs to maintain production networks. As the barter trade expanded, so too did debts for taxes. Local governments, faced with the revenue shortage, developed

mechanisms for in-kind taxation. As the vast fiscal implications of barter became clear, the federal government too, found itself forced to concede to the use of alternative means of payment of taxes, which it began to do from the fall of 1994. By 1996–97, non-cash tax collections accounted for around 40 percent of federal revenues and over 50 percent of provincial budgets (Woodruff 2000: 461–2).

By August 1998, the share of barter in total transactions had reached its peak of 54%; the rate of demonetisation in local and regional budgets was even higher (Woodruff 1999, 2000). Naturally, the demonetisation of the economy entailed severe social costs. As long as industrial enterprises were kept on the margin of bankruptcy, workers were not laid off, but they were not paid either. As of January 1998, the average industrial worker was owed nearly two months of back wages, and in agriculture the average delay was more than four months (Ershov 2000; Aslund 2002; Bedirhanoglu 2004: 31).

In the context of deepening economic recession, rising unemployment and prices, unpaid wages and pensions, the social costs of Russia's neoliberal transition became the most traumatic outcomes of the *laissez-faire* reforms. Comparisons with the late Soviet years, when the effects of a deep structural crisis had already been apparent, are staggering. In the last years of the USSR, its GDP per capita was ranked as number 43 in the world. In 2000, Russia ranked at number 135. In the ten years between 1989 and 1999, Russian GDP per capita was halved: from $2554 to $1249. If in 1989, around 11.5% of the population lived below poverty line; in 1999, the figure rose to more than 35% (Buiter 2000: 610–11; World Bank 2002a: 8–9). The social costs of the policy of marketisation – poverty and unemployment – unknown in Soviet Russia, along with humanitarian crises, environmental catastrophes and civil conflicts, became the most tragic outcomes of the Yeltsin reforms, which many scholars view as synonymous to 'market bolshevism' (Reddaway and Glinski 2001), or even genocide (Glaziev 2000).

The crisis

Notwithstanding the lingering socio-economic and political crises, Russia in 1997 was a world apart from Russia of 1991–1992. Moscow and other large cities were booming with investment, new financial companies and banks were hiring new staff, the country became more open to the global economy, and even in the area of policy reform, there was some progress to report. By 1997, the economy seemed to have overcome the macroeconomic instability of the early 1990s, although by ambiguous means. After five years of struggling with hyperinflation, the government succeeded in stabilising price levels (inflation was down to 11%) and the rouble exchange rate (pegged at around 6 roubles per dollar). The IMF, having registered a firm drop in inflation, supported a $10 billion restructuring programme (Blustein 2003) and praised the government's policies.

At the same time, in 1997 the federal government spending amounted to 18.3% of GDP, while revenues were only 10.8% of GDP, implying (on the IMF's accounting definitions) a deficit of 7.5% of GDP. Cash revenues were 9.1% of GDP, the rest being collected in the form of non-cash arrangements featuring the mutual clearance of tax and spending arrears (Fisher 1998).[4] In retrospect, it seems that in their search for cash inflows into the budget, the Russian reformers prioritised short-term stability at the expense of long-term structural and institutional balance. Unable either to monetise the deficit (i.e., print the roubles), or to collect enough taxes, the government opted for a third option: to borrow. The desperate need for new money, and the chosen technique of obtaining the finance, quickly drew the Russian state into a giant Ponzi pyramid scheme.

The Russian Ponzi game

Designed by Anatoly Chubais, the government debt market was set up in February 1993 (Klebnikov 2000: 279). Since then, the steady sale of high-yield government short-term bonds (GKOs) and long-term bonds (OFZs) became the major source of earnings for the Ministry of Finance, and of the federal budget revenue (Glaziev 1998). The hole in the federal budget was large and chronic, and given the constraints imposed by the rouble peg and IMF stabilisation programme, the deficit pushed the government to issue the debt paper continually. As a result, every Wednesday, new GKOs were offered to the eagerly awaiting market players.

---

4 http://www.imf.org/external/np/speeches/1998/010998.htm

In its early stages, the scheme operated within the frame of the Russian domestic financial system: the issuer of the obligations was the government, while the key purchasers of these bonds were young Russian financial institutions and banks, attracted by the extraordinarily high GKO yields. While initially, the debt market was open only to institutions resident in Russia, in February 1994 the central bank allowed non-residents to hold up to 10% of the nominal volume of the GKO issue. As the government's need for cash grew more urgent, the central bank deregulated the market further, making it easier for foreign buyers to participate in the GKO-OFZ auctions and repatriate profits. Eventually in January 1998, pressed for cash, the government removed all restrictions on foreign participation in the GKO market, thus liberalising it completely. Since the profits gained on GKO auctions were mostly re-invested into the financial market, and since there was no economic progress underpinning the growing yields on the commercial paper, the market which was initially envisaged as a temporary channel for additional funds into the budget quickly developed into a Ponzi scheme.

As noted above, in the inflationary climate of the early 1990s, the main and most profitable source of profits for financial companies were operations with foreign exchange: taking rouble deposits, converting them into dollars and gambling on exchange rate fluctuations. Yet with the introduction of the currency peg in 1995, inflation rates and the amplitude of exchange rate fluctuations decreased significantly, and banks' investment into foreign currencies became less attractive (Rud'ko-Selivanov 1998: 81). Thus from mid-1990s, commercial banks and investment companies switched to GKO-OFZ trade as a major source of profits (Ershov 2000). To those who knew how to play the game, the GKO scheme brought fantastic returns: profits of up to 120%, and higher returns were not unusual. On average, for every dollar invested into the Ponzi pyramid investors would get 18–36 dollars back.

In 1996, the investor euphoria was fuelled further. Boris Yeltsin won the 1996 presidential elections, thus signalling to the world that Russia stands firm on the road to the market and is not going back to the dark ages of its Communist past. By autumn 1996, Russia was engulfed in the emerging market financial fever. As Paul Blustein writes, that year, portfolio investment into the country surged to \$4.4 billion (up from a mere \$21 million in 1994 and minus \$378 million in 1993).[5] According to Blustein, the inflow of finance roughly equalled 10% of Russia's GDP, which stood at \$450 billion. Hundreds of newly emerged Russia-dedicated mutual funds swarm in foreign cash as the stock market, which began 1997 with its main index below 200, peaked at 571 in October. 'Having braved Russia's rickety air transport, western investment bankers developed a great appetite for risk by making syndicated loans and snapping up the bonds of local governments' (Blustein 2003: 245–6). In autumn 1996, Russia also received credit ratings from major world credit agencies, attracting more interest from foreign, and therefore, Russian, investors.[6]

Thus the GKO frenzy, and its key pillars – the fixed rouble rate and relatively low inflation – came to dominate the Russian political economy during the late years of the Yeltsin reign. Unwilling to compromise low inflation and stable (although overvalued) rouble, and unable to resolve the crisis in the economic reform, the government had no recourse but putting all its hopes and efforts into sustaining the GKO market turnover. By June 1996, the stock of T-bills alone surpassed the sum total of household deposits in the Russian financial system. By June 1997, the stock of GKOs and OFZs had surpassed all federal revenue. The Russian financial sector was, in effect, constructed around a vast GKO pyramid.

The debt pyramid was a classical Ponzi-scheme game. Russia was not alone in resorting to such senseless Ponzi schemes. Throughout the 1990s, Ponzi pyramids became common in all transition economies (Radaev 2000; Bezemer 2001); yet in Russia, Ponzi mentality spread not only through numerous private investment funds of dubious origin but became, in contrast to other transition economies, a key instrument of governmental economic policy. The sales of GKOs were backed up by negative rates of economic growth and shrinking budgetary revenues, an unsustainable practice as the

---

5 Data from the Central Bank of Russia.
6 In fall of 1996 major world rating agencies gave a new credit rating to Russia (Moody's – BA2, Standard & Poor – BB–, 1BCA – BB+) which implies solvency of the borrower while current political and economic stability is maintained. Similar ratings were enjoyed by Mexico and Hungary. http://www.fipc.ru/fipc/arch/whyrussia95.html

Russian policymakers must have known. On various short-term GKOs the government guaranteed fantastic returns – from 50 to over 200% per annum (Shmelev 1998: 6–7). As a result, all free (and not free) liquidity abandoned the real economy and poured into the GKO pyramid: who would invest for the average 5–10% profits in the real sector? The infamous Ponzi units such as *MMM, Chara, Khoper-Invest* stayed afloat for two years; the Russian government managed to do so for four years.

At the level of the macroeconomy, the growth of the GKO market substituted domestic debt finance for money creation, prompting a drastic increase in the domestic indebtedness. Between 1995 and mid-1998, the stock of outstanding Treasury bills jumped from 4 to 17% of the GDP (Commander and Mummsen 2000: 117). The state became the major debtor in the economy: by 1998, total outstanding debt of the Russian government stood at $218 billion, or 50% of GDP. By the end of 1998, it reached $242 billion, or 77% of GDP. In 1997, external indebtedness stood at $123.5 billion; by 1998 it has risen to $145.5 billion (Kheifets 2001). With its hands tied up by monetary restriction and the need to pay interest on the outstanding GKOs, the government started to suspend transfer payments and financing to enterprises. Thus the growing state indebtedness was paralleled by the spread of payment arrears and deteriorating tax collections.

The debt pyramid had far-reaching implications for the Russian economy and the financial system. The steady sale of forward dollar contracts to foreigners by the Russian banks in 1997 built up a huge exposure to contingent dollar liabilities. According to Perotti, the exposure represented up to 20 times of banks' (largely imaginary) capital. This allowed them to capture the interest rate differential without any real investment, nor any obligation they planned to honour. Thus effectively, Russian banks were bankrupt even before the crisis; they were pure legal fictions used primarily as conducts of capital flight, leveraging their speculation bets with borrowed funds (Perotti 2002). As revealed by one 'diligence' review conducted by the Russian central bank in 1998, out of the 18 large Moscow-based banks[7] reviewed, nearly all were deeply insolvent. Fifteen of the

---

7 Representing almost half of the privately owned banking system.

18 banks had negative net worth. Several of these banks had leverage ratios in excess of minus 400%. Only three banks actually had positive capital (Alexander *et al.* 2000: 6–7).

The Ponzi scheme became a shield that disguised many concomitant crises in the Russian economy. The most destructive impact of the growing pyramid had been the deepening gulf between Russia's financial and real economies and therefore, deepening financial fragility. The dangerously high pyramid of government debt disguised progressively growing illiquidity of the economy, both internally (as reflected in the growth of non-payments and barterisation) and externally (as seen in the highly overvalued rouble rate and rapidly diminishing hard currency reserves of the central bank). In reality, for about four years, the federal budget had been built on two fragile pillars: the GKO pyramid, including its dollar component; and the direct assistance of some external partners and international financial institutions (Perotti 2002; Shmelev 1998; Robinson 1999).

Fiscal austerity – i.e., the control of federal budget outflows – so vehemently demanded by the IMF advisers, in practice amounted to a series of sequestrations that were in turn linked to large accumulations of government arrears, over 5% of GDP by early 1998. Non-payments on the part of the government in turn, led to the proliferation of tax and budget offsets, as well as the widespread acceptance of settlements in kind. By 1996–1997, non-cash tax collections accounted for around 40% of federal revenues and over 50% of regional budgets. By 1998, only about 20% of the economy was serviced with cash; whereas the other 80% relied on barter and various kinds of monetary surrogates and IOUs. Blinded by the need to maintain the cash inflow into the budget, the Russian government was getting deeper and deeper into the trap of financial fragility and debt. The level of indebtedness inside the Russian banking system also indicated a systemically fragile situation. According to some estimates, the proportion of bad loans in bank credit amounted to 30% in 1996–1997, the share growing over time (Chapman and Mulino 2001: 14).

The rouble peg, in turn, imposed its own constraints on the sustainability of the financial boom. The rouble-dollar exchange rate band attracted foreign buyers into the GKO market and was one of the few achievements Yeltsin and his governments could boast. Yet in the context of falling oil prices at the world markets,[8] the currency peg became the key vehicle for transmitting the crisis into the Russian economy. In late 1997, refinancing the booming stock of short-term debt became extremely difficult: the fall of world oil prices hit Russian export revenues and hence foreign exchange reserves of the central bank; while the repercussions of the Asian crisis unnerved international investors. In light of market turbulence and especially following the collapse of the East Asian economies in late 1997, the government opened the market to foreign participants and thus shifted its borrowing abroad to push domestic yields lower (Sutela 1998: 110). Following the opening of the GKO market to non-residents in early 1998, the GKO market shares were split as follows: Russian commercial banks held around 30% of the market; Sberbank controlled 25%; central bank – 15%; foreign investors – 30%.[9] However in late 1997, foreign investors, increasingly anxious about the fate of emerging markets, began to abandon the Russian market, putting pressures on the rouble peg, and therefore on the vaults of the central bank. As a result of the massive sell-off, the official foreign reserves of the Russian central bank fell from $24.6 billion in mid-1997 to $12.7 billion in the third quarter of 1998.

As foreign investors were withdrawing their money, financial fragility in Russia, both domestically and internationally, became acute. Portfolio inflows dropped from their peak of $8.2 billion in 1997, down to $1 billion by the middle of 1998 and to a mere $0.7 billion by the end of the year. In the first quarter of 1998, Russia's trade balance fell to a deficit of $1.5 billion; the year before it was $3.9 billion in surplus (Blustein 2003: 248). A new government, headed by a young prime minister, Sergey Kirienko, was brought in March 1998 on a mandate to restore stability. Kirienko's few reforms went unimplemented, tax collection failed to improve and banks' coffers were emptied (Perotti 2002: 373). Concerns about the sustainability of the rouble peg mounted, and capital flight continued apace. During June alone, the central bank's reserves had dwindled by more than $3 billion as investors swapped their roubles holdings for dollars (Blustein 2003: 255).

---

8 The world price for Urals crude dropped from $18 a barrel in early 1997 to approximately $15 at the year of the year (Freeland 2000: 285).
9 Figures for the summer of 1998 (*Source*: Aton Capital Group, 4 September 1998).

Amidst the panic, the government made two desperate attempts to keep the Ponzi game up. First, in January 1998, when the GKO debt pyramid had outgrown the internal financing facilities, all restrictions on capital expatriation were removed and foreign participants were encouraged to buy state securities. Estimates at the time put the share of foreign investors in the GKO pyramid at around 30–32% for August 1998. In reality, if we include assets employed by the foreign banks resident in Russia and hence operating like Russian banks, the share of foreign participation in the GKO pyramid was closer to 50%. By mid-1998, foreign institutions owned around one-third of the government securities market and two-thirds of the equities market. The increased dependence of the Russian market on foreigners was a direct consequence of the deregulation of the financial market in 1996–1998 (Zagashvili 1999: 24–5).

The liberalisation of the financial market and the withdrawal of the Russian central bank from intervention in the foreign exchange operations aggravated the fragility of the Russian banking sector. In practice, Russian banks could do little more than follow the market trend formed by the foreign investors' sentiments (Ershov 2000: 294–5). Foreign sentiments, in turn, were not good at all in 1998. Out of the three regions of emerging economies – Latin America, East Asia and Eastern Europe – Russia probably featured least favourably. The shallowness of the Russian financial market implied an acute vulnerability to even small fluctuations in capital movements. Given the low capitalisation of the Russian banking and financial sectors, it was foreign operators who provided the main support to the GKO-OFZ market. Any, however small, deviation from the dominant trend in prices immediately impacted upon general market indices. The speculative character of the majority of capitals on the Russian financial market rendered it especially unstable and increased its dependence on foreign markets.

In this climate of domestic financial fragility, the liberalisation of the GKO market was a decisive policy mistake: it severely restricted the opportunities for debt management and restructuring. Fearing the possibility of rouble devaluation, foreign investors, seemingly unaware of the deep-seated fragility of the Russian banking system and near-bankruptcies of many key institutions,[10] had hedged their investments

---

10 Even the largest banks – SBS Agro, Menaptep, Imperial and Inkombank would default in August 1998.

with the Russian banks. Thus the GKO debt was effectively dollarised by hedging: when a US bank went in and purchased GKOs, it offset its rouble exposure through dollar hedge positions with several big Russian banks. Concurrently, the debt pyramid was getting higher: by mid-1998, the GKO market turnover had surpassed 300 billion roubles; while the existing money mass (M2) stood only at 370 billion roubles. If in 1994 internal sources represented 90% of the federal budget deficit financing, by 1998 the debt was financed almost entirely from external borrowings. Such heavy bias towards external financing channels started to distress both individual banks' portfolios, and the country's levels of indebtedness as a whole. With the growing portion of the debt financed through foreign borrowings, a collapse of the pyramid was inevitable, if unpredictable as to timing (Ericson 1999; Ershov 2000: 289; Federal Council 1999). By the summer of 1998, the total debt of the Russian government represented 77% of the country's GDP. With dwindling hard currency reserves, and no tangible inflows of cash, Russia was literally living on borrowed time.

In July 1998, the government made a second, and, it would turn out, last fruitless attempt to secure additional cash inflow into its Ponzi scheme. Desperate for help, Moscow turned to the IFIs for a loan. Under a severe pressure from the Clinton administration, the IMF reluctantly assembled a $22 billion rescue package for Russia. The deal was finalised on July 13th, with the first disbursement of $4.8 billion. Encouraged by Western support, president Yeltsin, largely detached from the events at the market, repeatedly reassured the public that 'there will be no devaluation of the rouble'.

However, despite the efforts to calm the storm, the IMF rescue package failed. There are many reasons behind the failure. Joseph Stiglitz (2002) cites the highly overvalued rouble peg and structural crisis as chief among them; others point to market pressures and herd-like mentality of investors who got particularly anxious after George Soros published a letter in *Financial Times*, calling for rouble devaluation. Moreover, there are speculations that part of the IMF July loan itself ended up in foreign bank accounts of members of the Russian government (Federal Council 1999). Since 1998, the 'vanishing billions' of the IMF credits have been the subject of investigations by the FBI and Swiss officials linked to the larger Bank of New York scandal involving the alleged laundering of up to

$10 billion in dirty Russian money (Whittle 2000). Investigators suspect that elaborate money laundering schemes, involving foreign bank and offshore accounts, were constructed with the assistance of Russian oligarchic structures such as Menatep and Yukos (World Bank 1999).

With no sources of cash, the market continued to crumble. 'Russian stocks, the highest of flyers among emerging market investments a year earlier, had fallen 48% in the four weeks after the IMF programme's approval. Investors were dumping Russian treasury bills like hot potatoes, and the government was forced to cancel its weekly sales of GKOs because it could not pay the 100 plus % interest rates the markets would have demanded. 'The turmoil threatened to undo one of the most cherished accomplishments of Yeltsin's regime, the stability of the rouble against the US dollar' (Blustein 2003: 235). Still however, despite the stupefying size of the Ponzi scheme, like in East Asia a year earlier, few expected a large-scale financial collapse: bond markets had envisioned devaluation, but not a complete default (Perotti 2002: 373).

According to Freeland (2000: 304), the decision to repudiate on the debt and to devalue the rouble was taken by Kirienko, Dubinin, Alexanshenko, Chubais and Gaidar over the weekend of 14–16th of August. Boris Yeltsin, away at his dacha retreat near Moscow, was not involved in the discussions, and was informed only after the technical questions of the default had been finalised. After weighting the options available to them, the team opted to default on the government's domestic debt and to restructure the terms of foreign indebtedness. With controlled devaluation and some breathing space for interest repayments, the government could, in principle, control the financial stability. The problem, however, was that this scenario implied ripping off both domestic and foreign investors; if implemented, Russia's reputation as a capitalist economy and a responsible participant in the global financial game would be severely damaged. In the words of Gaidar himself, the path of action the young reformers took was a 'bastardly, disgusting scenario' (Freeland 2000: 305). Crucially, the plan angered the oligarchs who had been calling for devaluation for months. In the end, the scheme was tweaked so that the government ordered a moratorium on debt payment by commercial banks to their creditors (Freeland 2000: 305–6, 309).

On Monday morning of August 17th 1998, Kirienko announced the final scheme: the government relaxed the currency peg from 6 to 9.5 roubles per dollar, froze all domestic bonds maturing to the end of the year, thus defaulting on $40 billion, one-third of which was owned by foreign investors; and imposed a moratorium on the payments of all foreign debts by Russian companies and the public (Freeland 2000: 309; also Buchs 1999; IMF 2002a: 69). The giant Russian Ponzi game was over.

A Minskyan crisis?

Economic and social scientists continue to debate the nature, causes and lessons of the 1997–1998 crises. Yet if we want to inquire into the processes and mechanisms that drove the economies into crises, it is the framework that Hyman Minsky suggested some 30 years ago that proves to be most revealing. Under the regime of pegged exchange rates, the construction of speculative and Ponzi pyramids (bad lending practices in East Asia; government debt pyramid in Russia), led to acute crises of illiquidity, ultimately bringing private firms in East Asia and the Russian government to insolvency.

In the analyses of the political economy of the Russian crisis of 1998, it is difficult to isolate a single factor that accounted for the devastating economic collapse. On the one hand, considering the complexity of the problems inherited from the USSR, as well as difficulties in implementing the reforms during the 1990s, it seems that it was only a matter of time before problems in the real economy manifested themselves in the financial sphere. On the other hand, in a 'disjuncture framework', the 1998 crisis was largely a consequence of the disjointed development of the booming financial markets and the 'real' economy of industrial production, stagnating agriculture and services, rather than a mere outcome of progressive budget deterioration, as some economists claim (e.g., Aslund 2002).

Many of the causes of the 1998 crisis lay in the financial sphere. The underdeveloped state of the financial market and the banking system; the lack of legal norms and regulatory oversight; pervasive cronyism and corruption; misapplication of the monetary restriction, all made the Russian financial market extremely vulnerable to fluctuating prices, volumes of trade and exchange rate risk. With banks engaged mostly in GKO and foreign exchange trading, monetary tightening unleashed a vicious circle: the banking sector did not advance credit to the real economy; the real sector, in turn, lacking liquidity, technology and investment, deteriorated fast. This, in turn, led to the growth of overdue payments in the structure of banks' balance sheets, and the fall in overall banks' liquidity, which further diminished the banks' investment potential (Rud'ko-Selivanov 1998: 80).

Internationally, the Russian economy was extremely vulnerable to speculative fevers and changes in foreign sentiment. The reforms of 1991–1992 opened Russian markets prematurely and prioritised the liberalisation of finance and trade over the progress of reform in the real economy. Lacking any internal foundations of economic stability and growth, Russia's integration into global capitalism relied almost exclusively on the financial sector. Here, finance, just as it does elsewhere, provided Russia with an attractive window of opportunity to flirt with foreign investors and international financial institutions; but it did this at a high price of systemic illiquidity and a *de facto* debt trap.

It would be a mistake to overlook the role of the state policies in the 1990s transition generally, and in the 1998 crisis in particular. Since the early 1990s, the succession of Russian governments had committed numerous errors and miscalculations, many of which were overlooked, or sometimes even encouraged, by foreign advisors and the IFIs. And yet seen in the context of the globalising market of speculative capital, driven by private actors and the process of financial innovation, the Russian crisis clearly would not have been so severe had it not occurred in the country open to global markets and financial capital.

In this respect, despite the many idiosyncrasies of the Russian socio-economic and political system that continue to baffle social scientists to this date, the August crisis of 1998 is far from being unique. In its dynamics, it was similar to the Asian collapse that preceded it a year ago; bewilderingly, as we will see later, the centrality of Ponzi finance in the August 1998 crisis also makes its dynamics close to the subsequent crises in advanced markets, such as the crash of the LTCM fund in 1998, or the dotcom bubble burst in 2000–2001. With these considerations in mind, it is possible to identify three major factors that shaped the nature of the 1997–1998 crises in emerging markets: the negative consequences of financial liberalisation, reinforced by the regimes of currency pegs; progressive illiquidity of domestic economies, amplified by the effects of financial innovation; and the levels, and nature, of incurred indebtedness.

8
Ponzi Finance Goes Global

Each one of the crises analysed in the previous chapters was unique in many respects. It is important, however, to try and understand why each of these crises spread so fast throughout the entire financial system. Orthodox theories tend to see each crisis in isolation, as specific to a country and attributed mostly to human error and/or market shocks. Alternative explanations, originating in the 'disjuncture' paradigm of financial capitalism view the crises as symptoms of the fissure between the overblown financial market and the stagnating 'real' economy. A Minskyan framework provides an insight into the inner mechanisms of financial fragility in crisis-hit countries, while allowing for important institutional and structural differences between them.

It would be naïve of me to claim that financial crisis today is necessarily a Minsky-type one. Minsky himself recognised that financial fragility has many causes, structural and idiosyncratic. In many cases, the economic and political circumstances in the run-up to the crisis are so complex and uncertain that a comprehensive analysis of all the precipitating factors is only possible retrospectively, *after* the collapse, if at all. Yet at the same time, the central role of financial speculation, reckless borrowing and especially, arising progressive illiquidity of credit pyramids in the recent wave of crises, have exposed the limits of conventional economics in understanding financial fragility and crisis management.

Financial crisis has become a veritable curse of the 1990s. Volatility and shocks no longer discriminate between the traditionally 'problematic' emerging market economies, and the highly sophisticated financial systems of advanced industrialised countries. Financial volatility has affected most participants of the global economy, from households to corporations to national and regional economies. Emerging markets, nonetheless, whose relatively small economies could easily be overwhelmed by macroeconomic shifts on such scale, took the brunt of the impact (Pettis 2001: 31). When a country, or even a whole region, becomes a favourite of international investors, it often experiences a temporary boom. Mexico in the late 1970s and early 1990s, East Asia throughout the 1980s and first half of the 1990s, Russia in 1995–1998, all lived through feverish consumption booms driven by foreign investment, only to end up in crashes when in a couple of years or so, the very same foreign investors concluded that the economic 'fundamentals' failed to justify their initial euphoria (Krugman 2000: 26; Bello *et al.* 2000).

The results of these investment booms were unfortunately all too familiar: irrespective of the economic fundamentals, whether they were sound or not, progressively illiquid financial pyramids triggered a financial crisis. This was precisely the case of East Asia. Naturally, when the fundamentals are weak, illiquidity makes a bad situation worse, as was the case in Russia. Once it becomes a problem, international illiquidity further undermines the confidence of international capital markets in a stricken country. Capital outflow increases, reducing liquidity further, thereby depleting reserves and precipitating default. Thus just like investment booms in advanced economies, the foreign decision to invest in an emerging market, while often justified by perceived changes in the economic policy, tends to follow its own rhythm and pattern, somewhat independent from the 'fundamentals' of the country (Pettis 2001: 47; Bird and Rajan 2002). Therefore, one of the lessons of the late 1990s suggests that 'countries and even regions are increasingly subject to market-related risks and shocks that can disrupt their behaviour, just as companies are, and these risks are transmitted in a similar way: through their capital structures' (Pettis 2001: ix).

Changes in investor sentiment and abrupt capital outflows are often motivated by concerns over mounting public debt or financial imbalances. The crises of the late 1990s have been aggravated by cross-border financial contagion, where market liquidity suddenly dried up – again, not because of economic fundamentals in these countries, but because they shared some characteristics with another economy, suffering as a result an unfortunate loss of confidence (OECD 2002). According to Woodward (2001: 9, 187), speculative investment played three distinct roles in the financial crises in Mexico, East Asia and Russia, although their relative importance varied markedly:

- It helped to inflate speculative bubbles in asset markets;
- It contributed to the reversal of capital flows which precipitated and intensified the crises;
- It was a key factor in the contagion process spreading crises between countries.

A Minskyan crisis scenario centred on financial expansion, debt and illiquidity, was played out in almost all cases of financial fragility over the past decade and a half. The scope of this book does not permit us to delve into the details of each of the episodes and their consequences, but it will be useful to briefly review some of the cases in the late 1990s' chain of financial fragility in key emerging markets: Brazil, Turkey and Argentina.

Brazil, 1999

A large, open, but historically unstable economy, Brazil in the 1990s shared many attributes of the Russian economy. Just like Russia, Brazil embarked in the second half of the decade on a recovery plan after a long period of economic stagnation. By 1995, economic growth had reached 10.4% (Palma 2002: 411). And although Brazil was running a deficit (3%) on its current account in 1995 (just like Russia), a fixed exchange rate of the Real to the dollar encouraged an inflow of foreign capital into the economy. In the ensuing investment euphoria, Brazil had attracted a large share of foreign investment. During this period, between 1994 and 1998, real interest rates remained high and averaged around 23% per year. By 1998, the net inflow of capital into Brazil reached $50 billion a year, a marked increase from a net outflow of over $3 billion the year before the Collor plan was introduced in March 1990 (Palma 2002: 397; Cardoso and Helwege 2001: 161). It was in these circumstances, that just like Russia in 1995–1998, Brazil became another emerging market to get carried away in a giant Ponzi gamble (Kregel 2000).

Despite the apparent success of the stabilisation programme, there were several macroeconomic factors that contributed to the build-up of financial fragility in Brazil. Successful stabilisation of the inflation rate was anchored in the policy of high interest rates; while the liberalisation of the capital markets fuelled a sense of optimism about the prospects of the national economy (Palma 2002: 393). At the same time, the overvalued Real had been distorting the export-led growth strategy; coupled with growing inflows of foreign capital, exchange rate policy affected the pattern of growth, re-orientating it towards a dangerous combination of private consumption dependent on externally financed private investment (Palma 2002: 397–9).

In late 1997, again, just like in the Russian case, the country's creditors got anxious about the Brazilian policy mix and prospects of emerging markets in general, and began to withdraw their funds from the country (Cardoso and Helwege 2001). Faced with the danger of investor panic, a massive withdrawal of funds, and potentially, a domestic banking collapse, the Brazilian authorities introduced all the necessary restrictive measures to try and avoid these types of crisis. In order to keep reserve losses down and support the exchange rate, interest rates were raised to 50% (Eatwell and Taylor 2000: 175). Yet in implementing these measures, Brazilian policymakers in fact 'ended up creating a different type of crisis': a Minskyan Ponzi-type collapse (Palma 2002: 393).

In the midst of global financial turbulence of 1997–1998, the combination of fixed exchange rate and high interest rates made the Brazilian economy particularly vulnerable to a financial shock. In another parallel to the Russian experience, domestic budget deficit doubled from 4% of GDP in 1997 to 8% in 1998. And although the IMF provided a loan to support the Real, this measure was insufficient to sustain confidence in the currency and the country's financial system (Eatwell and Taylor 2000: 175). In these circumstances, 'a deregulated, but badly supervised financial market, closely linked to a highly liquid, but under-regulated and unstable international financial market, coupled with a domestic economy characterised by large imbalances, a weak state, and even a weaker government coalition, made a sudden collapse of confidence and withdrawal of funds a real possibility' (Palma 2002: 428). By February 1999, foreign reserves had fallen to $25 billion and the exchange rate came close to 2.0 Reals per dollar as opposed to 1.2 in October (Eatwell and Taylor 2000: 175). A Ponzi-type crisis ensued.

Turkey, 2000–2001

While often seen in isolation, and not centred on a Ponzi scheme, the next collapse of an emerging market, the Turkish financial crisis of 2000–2001, echoed some of the dynamics identified in this book. Like most economies undergoing structural reform, macroeconomic conditions in Turkey in the late 1990s were not particularly robust. However despite macroeconomic difficulties, in anticipation of a new stabilisation programme, in November 1999, Turkey's investment status had been upgraded to positive (Alper 2001: 61). Soon afterwards, the fragile banking system of the country was shaken by rumours of instability of several commercial banks, and foreign capital began to flee. Just like in Russia and Brazil, the IMF $7.5 billion loan to Turkey proved inadequate to eliminate the exchange rate risks (Alper 2001: 78).[1]

A vicious Minsky-type cycle of debt deflation unfolded: banks in need of short-term credit rapidly sold government securities, raising the interest rates in the process. Growing demand for foreign exchange fuelled capital outflow further and put pressure on the currency markets (Alper 2001: 69). The capital flight and high interest rates eroded the equity of many commercial banks and reduced the value of government securities, increasing the market risk. As a consequence, the year 2000 saw an increase in the ratio of short-term foreign debt to the foreign exchange. This ratio had reached 1:1 by the end of August, and 1:44 by the end of the year, which was far above the corresponding pre-crisis levels of Malaysia (0.61)

---

1   In December 2000, the IMF provided a support credit of $7.5 billion for the period of three years but the conditions of the loan meant that interest rates remained high in early 2001, eroding the equity of commercial banks and ultimately, precipitating a second liquidity crisis in February 2001 (Alper 2001).

and the Philippines (0.85), and almost equivalent to that of Thailand (1.45) before the Asian crisis (Orhangazi 2002: 338).[2] At the end of 2001, the total debt stock in Turkey rose from 75.8% of national income to 88.5%. According to Orhangazi, the costs of the crisis had been $45 billion for additional domestic debt, $22.4 billion for additional foreign debt, and $52 billion lost in national income; the cost of the IMF-directed programme has reached almost 80% of GNP, or $1,800 per capita (2002: 339).

Argentina, 2001

Again, like Russia, Brazil and Turkey, the Argentine crisis of 2001 became a product of a dangerous combination of domestic financial fragility and destabilising influence of foreign capital inflows, and specifically, of high short-term borrowing by domestic firms. During the 1990s, the build-up of liabilities in many Latin American economies generally resembled a Ponzi scheme, justified only by the waves of investor optimism in 1990–1993 and 1997–1999. This process generated many imbalances, as under the policies adopted in most countries, for instance, in Brazil, only restrictive measures were available to respond to deteriorating investor confidence. In addition, the induced dollarisation of domestic financial assets and liabilities aggravated currency mismatches and domestic financial fragility (Ffench-Davis and Studart 2003: 78).

Although for most of the 1990s Argentina had been a 'star' student of the Washington Consensus paradigm, in the wake of the 1997–1998 crises, growth expectations rapidly declined. In large part, this was caused by the monetary and fiscal measures that were adopted to sustain credibility and investor confidence. At the same time, the need to maintain high levels of reserves and the nature of the financial reforms stimulated short-term borrowings, thus contributing to the build-up of systemic financial fragility (Ffench-Davis and Studart 2003: 71–3). As Abeles (2005) details, external capital inflows into Argentina were gradually transformed into a Ponzi scheme: between 1995 and 2001, along

---

2 A similar deterioration was also observed in the ratio of short-term foreign debt to exports.

with the general increase in leverage ratios, foreign liabilities as a share of total liabilities has increased from 0.39 to 0.51. This increase in short-term indebtedness threatened many firms with illiquidity and insolvency. Between 2001 and 2002, Argentina's peso depreciated by more than 70% (Abeles 2005: 16, note 21). At the same time, the ratio of current account balance and external debt[3] was not only negative throughout the period, but deteriorated rapidly during the two periods of investor euphoria: from 1990 to 1994, and again from 1996 to 1997 (Ffench-Davis and Studart 2003: 70). The ensuing crisis of 2001 in Argentina entailed a painful macroeconomic austerity programme domestically, and the biggest restructuring of foreign debt in history (Helleiner 2005).

Financial fragility in the emerging markets: some lessons

The emerging market crises in the late 1990s presented the world of finance and economics with many sobering lessons. The collapse or near collapse of economies as diverse as East Asian 'tigers', Russia, Brazil, Turkey and Argentina undermined many of the principles of the Washington Consensus of the 1990s and spurred a debate of the whole framework of the international financial architecture (Eichengreen 1999; Kenen 2001; Soederberg 2002b, 2005). One particular lesson from the 1990s stands out: the eruptions of fragile finance have shown that blaming a set of macroeconomic policies for financial crises is simply, misguided (see Pettis 2003). On the contrary, a Minskyan reading of finance and crisis shows that the crises in East Asia, Russia and other economies were not mere accidents. At the heart of financial fragility in all crisis-hit countries lay poor liability management, excessive borrowing and structural fragility of economies open to global capital. In its contemporary setting, crisis is caused by speculation, over-borrowing and progressive illiquidity of companies and, in the case of emerging markets dependent on currency pegs, national economies.

Of these three factors precipitating fragile financial structures today, it is the problem of progressive illiquidity that proves to be

---

3 A key indicator of the capacity of an economy to repay its external liabilities.

most complex. Indeed, with the expansion of private credit to the terrain of emerging markets, in addition to the characteristics of domestic financial fragility mentioned by Minsky in his original work, foreign exchange has become a crucial component of financial fragility in the global context (Wolfson 2002). The core of the illiquidity problem is a mismatch between assets and liabilities, and a general loss of money-liquidity poses a great danger in all capital markets, national or international. As most of heterodox crisis models document, the illiquidity of the financial system is typically rooted in a previous bout of financial liberalisation, which accentuates the maturity mismatch between international assets and liabilities (Eatwell and Taylor 2000: 112; Chang and Velasco 1998). The rapid rise of short-term borrowing reflected speculative asset booms in many developing countries. Financial deregulation and capital account liberalisation, combined with distortions in international capital-adequacy regulations, also favoured short-term lending. These, in turn, increased the vulnerability of many countries, as in East Asia and Russia, to liquidity crises, especially as short-term borrowing tended to reverse rapidly during adverse economic shocks (Dadush *et al.* 2000).

Today's combination of a liberalised financial system, a monetary standard with no exogenous anchor such as gold, and a monetary policy prioritising short-term price stability increases the risk of longer and bigger build-ups in credit. That makes asset-price and debt bubbles more likely (*The Economist*, 26 September 2002: 29). Therefore increasingly, financial crisis in an emerging economy occurs at a nexus of foreign exchange market disturbances, debt defaults (sovereign or private), and banking system failures (Eichengreen and Portes 1987). Indeed crises in recent years have all involved countries or companies in which debts were run up to excessive levels which then, when circumstances suddenly changed, caused acute pain. Excessive borrowing by firms, households and governments lay behind the economic crises in Mexico, East Asia, Russia, Brazil and Argentina.

A situation of international illiquidity in an emerging market is often critical, because it involves a fragile situation: it is a necessary and often sufficient precondition for financial crashes and debt crises. If initially financial systems are relatively illiquid, a 'small' real shock can push the economy into a region where a financial crisis is inevitable. If a crash does occur, bankruptcies and the liquidation of investments entail systemic consequences that multiply the harmful effects of the initial shock. Making payments on existing debt restricts investment and dampens growth, due to a liquidity shortage. This shortage arises, in turn, because expectations of continuing future debt burden reduce incentives for current investment and dissuades external lenders from new financing (Dymski 2003: 4). And although they may seem as less serious than solvency crises, liquidity crises can be extremely damaging. As Pettis (2001: 25) reminds us, liquidity crises, especially at a system level, entail detrimental socio-economic repercussions.

Minskyan crises in the U.S. economy

LTCM, 1998

The scandal and the collapse of the Long Term Capital Management (LTCM) Fund in the USA became an almost immediate, and direct, consequence of the Russian debt default of August 1998, and a legend of recent financial history in its own right. Although conceived by three champions of financial mathematics and operating like diversified fund aiming to outguess the bond markets, the fund, in fact, operated (and collapsed), as we will see, like a giant Ponzi scheme. LTCM was formally established in Greenwich, Connecticut, in 1994. In the words of Nicholas Dunbar (2000: 124) 'the apparent obscurity of this location would later add to the sense of mystery surrounding' the fund. LTCM's starting capital (equity) was $1.3 billion. Of this sum, over $100 million was contributed by the LTCM general partners, who included, among others, Myron Scholes and Robert Merton, who both won Nobel prizes for their work in the pricing of financial instruments (Edwards 1999: 199; Dunbar 2000).

The fund's operations were mostly focussed on the arbitrage in the bond markets. The principal idea guiding the operations was simple enough: it was a belief that some of the bonds, particularly the so-called junk papers, were under-priced in the markets. And LTCM, through clever use of arbitrage, would correct this, while making profits by using its dynamic models of option pricing (Dunbar 2000). To this end, the fund held long positions in less liquid bonds that it considered undervalued, and short positions in liquid, lower-yielding securities that it considered overvalued (Edwards 1999: 198).[4]

For several years, the chosen strategy had worked smoothly for LTCM and its investors. Conceived by the geniuses of financial economics, LTCM, operating with a high leverage ratio, brought excellent returns to its investors: nearly 20% in 1994, 42.8% in 1995, 40.8% in 1996 and another 17.1% in 1997 (Edwards 1999: 198). The institution became a 'pinnacle of a 30-year-long revolution in finance, which had done for trading what the Apollo space programme had done for lunar exploration' (Dunbar 2000: xi) At any fixed point in time, the wide range of different trades open by LTCM made it look as if its portfolio was diversified, and thus the exposure to risky assets and market shocks had been minimised. Deceptively, LTCM had about 20 different trades on at any moment, and the long/short balance meant that they were not exposed to the risk of bond prices rising or falling. Yet from a Minskyan view, Mehrling argues, LTCM was not diversified at all. In fact, the fund made only one bet – that liquidity spreads would narrow (Mehrling 2001: 154). Confident in its own arbitrage strategy as liquidity creating, LTCM seems to have been unaware of its vulnerability to a short squeeze and an eventual evaporation of market liquidity (Mehrling 2001: 154–6; Dunbar 2000: 203–6). And although the use of computer models and dynamic trading techniques had supported the partners' hypotheses for several years, by 1998, excessive reliance on leverage and derivatives contracts had made LTCM's position particularly fragile.

During its relatively short life in the market, LTCM had reportedly borrowed more than $125 billion from banks and securities firms, having only around $5 billion in equity. This 20-to-1 ratio, Edwards stresses, was exceptionally high and unusual even for hedge funds. Although clever use of leverage and mathematics made LTCM's trading technique particularly successful, in the wake of the Asian financial crisis the fund encountered difficulties in sustaining profitability. In early 1998, its equity stood at only $4.8 billion, down from $7 billion in late 1997 (Edwards 1999: 198). Reacting to market

---

4 Specifically, LTCM bought high-yielding, less liquid bonds, such as Danish mortgage-backed securities, bonds issued by emerging market borrowers, and 'junk' corporate bonds, and sold low-yielding, more liquid bonds, such as US government bonds (Edwards 1999: 198).

stress and contagion, the fund calculated that the yield spread between high- and low-risk bonds (or less liquid and more liquid securities) was excessively wide – for example, the spread between high-yield corporate bonds and US Treasuries was close to 4 percentage points in early 1998 – and so would narrow as investors reassessed the risks (Edwards 1999: 198).

Relying on these calculations, LTCM entered into derivative contracts in Russia. Dunbar (2000: 199–200) explains the mechanism as follows. A friendly investment bank would buy the Russian GKOs for LTCM. In return for paying the bank a dollar floating rate, LTCM would receive the high GKO coupons, in roubles, which could be converted back into dollars again (Dunbar 2000: 199). Simultaneously, LTCM entered into a forward contract (with a different investment bank) so that as soon as it received a rouble payment in a few months time, it could exchange the roubles for dollars at today's exchange rate.[5] This hedging mechanism ensured that if the rouble was devalued in the meantime, LTCM would be protected (Dunbar 2000: 199).

But the fund's strategists badly miscalculated risk. Already by early 1998, contagion had spread from the East Asian financial markets to other economies. While other financial institutions began to unload their risky, illiquid positions, LTCM's trading models still predicted that liquidity spreads would narrow. However, as investors across the world were growing increasingly fearful of emerging markets, buyers of junk bonds disappeared: within a few months, there was virtually no bids and hence, market, for junk bonds, as buyers vanished and yields on high-risk bonds soared. With the disappearing buyers, liquidity also evaporated. And then politics interfered with the markets.

On 17 August, Russia defaulted on 281 billion roubles ($13.5 billion) of its Treasury debt and devalued the rouble. That decision came as a shock to global financial markets generally, and as a particularly nasty surprise to LTCM and its partners. In a somewhat delayed attempt to protect the Russian financial system from complete collapse, the Kirienko government issued a decree forbidding domestic banks from

---

5 This second bank would earn its fee on the transaction, which it would hedge by trading in the Russian domestic currency markets. To make life even simpler for hedge funds like LTCM, both halves of the money machine could be expressed as a value in dollars, so save the trouble of having to deal in actual roubles (Dunbar 2000: 200).

honouring their foreign exchange obligations for a month. As a result, Russian banks and securities firms exercised the *force majeure* clause in their derivatives contracts and refused to honour their contracts (Edwards 1999: 199). LTCM was one of the high-profile clients in the unfortunate group of foreign investors caught in the cross-fire: holding large open positions in junk bonds of emerging markets, the fund lost about $430 million on to the Russian default.

And although LTCM's own exposure to the Russian market was not particularly large (Mackenzie 2007), the spread of financial panic across global financial markets has turned the fortune of the fund around. Across the world, panicking investors adjusted their portfolios to safer assets, grabbing US treasury bonds and selling other securities. As a result, contrary to LTCM's initial calculations, the values the bonds diverged, and already by late August 1998 the fund had lost $1.85 billion in capital. By mid-September 1998, LTCM's equity had dropped to $600 million, a loss of more than $4 billion (Edwards 1999: 199). Over-leveraged, and having lost its key source of profits, the fund was *de facto* bankrupt.

Although the giant fund had around a dozen or so big counter-parties, its collapse could have unleashed serious systemic risk for the US economy. The Fed had little choice but to step in with a rescue operation, organising a consortium of creditors to inject additional capital into the sinking fund.[6] On September 23 1998, a 16-member consortium arranged a $3.625 billion package in exchange for 90% of the remaining equity in LTCM. By the end of 1998, the stakes of the 16 general LTCM partners were reportedly worth about $30 million, down from $1.6 billion earlier in the year (Edwards 1999: 200). Since the creditor bailout, LTCM have reportedly made profits of more than $70 million, and the old LTCM partnership was said to collect annual fees of as much as $50 million (Pacelle 1998, in Edwards 1999).

The rise and fall of LTCM has become a legend of recent financial history (see de Goede 2001; Mackenzie 2007; Lowenstein 2002). Among the many lessons that the scandal of the fund offers to

---

6 The consortium included: Goldman Sachs; the Travellers group, Merrill Lynch, JP Morgan, Morgan Stanley, Dean Witter, Union Bank of Switzerland, Barclays, Bankers Trust, Chase Manhattan, CSFB, Deutsche bank, Lehman Brothers, Paribas, and Soceite Generale (Edwards 1999).

students of finance, one stands out in particular. From a Minskyan point of view, LTCM was essentially a Ponzi scheme. Relying on leverage, it held long positions in illiquid securities and short positions in lower-quality, but more liquid securities. Since LTCM's theory of security valuation completely abstracted from the problem of liquidity, such an exposure entailed serious systemic risk (Mehrling 2001). The EMT of finance tends to assume all tradable assets as equally and completely liquid. This assumption makes the dealer's role of 'completing the market', of tying together the various tiers of the system, relatively straightforward (Mehrling 2001: 154–6).

Minsky, in contrast, believed that financial intermediation entails complex structures of claims and liabilities that require accommodating cash flows to keep them from collapse. Indeed, in the real world, capital markets are used to refinance the reserves and productive capital of companies, rather than as initial finance for new fixed capital investment. This refinancing mechanism can cause extreme shifts in corporate liquidity over the period of the business cycle (Toporowski 1999: 22; 2000: 7). Ignoring the problem of liquidity and its systemic implications has become a fatal mistake of LTCM and a personal drama for its founding partners. At a broader level, the crash of the fund has highlighted a more serious challenge for modern finance theory: as the preceding crashes in East Asia and Russia, as well as subsequent crises in other emerging markets, the story of LTCM suggests that financial crisis today is a crisis of liquidity and over-borrowing far more than it is a crisis born of information, market failures or policy mistakes (Bookstaber 2000).

The 'new economy' crash, 2000–2001

For a short period in the wake of the LTCM crisis, the US financial system, supported by systemic liquidity assurances, remained the safe haven for the expansive global speculating community. Yet in late 2000–early 2001, US energy and electric utility companies using derivatives, such as Enron, shocked the world of investors when they unsuccessfully tried to convert the derivatives-related receivables on their balance sheets into cash (Hughes 2003). The Minskyan pattern of systemic financial fragility centred on financial innovation, access to new credit and speculation, repeated itself yet again, in the so-called 'new economy' mania in 1995–2000. The story behind the rise and fall of the dotcom bubble in the American economy in the late 1990s is now well known (Bootle 2003; Henwood 1997; O'Hara 2003; Rennstich 2002; Shiller 2000; Aysha 2001).

In the USA, like in East Asia prior to the 1997–1998 crises, along the classic Minskyan lines, much of the surge in borrowing in the late 1990s was based on overly optimistic and unwarranted forecasts of income. In the first quarter of 2000, the value of US corporate equities, their market capitalisation, had soared to $19.6 trillion, up from $6.3 trillion in 1994. The incongruity of this figure, and its ascent, was evident from many angles. Most definitive was the lack of connection between the rise of share prices and the growth of output – and particularly of profitability – in the underlying economy. Market capitalisation as a percentage of GDP had needed just five years between 1995–2000 to triple from 50% to 150% of GDP – despite the fact that after-tax profits had risen by only 41.2% in the interim (Beams 2002). In the first quarter of 2000, the ratio of stock market value of US non-financial corporations to their net worth – known as Tobin's Q – reached 1.92, up from 0.94 in 1994 and 1.14 in 1995, and from an average of 0.65 for the 20th century as a whole. As Brenner (2000) argues, from 1998 onwards, the growth of debt-driven consumption came to substitute for increasing manufacturing competitiveness and rising exports in pushing the US economy forwards, enabling it to 'finesse the system-wide problems'.

As Rima (2002) observes, the mystique that surrounded the issues of dotcom shares was in large part a reflection of first-day gains. Some dotcom stock prices soared in excess of 1000% within a very short time of the date of their initial public offering. Their spectacular performance confirms Minsky's expectation that a regime in which capital gains are expected generates an environment for engaging in speculative and/or Ponzi finance. Rising values served as collateral for debt on the premise that the rise in equity prices would continue. Yet by the spring of 2000, as the confidence in 'new economy' stocks evaporated, the dotcom bubble had started to deflate, leaving mountains of unpayable debts behind (Rima 2002: 407–14).

According to S&P's there were more defaults worldwide in 2001 than ever: 216 companies defaulted on $116 billion of debt.[7] That

---

7 The figure reflects a specific method chosen by S&P. The actual number of bankruptcies is likely to be much higher.

trend continued into the first quarter of 2002, when defaults reached $34 billion. The rate of failure among large corporations was higher relative to smaller companies than in the past, suggesting that the ability of larger companies to generate and retain more debt – and exploit derivative markets and off-balance sheet vehicles – has resulted in the higher default rates. Only in the period between 2000 and 2002, 25 large US corporations have filed for bankruptcy, with the total cost of the five largest defaults around $230 billion (Data from the *Financial Times*).

The crash of the 'new economy' bubble in the USA has brought the world economy into recession, raising further concerns about a possible global spread of a debt deflation process. In many ways, the euphoria associated with the rise of the Internet and 'new economy' age of prosperity mirrored previous financial manias, such as the Dutch tulip mania of 1636, the South Sea bubble of 1720, the technology revolution of the 1920s, or the stock market crash of 1987. In each of these episodes, investors got carried away on the promise of high and easy profits, yet the speculative drive of 'new economies' stretched the financial pyramids too far away from the underlying foundations of growth. Each mania was followed by a severe recession and, in the case of the 1920s economic boom, a Great Depression. And although history knows of too many painful consequences, observers are baffled by how easy the lessons of history can be forgotten...

After the crises

Indeed, ten years onwards, most of the crisis-hit economies managed to recover from the traumas and outperform their pre-crisis growth. Since 2000, the East Asian region has been growing on average at around 6–7% per year. Asian emerging economies have benefited from a surge in external demand for the region's products, particularly electronics. Corporate governance reforms that ensued in the wake of the crises of 1997–1998 have facilitated a renewed surge of investments into the region, while domestic technological, legal and economic reforms are said to have transformed Asian industries from old-style type of industrial concentration to more innovative, IT-driven mode of competition (IMF 2006; Lee and McNulty 2003).

In Russia, similarly, the August 1998 crisis marked a start of a new era of prosperity. Since 1999, the country's GDP has been growing steadily, averaging 6–7% per year. Employment and real wages have been rising. Supported by the rouble devaluation and high oil prices, Russia's current account and federal budget have been in surplus since 2000; the Russian central bank has accumulated more than $311 billion of hard currency reserves, one of the highest levels in the world today. In 2006, the Russian rouble was made a convertible currency. Russia's fiscal health is among the best in the world. In August 2006, Russia paid off its debt to the Paris Club ahead of schedule, 12 years before the due date, thus saving around $7 billion. The contrast between the Russian economy today and its pre-1998 situation, structurally disjointed and financially fragile, seems striking indeed.

Across the world, the emerging markets, having suffered from the exhaustion of capital inflows in the wake of the 1997–1999 crises, have been again attracting large inflows of capital. In 2003–2005 emerging market shares more than doubled, with total returns of 165%. East European markets returned 226%, Latin American markets 265% and Asian markets[8] 122%. While in the late 1990s, these countries were suffering from domestic and international financial fragility,[9] as reflected in weak balance sheets, opaque accounting and murky governance, at present, their positions seem rather different. Today, emerging markets have strong current account surpluses, vast reserves and undervalued currencies. If ten years ago, emerging economies had an average current account deficit of 2% of gross domestic product; today the figure is a 2% surplus. Fiscal deficits, which averaged 3% of GDP ten years ago, now fluctuate at around modest 1%. Inflation, 14% on average a decade ago, is now only 4%. Reflecting the 'rehabilitation' of many emerging markets, international rating agencies upgrade their sovereign debt frequently (figures from the *Financial Times*).

It is important however, not to get away amidst the current wave of optimism. In the East Asian economies, the post-crisis restructuring and financial reforms have been paralleled by a widening of the financial services sector: previously 'unbanked' layers of the population have been drawn into the private-sector credit boom. Korea, a champion of post-1998 economic recovery, in fact already suffered

---

8 Outside Japan.
9 Deficits, overvalued currencies and insufficient foreign exchange reserves.

a credit-card crisis in 2002. Korea's credit-card industry expanded rapidly from 1999 to 2002, with the number of active cards more than doubling to over 100 million. The consequences of this excessive expansion were a large number of household delinquencies[10] and several credit-card companies in financial distress.[11] The subsequent consumer credit crunch put the economy into a recession (IMF 2006: 62–3).

Throughout the Asian region, the IMF continues, consumer credit boom creates more risks. For example, as the upturn in the global interest rate cycle increases debt service costs, consumption and asset prices may be threatened. Banks may have loosened lending standards to compete for market shares in what they perceived as a strategic market for the medium term, while at the same time they may have struggled to process large numbers of applications for products for which they, as well as the borrowers, had little experience. In addition, although credit-card loans are still a small fraction of total credit in most Asian countries, they are often concentrated at a small number of institutions relying on interbank and wholesale markets for financing. As such, instability associated with these segments may be of systemic relevance (IMF 2006: 62; Ward 2003; Fifield 2004).

In Russia, where mortgage markets and credit card industry are still miniscule by international standards, private sector indebtedness is growing rapidly. Worryingly, there are signs that the state-led borrowing of the Yeltsin era has been replaced by the private sector debt during the Putin regime. While the external indebtedness of the Russian state has been decreasing under Putin; the debt of Russian private companies to international creditors has grown more than six times: from $31 billion in 2000 to $176 billion in 2006. Paradoxically, although the country has been striving to repay its major foreign debts before the deadlines, the total foreign debt of the country continues to rise: from $186 billion in 2004 to $275 billion in 2006. The new loans go to Russian banks and private companies (including those that are partially owned by the government). The interest on these new loans is high: 1.5–2% higher than on state debts. While there are few

---

10 An average of four cards per adult. About 17% of the economically active population.
11 The largest, LG Card, eventually was the object of a bailout.

worries about the Russian oil giants' ability to repay their debts amid high world oil prices, the sustainability of these debts may be shattered once raw materials prices fall, or if the world markets suffer from a different kind of shock, or if the Russian financial market suffers from a systemic crisis.

But nowhere has the growing fragility of the consumer finance industry has been more pronounced than in the Anglo-Saxon economies (Montgomerie 2006, 2007). The deregulation of lending and the removal of capital controls that accompanied the emergence of large-scale institutional investors, have prompted the public to detach themselves from state welfare and pension provisions. As Pettifor (2003) claims, the abrogation of responsibility by the government for the welfare of the elderly led to today's pension crisis. Both in the UK and USA, household savings are channelled into corporate savings. As a result, the Anglo-Saxon stock markets operate like giant Ponzi schemes (Froud *et al.* 2001).

The UK's personal debt burden recently topped £1 trillion; the total household debt servicing, including secured debt, is now above 20% of incomes; the country's credit card debt accounts for two-thirds of the EU's total. While the bulk of the debt is mortgages, more than a fifth is unsecured debt – on credit cards and personal loans. 'Middle-income Britain is locked into a cycle in which periods of excessive spending are followed by remortgaging and other debt consolidation.' Essentially, an average household has unsecured loans of £7650 (Halligan 2005: 12). Consumer bankruptcies have hit record levels: at the time of writing, individual insolvencies are twice as common as when Labour took office in 1997.

In the USA, new, riskier forms of mortgage finance also allowed buyers to borrow more. In 2004, 42% of all first-time buyers and 25% of all borrowers made no down payment on their home purchase. In 2005, adjustable-rate mortgages have risen to 50% of all mortgages in those states with the biggest house price rises (*The Economist*, 18 June 2005). American banks have been lending to 'marginal' debtors, unloading many of the loans either on one of the quasi-governmental housing agencies (Fannie Mae, Freddie Mac) or to private investors in asset-backed securities. Much of the lending took the form of 'subprime loans', variable-rate, interest-only and negative-amortisation loans. As a result, both debtors and creditors have become more exposed to interest-rate changes, and the continuing souring of the

US housing market reflects the deepening fragility of debt-driven economy in the USA (*The Economist,* 18 August 2005).

Against this worrisome background, it is important to learn from the wave of the financial crises of the late 1990s–early 2000s. The scandals of LTCM, the collapse of the dotcom bubble in 2001, as well as many other corporate scandals over the past few years, do offer many sobering lessons to students of finance and financial policymakers. While disagreements about the nature and long-term significance of these crises persist, most post-crisis assessments converge around the following: the global financial system has become inherently volatile; financial markets are prone to information failure, moral hazard and herd-like tendencies, and thus can be inefficient. Financial contagion is a new and serious danger emanating from the tight interconnectedness of global credit networks. Investment and capital inflows are crucial for development and economic growth, yet the experience of the 1990s shows that financial liberalisation can be a very mixed blessing (c.f. Bordo *et al.* 2001; Eatwell and Taylor 2000; Kaminsky and Reinhart 1998; Stiglitz 2003; Soederberg 2005; Woodward 2001; Rogoff *et al.* 2003).

The crises that occurred in an environment of low inflation and often did not involve major fiscal deficits,[12] posed severe intellectual challenge to neoclassical models of finance and crisis; casting doubts on the validity of the underlying paradigm of monetary economics (Rajan 2002; Eatwell and Taylor 2000; Bello *et al.* 2000; Mishkin 1999; Toporowski 2001; Eichengreen and Mitchener 2003). As a result, perhaps rather painfully, financial policymakers have had to face the fact that in today's climate of privatised credit and financial expansion, their intellectual and theoretical apparatus may be insufficient when dealing with the issues of financial volatility and its threats to the economic stability and societies across the globe. One of the responses to financial fragility was the so-called New International Financial Architecture (NIFA). Increasingly, along with routine problems of development finance and policy implementation, the NIFA designers have recognised the need to tackle much more fundamental issues of the nature of finance and credit itself (Kapstein 2006; Knight 2005; Borio *et al.* 2003; White 2006a, b; Kaufman 1998). In the concluding chapter, we review some of these shifts.

---

12 Russia in 1998 and Turkey in 2000 are notable exceptions.

Conclusion

The spate of financial crises and financial volatility of the last decade have not gone unnoticed, but have alerted policymakers and academics to many, often hidden, hazards of liberalised finance. If one thing was learned from the experience of the past two decades, then it was that liquidity management and control are among the most difficult challenges to financial orthodoxy and policy apparatus today. At the same time, although the causality of the build-up of progressive illiquidity has recently been noted by a number of market practitioners and financial regulators, it remains extremely unclear what is the best way to gauge and tame illiquidity at a systemic level, and how to enforce measures of crisis prevention. Hyman Minsky did not live to witness the dramas of the late 1990s–early 2000s. Yet it is telling that among the wide variety of economic perspectives on finance, it is the work of Hyman Minsky that has been revived in the wake of the recent financial explosions (Warburton 2000; Persaud 2002; Myers and Rajan 1998; Felix 2003; Kregel 2000, 2001; Pettis 2001, 2003; Wolfson 2000, 2002).

Central banks and illiquidity

When confronted with systemic crises brought on by excessive speculation, it is the central banks that have to accommodate the market's need for monetary base and provide the needed liquidity (Savona 2002: 181; Ferguson 2003: 8). There are, however, at least two problems related to the existence and functions of the lender of last resort in the global financial system. First, at the national level, central banks in emerging markets – the most common victims of financial crisis – have a very limited ability to tame financial volatility in time and avert a crisis. Central bank intervention at an early stage of crisis evolution raises the risk that it will set off currency depreciation, and possibly, raise interest rates, thus pushing the economy into a deeper structural crisis (Mishkin 1999).[1]

Second, the presence of a lender of last resort (LLR) propagates moral hazard, encouraging excessive risk-taking and speculation (Mishkin 1999: 18). The traditional remedy for a financial collapse, as we have seen in the cases of the Mexican, Asian and Russian crises, was to provide new loans to governments, with disbursements conditional on macroeconomic targets and specific policy changes. However, as illustrated by the East Asian case most persuasively, foreign loans tend to be directed to bailing out foreign financial institutions, and do little, if anything, to solve the underlying problems of the domestic economy itself (Hart-Landsberg and Burkett 1999). Third, Barry Eichengreen notes that the distinction between illiquidity and insolvency is especially difficult to draw for countries (also Kenen 2001). In recent defaults of Ukraine and Pakistan, for example,

> the markets' unwillingness to defer their claims in the absence of IMF support sounds like a classical liquidity problem. But the reluctance of (creditors) to meet the countries' requests [to restructure the debts] ... reflected the existence of policy problems... that raised concerns about the willingness and ability of their governments to service their obligations... In other words, it was hard to categorise Pakistan and Ukraine as cases of either pure insolvency or pure illiquidity (Eichengreen 2002: 58).

Meanwhile, lending to governments still operates on the principle that 'countries do not go bankrupt'. As a result, the IMF – the current international 'quasi-LLR' – still experiences problems adju-

---

1   As F. Mishkin explains it, particularly in an emerging economy, central bank's lending in the wake of a financial crash may fuel fears of high inflation, with the effects of higher nominal interest rates, currency depreciation and further deterioration of balance sheets (p. 15).

dicating when a country is insolvent or illiquid. As a result, lending to governments in crisis involves a considerable degree of political judgement and again, propagates moral hazard (Eichengreen 2002: 56–66).

Given the complexity of financial trades today, the need to distinguish illiquidity from insolvency, difficult even in the context of a closed economy, poses an arduous challenge at the international level (Fratianni and Pattison 2002). As both Asian and Russian crises showed, macroeconomic illiquidity has ramifications through its impact on domestic and global markets and settlement mechanisms.[2] Similarly, recent increases in foreign reserves of many emerging markets boosted central bank liquidity in the domestic currency. To the extent that this additional liquidity is not sterilised by the central bank, excess liquidity can spill over to another country, destabilising the financial situation there (IMF 2005a, Chapter 2, Box 2.1: 15). These hidden interconnectivities make it almost impossible for monetary and financial authorities to diagnose the type of crisis accurately and introduce relevant policy measures in time.

Thus along with academics, policymakers increasingly confront the need to understand the process whereby perceptions about the behaviour of the products of financial innovation tend to affect the systemic balance and precipitate crises of confidence and valuation. Being at the heart of the process of asset price inflation, over-the-counter trading and speculation, liquidity has become a key focus in regulatory attempts to capture and mitigate the problem of systemic risk. Given the growing awareness of the problems of credit endogeneity, it is unsurprising that many recent attempts to resolve the puzzles encrypted in the dilemmas of liquidity seem to gravitate to the ideas of financial Keynesianism. Interestingly in this case, back in 1995, one post-Keynesian scholar predicted that soon, Hyman Minsky 'may be reclaimed by economic orthodoxy' (King 1995: 13). In 2001, Perry Mehrling noted that the key debate

---

2 In the East Asian countries and in Russia, the lack of foreign exchange reserves undermined the currency pegs, translating into the inability of banks and firms to settle foreign currency-denominated contracts. The use of financial derivatives added to the spread of financial panic and international contagion.

in finance today is no longer between Keynesians and monetarists, but between Minsky and central bankers on the one side, and modern finance on the other.

Claudio Borio and the thinking at the BIS

In this regard, along with academics working in the post-Keynesian tradition, one of the most prolific analysts of the problem of liquidity and its systemic implications has been a chief economist at the BIS, Claudio Borio. In his insightful studies of the behaviour of financial markets, some of which closely parallel Keynesian notions of the 'illusion of liquidity', Borio developed the notion of *artificial liquidity* as an intuitive, yet useful, gauge of financial fragility. Here, one of the most important lessons from the past wave of crises is the recognition that the fluidity, or velocity of financial circulation – the key products of financial deregulation and liberalisation of credit – are, just as Minsky warned, not synonymous with liquidity of the system as such (cf. Warburton 2000).

According to Borio, the interaction between cash and market liquidity is a critical determining factor for gauging the robustness of financial markets. The dislocations generated by the evaporation of liquidity in systemically important markets in 1998–1999 are clear illustrations of the heightened significance of systemic liquidity for financial stability (Borio 2000: 38–9; 2004; Pettis 2001, 2003). This dark side of liquidity – its disappearance during times of stress – has received attention of scholars and market analysts in the past few years. As a consequence of such liquidity illusions, the fragility associated with liquidity strains often leads to systemic changes in the behaviour of both public and private sectors, as both investors and regulators become more aware of the dangers associated with the proliferation and transfer of credit risk. Thus increasingly in the debate on global financial regulation, systemic risk relates to concerns about solvency of financial institutions, as well as failures of market liquidity and breakdowns of market infrastructure (Davis 2003; Large 2005).

In their attempts to formulate a more nuanced understanding of liquidity within a financial cycle some central bankers and market analysts have distinguished between several types of risk associated with liquidity. The Basel committee, for instance, has identified two types of liquidity risk. First, *market liquidity risk* concerns a party's ability to liquidate a position. This depends on a number of factors, including the markets for the product, the size of the position, and the creditworthiness of the counterparty. Second, *funding liquidity risk* relates to the ability to fund a position. In addition, there is a residual category of operational risk ('other risks') that covers fraud, legal negligence, misconduct, and technology failure (Alexander *et al.* 2006: 25).

Recent research at the European Central Bank (ECB) has identified two corresponding types of liquidity within a financial cycle: *search liquidity* and *systemic liquidity*. While 'search liquidity' describes the behaviour of market institutions during 'good' times, systemic liquidity matters in times of stress. In 'quiet times', the liquidity premium[3] is driven by 'search' costs: time, information, capital, funding, inventory and research costs required for a trader to locate a buyer for a 'stock' that it has recently purchased. In stress times on the other hand, liquidity premium is determined by the homogeneity of investors. Thus systemic liquidity relates to the collective behaviour of investors. If investors are similar in reacting to information, in valuing and managing risks, and are reducing their risk exposures simultaneously, finding a buyer is almost impossible. The liquidity to sell disappears down a 'black hole' (Persaud 2002; Lagana *et al.* 2006).

It appears that the new approaches to understanding risks and market dynamics outlined above award greater importance to the subjectivity of investors' actions, as well as certain scepticism about the ability of existing regulatory frameworks to capture the complexity of financial risks (Lagana *et al.* 2006: 15). These nascent shifts sketched out above point to a remarkable transformation within the existing framework of financial regulation. Intriguingly, it transpires that many of the post-crisis views on the problem of financial fragility and liquidity illusions are grounded in Keynesian and post-Keynesian economic traditions. Given the otherwise intact hegemony of neoclassical economics, this is a remarkable development indeed. Can the ideas of Keynes, Minsky and their followers help re-establish some order in the complex and increasingly opaque world of finance and credit today?

---

3 The liquidity premium approximates the difference between the observed corporate bind yield spreads and the smaller theoretical spreads derived from default probabilities.

Towards a new post-Keynesian financial architecture?

This is not the first study to have observed certain parallels between the design of global financial regulation today and a vision of financial markets Keynes proposed some 70 years ago (e.g., Gnos and Rochon 2004). Following the Enron débacle, many analysts recognised the need for an internationally coherent plan for reform of the financial system. The so-called New International Finance Architecture (NIFA) is an umbrella term that refers to a myriad of coordinated policy responses at the international level to the wave of crises that engulfed emerging economies and threatened the stability of advanced capitalism (Blinder 1999; Summers 1998; US Treasury 1999; Feldstein 1999). A full discussion of NIFA is beyond the scope of this study, but as Cartapanis and Herland (2002) point out, both NIFA and the Keynesian theory of finance share a built-in scepticism of the role of foreign investors and the necessity to subject them to certain standards of behaviour.

The ostensible change in the global financial paradigm is supported by the growing interest in Keynesian political economy on the part of some representatives of global policy elite (Felix 2003; Brealey *et al.* 2001). The self-professed 'global Keynesians' include Joseph Stiglitz and George Soros, both of whom have recommended the introduction of a new form of global money[4] to support wider developmental goals (Gnos and Rochon 2004). Stiglitz, in particular, has noted that the practical challenges of distinguishing between illiquidity and insolvency today expose the inability of monetarist orthodoxy to tame financial fragility: 'the distinction [between illiquid and insolvent institutions] itself is evidence of the belief that markets do not work in a manner described by the neoclassical model, in which any firm which had a positive net worth could gain access to credit' (Stiglitz and Bhattacharya 1999).

As an institutional alternative, Stiglitz suggests an establishment of an international body that would provide 'global greenbacks' to the countries facing deficits and financial distress (in Duncan 2005: 257). In a similar vein, asserting that 'the private sector is ill-suited to allocate international credit', Soros has suggested the

---

4   An SDR-based currency.

creation of an International Credit Insurance Corporation (ICIC) to guarantee international loans. The ICIC would help control crisis-prone credit expansions and contractions inherent in the current market-dominated system (*Financial Times*, 31 December 1997). He added that 'the IMF has to become more of a lender of last resort, on an international scale... [it should] develop in the direction of an international central bank' (Soros 2000).

In the wake of the crises, financial regulators stressed the need for convergence and transparency, prioritising identical rules on accounting, auditing and governance across the world. But gradually, it has transpired that this programme was far too ambitious: as a result, financial watchdogs are switching their attention to more achievable principles of 'mutual recognition' of regulations that affect accountants and companies operating in multiple jurisdictions. This change, *Financial Times* argues, reflects a pragmatism borne of futile attempts to achieve full convergence. 'Talk of mutual recognition at least signals that the objectives are maturing, away from the idealism of full convergence towards a more realistic attempt to get along' (Jopson 2006: 1–2).

Yet despite some notable shifts from the financial consensus of the 1980s and early 1990s, the 'new macroprudential framework' of financial regulation is still limited in its ability to account for the link between microeconomic risk-taking and macroeconomic performance. The existing approach to financial regulation focusses on payment and banking systems within their national jurisdictions; it largely ignores the evolution of the non-bank financial institutions, leaving the global interconnectedness of private credit networks outside the frame of regulation (Alexander *et al.* 2006: 268). As a result, notwithstanding recent advances in regulation and some improvements in the balance sheets of companies and banks, the global financial system is more opaque and complex than ever. In this sense, the new post-Keynesian insights into the dynamics of financial markets, although signifying an interesting methodological shift, offer little pledge of financial stability: when it comes to detecting new strains in the system, 'policymakers are increasingly flying blind' (Tett 2005).

Ironically, it transpires that if the recent insights into the behaviour of financial markets brought something qualitatively new to the policy consensus compared to its formulation in the 1980s and

1990s, it is in the growing realisation that today, financial regulators are often helpless in the face of outbreaks of financial volatility and crises. The recent crises have cast new light on many of the previously ignored processes of financial evolution; yet many dangers of credit expansions still remain hidden from the regulators' lens. And while the global financial system seems to have withstood the shocks of the recent years, largely with the help of timely interventions by monetary authorities, the sustainability of current global capital boom is not certain...

As the process of private financial expansion continues, as Minsky forewarned, 'innovations, particularly in finance, assure that problems of instability will continue to crop up; the result will be equivalent but not identical bouts of instability to those that are so evident in history' (1986: 287). At the time of writing, the confidence associated with relative stability of advanced economies complicates the challenge to discern the risks posed by the global spread of financial innovation.[5]

In this instance, as in others, Hyman Minsky cautions: one of the causes of financial instability is...stability itself. Stability encourages optimism, financial experimentation, innovation and excessive risk-taking. Therefore unfortunately, any endeavour to stabilise the financial markets and an attempt at 'restructuring will enjoy only transitory success'. The current relative stability of global financial markets does offer some breathing space for national and global policymakers. It is important to use this space in order to prepare for the next, and unfortunately, inevitable cycle of distress and crises, and to learn the ways to minimise their social costs. A closer focus on the dilemmas of liquidity, fragility and systemic risks in the emerging regulatory framework is a right step in that direction, and the scholarship of Minsky and his

---

5   As one shrewd observer notes: 'Until very recently, we have seen an unusual dynamic in financial markets, in which low realised volatility in macroeconomic outcomes, low realised credit losses and low uncertainty about future inflation and interest rates have worked together to bring risk premia down across many asset prices. There is a self-reinforcing character to this pattern, with past stability seemingly increasing confidence in future stability, and this dynamic itself can magnify the risk of a more damaging reversal' (Geither 2005).

followers offers a fertile pool of knowledge for such an exercise. And yet among the many lessons that Minskyan and post-Keynesian readings of financial fragility have to offer, one stands out in particular. It may well be that along with many other products of the three decades of private financial innovation – such as the emergence risk management tools, new techniques of investment and greater variety of financial strategies and institutions – it is uncertainty and therefore, endemic fragility, that are the most lasting legacy of the post-Bretton Woods financial revolution.

Bibliography

Abeles, M., 2005, 'Economic Openness, Financial Fragility and Corporate Finance: A Minskyan Perspective on Argentina's 2001 Crisis', paper to the Annual Conference for Development and Change, New School University.

Aglietta, M. and R. Breton, 2001, 'Financial Systems, Corporate Control and Capital Accumulation', *Economy and Society*, 30(4): 433–66.

Akira, S., 1989, *Capital Accumulation in Thailand 1855–1985*, Tokyo: The Center for East Asian Cultural Studies, pp. 154–72.

Akyus, Y., 1998, 'The East Asian Financial Crisis: Back to the Future', in J. Jomo (ed.) *Tigers in Trouble. Financial Governance, Liberalisation and Crises in East Asia*, London, New York: Zed Books.

Alexander, K., R. Dhumale and J. Eatwell, 2006, *Global Governance of Financial Systems. The International Regulation of Systemic Risk*, Oxford: OUP.

Alexander, W., D. Hoelscher and M. Fuchs, 2000, 'Banking System Restructuring in Russia', Washington DC: International Monetary Fund, www.imf.org/external/pubs/ft/seminar/2000/invest/pdf/alexander.pdf

Allen, F. and D. Gale, 1999, 'Bubbles, Crises and Policy', *Oxford Review of Economic Policy*, 15(3): 9–18.

Allen, R., 1999, *Financial Crises and Recession in the Global Economy*, Cheltenham: Edward Elgar.

Alper, E., 2001, 'The Turkish Liquidity Crisis of 2000', *Russian and East European Finance and Trade*, 37(6).

Altvater, E., 1997, 'Financial Crises at the Threshold of the 21st Century', *Socialist Register*.

Altvater, E., 2002, 'The Growth Obsession', *Socialist Register*, 73–92.

Arestis, P. and M. Glickman, 2002, 'Financial Crisis in Southeast Asia: Dispelling Illusion the Minskyan way', *Cambridge Journal of Economics*, 26: 237–60.

Arestis, P. and M. Sawyer, 1999, 'The Tobin Tax', in J. Michie and J. Smith (eds) *Global Instability. The Political Economy of World Economic Governance*, London: Routledge.

Arestis, P. and M. Sawyer, 2001, *Money, Finance and Capitalist Development*, Cheltenham, Northampton, MA: Edward Elgar.

Arestis, P., 2001, 'Recent Banking and Financial Crises: Minsky vs. the Financial Liberalisationists', in R. Bellofiore and P. Ferris (eds) *Financial Keynesianism and Market Instability. The Economic Legacy of Hyman Minsky*, Vol. 1, Cheltenham: Edward Elgar.

Arrighi, G., 1994, *The Long Twentieth Century*, London: Verso.

Armijo, L. (ed.), 2001, *Financial Globalisation and Democracy in Emerging Markets*, Basingstoke: Palgrave.

Aslund, A., 1998, Russia's Financial Crisis: Causes and Possible Remedies', *Post-Soviet Geography and Economics*, 39(6).

Aslund, A., 1999, 'Russia's Virtual Economy: A Comment', *Post-Soviet Geography and Economics*, 40(2).

Aslund, A., 2002, *Building Capitalism*, Cambridge: Cambridge University Press.

Aysha, E., 2001, 'The US Boom, 'Clintonomics' and the New Economy Doctrine', *New Political Economy*, 6(3).

Aziz, J., F. Caramazza and R. Salgado, 2000, 'Currency Crises: In Search of Common Elements', IMF Working Paper, WP/00/67.

Baddeley, M. and J. McCombie, 2001, 'An Historical Perspective on Speculative Bubbles and Financial Crises: Tulipmania and the South Sea Bubble', in P. Arestis *et al.* (eds) *What Global Economic Crisis?*, Basingstoke: Palgrave.

Bartholomew, P. and R. Phillips, 2000, 'Dealing with Financial Crises: Lessons from Minsky,' paper presented at the 10th Annual Hyman P. Minsky Conference on Financial Structure at the Jerome Levy Economics Institute of Bard College, 27–28 April.

Beams, N., 2002, 'The World Economic Crisis: 1991–2001', *World Socialist Web Site*, 15 March.

Bedirhanoglu, P., 2004, 'The Nomenklatura's Passive Revolution in Russia in the Neoliberal Era', in L. McCann (ed.) *Russian Transformations. Challenging the Global Narrative*, London, New York: RoutledgeCurzon.

Beeson, M. and R. Robison, 2000, 'Introduction. Interpreting the Crisis', in R. Robison, M., Beeson, K., Jayasuriya and H. Kym (eds) *Politics and Markets in the Wake of the Asian Crisis*, London: Routledge.

Beeson, M., 1998, 'Indonesia, the East Asian Crisis and the Commodification of the Nation-State', *New Political Economy*, 3(3).

Bell, S., 2001, 'The Role of the State in the Hierarchy of Money', *Cambridge Journal of Economics*, 25: 149–63.

Bello, W., N. Bullard and K. Malhotra (eds), 2000, *Global Finance. New Thinking on Regulating Speculative Capital Markets*, London, New York: Zed Books.

Bello, W., K. Malhotra, N. Bullard and M. Mezzera, 2000, 'Notes on the Ascendancy and Regulation of Speculative Capital', in W. Bello, N. Bullard and K. Malhotra (eds) *Global Finance. New Thinking on Regulating Speculative Capital Markets*, London, New York: Zed Books.

Bellofiore, R. and P. Ferris, 2001, *Financial Keynesianism and Market Instability. The Economic Legacy of Hyman Minsky*, Vol. 1, Cheltenham: Edward Elgar.

Ben-Ami, D., 2001, *Cowardly Capitalism*, New York: John Wiley & Sons.

Bernard, M., 1999, 'East Asia's Tumbling Dominoes: Financial Crises and the Myth of Regional Model', *Socialist Register*.

Best, J., 2005, *The Limits of Transparency. Ambiguity and History of International Finance*, Ithaca and London: Cornell University Press.

Bevacqua, R., 1998, 'Whither Japanese Model? The Asian Economic Crisis and the Continuation of Cold War Politics in the Pacific Rim', *Review of International Political Economy*, 5, 410–23.

Bezemer, D., 2001, 'Post-Socialist Financial Fragility: The Case of Albania', *Cambridge Journal of Economics*, 25: 1–23.

Bies, S., 2002, 'The Challenge for Corporate Governance Posed by Financial Innovation', Federal Reserve Board, October 2002.

Binswanger, M., 1999, Stock Markets, Speculative Bubbles and Economic Growth: New Dimersions in the Co-evolution of Real and Financial Markets, Cheltenham, UK and Northampton, MA: Edward Elgar.

Bird, G. and A. Milne, 1999, 'Miracle to Meltdown: A Pathology of the East Asian Financial Crisis', *Third World Quarterly*, 20(2): 421–37.

Bird, G. and R. Rajan, 2002, 'Regional Arrangements for Providing Liquidity in a Financial Crisis: Developments in East Asia', *The Pacific Review*, 15(3): 359–79.

BIS, 1986, Annual Report, Basel: Bank for International Settlements.

BIS, 2000/2001, 71st Annual Report, 1 April 2000–31 March 2001, Basel: Bank for International Settlements.

BIS, 2001/2002, 72nd Annual Report, Basel: Bank for International Settlements.

BIS, 2003, *Quarterly Review*, December, Basel: Bank for International Settlements.

BIS, 2005a, *Annual Report* (75), Basel: Bank for International Settlements.

BIS, 2005b, Derivatives Statistics, Basel: Bank for International Settlements.

Bisigano, J., 1999, 'Precarious Credit Equilibria: Reflections on the AFC', BIS Working Paper No. 64, Basel: BIS.

Blinder, A., 1999, 'Eight Steps to a New Financial Order', *Foreign Affairs*, September/October.

Blustein, P., 2003, *The Chastening: Inside the Crisis that Rocked the Global Financial System and Humbled the IMF*, New York: Public Affairs.

Board of Investment, 2000, *A Guide to the Board of Investment*, Bangkok: The Office of the Board of Investment.

Bonner, W. and A. Wiggin, 2005, *Financial Reckoning Day. Surviving the Soft Depression of the 21st Century*, New York: John Wiley and Sons.

Bookstaber, R., 2000, 'Understating and Monitoring the Liquidity Crisis Cycle', *Financial Analysts Journal*, September/October.

Bootle, R., 2003, *Money For Nothing*, Yarmouth, Maine: Nicolas Brealey.

Bordo, M., 2002, 'The End of Globalization, by J. James', Review, *Finance and Development*, Washington D.C.: IMF.

Bordo, M., B. Eichengreen, D. Klingebiel, M.S. Martinez Peria and A.K. Rose, 2001, 'Is the Crisis Problem Growing More Severe?', *Economic Policy*, No. 32, April, 51–82.

Bordo, M., B. Mizrach and A. Schwartz, 1995, 'Real vs Pseudo-International Systemic Risk: Some Lessons from History', NBER Working Paper 5371, December.

Borensztein, E. and Lee Jong-Wha, 1999, 'Credit Allocation and Financial Crisis in Korea', International Monetary Fund Working Paper No. 99/20, Washington D.C., February, 1999.

Borio, C. and P. Lowe, 2002, 'Asset Prices. Financial and Monetary Stability: Exploring the Nexus', BIS Working Paper No. 114, Basel: BIS, July.

Borio, C., 2000, 'Market Liquidity and Stress: Selected Issues and Policy Implications', in *BIS Quarterly Review*, November, Basel: Bank for International Settlements.

Borio, C., 2004, 'Market Distress and Vanishing Liquidity: Anatomy and Policy Options', BIS Working Paper No. 158, Basel: Bank for International Settlements, July.

Borio, C., W. English and A. Filardo, 2003, 'A Tale of Two Perspectives: Old or New Challenges for Monetary Policy?', BIS Working Paper No. 127, Basel: Bank for International Settlements.

Boyer, R., 2000, 'Is a Finance-led Growth Regime a Viable Alternative to Fordism?', *Economy and Society*, 29(1): 111–45.

Braudel, F., 1982, *Civilization and Capitalism*, London: Collins.

Brealey, R., A. Clark, Ch. Goodhart, J. Healey, G. Hoggarth, D. Llewellyn, C. Shu, P. Sinclair and F. Soussa, 2001, *Financial Stability and Central Bank: A Global Perspective*, London: Routledge.

Brenner, R., 1998, 'The Economics of Global Turbulence', *New Left Review*, May/June.

Brenner, R., 2000, 'The Boom and the Bubble', *New Let Review*, No. 6, November/December.

Brenner, R., 2001, 'The World Economy at the Turn of the Millennium toward Boom or Crisis?', *Review of International Political Economy*, 8(1).

Brown-Humes, Ch., 2006, 'Emerging Markets are Vigorous – For Now', *Financial Times*, 1 March.

Bryant, R., 1987, *International Financial Intermediation*, Washington D.C.: The Brookings Institution.

Buchs, T., 1999, 'Financial Crisis in the Russian Federation', *Economics of Transition*, 7(3): 687–715.

Buiter, W., 2000, 'From Predation to Accumulation? The Second Transition Decade in Russia', *Economics of Transition*, 8(3): 603–22.

Burgess, K., 2002, 'The Wheel is Spinning, Once Again', *Financial Times*, 30/31 March.

Burke, M., 2001, 'The Changing Nature of Imperialism: The US as Author of the Asian crisis of 1997', *Historical Materialism*, Vol. 8.

Burkett, P. and M. Hart-Landsberg, 2001, 'Crisis and Recovery in East Asia: The Limits of Capitalist Development', *Historical Materialism*, 8.

Burn, G., 1999, 'The State, the City and the Euromarkets', *Review of International Political Economy*, 6(2): 225–61.

Burn, G., 2006, *The Re-emergence of Global Finance*, Basingstoke: Palgrave Macmillan.

Caprio, G., J. Hanson and R. Litan (eds), 2005, *Financial Crises. Lessons from the Past, Preparation for the Future*, Washington D.C.: Brookings Institution Press.

Cardoso, E. and A. Helwege, 2001, 'The 1990s Crisis in Emerging Markets: The Case of Brazil', in D. Dasgupta, M. Uzan and D. Wilson (eds) *Capital Flows Without Crisis?*, London, New York: Routledge.

Cartapanis, A. and M. Herland, 2002, 'The Reconstruction of the International Financial Architecture: Keynes' Revenge?', *Review of International Political Economy*, 9(2): 257–83.

Castells, M., 1993, 'The Informational Economy and the New International Division of Labour', in M. Carnoy, M. Castells, S. Cohen and F. Cardoso, *The New Global Economy in the Information Age*, London: Macmillan.

Castells. M., 1996, *The Rise of the Network Society*, Oxford: Blackwell.

Castells, M., 2000, *End of Millennium*, Oxford: Blackwell.

Cerny, P., 1994, 'The Infrastructure of Infrastructure', in R. Palan, B. Gills (eds) *Transcending the State-Global Divide*, Boulder Co: Lynne Publishers.

Chandrasekhar, C. and J. Ghosh, 1998, 'Hubris, Hysteria, Hope: The Political Economy of Crisis and Response in Southeast Asia', in K.S. Jomo (ed.) *Tigers in Trouble: Financial Governance, Liberalisation and Crises in East Asia*, London: Zed Books.

Chang, H., H. Park and C. Yoo, 1998, 'Interpreting the Korea crisis: Financial Liberalisation, Industrial Policy and Corporate Governance', *Cambridge Journal of Economics*, 22: 735–46.

Chang, H-J., 2000, 'The Hazard of Moral Hazard – Untangling the Asian crisis', *World Development*, 28(4): 775–88.

Chang, H-L., 1998, 'Korea: the Misunderstood Crisis', *World Development*, 26: 1555–61.

Chang, R. and A. Velasco, 1998, 'The Asian Liquidity Crisis', Federal Reserve Bank of Atlanta, Working Paper 98-11, July.

Chang, R. and A. Velasco, 1999, 'Liquidity Crises in Emerging Markets: Theory and Policy', NBER Working Paper No. 7272, July.

Chapman, S. and M. Mulino, 2001, 'Explaining Russia's Currency and Financial Crisis', *MOST*, 11: 1–26.

Cheng, I., 2002, 'Survivors Who Laughed All the Way to the Bank', *Financial Times*, 30 July.

Chinyaeva, E., 2003, 'The Russian Economy, Lost in the Dark', *Russia and Eurasia Review*, 2(3), 4 February.

Clarke, S., 1994, *Marx's Theory of Crisis*, New York: St. Martin's Press.

Clarke, S., 2001, 'Class Struggle and the Global Overaccumulation Problem', in R. Albritton (ed.) *Phases of Capitalist Development*, Basingstoke: Palgrave.

Clarke, S., 2003, 'Globalisation and the Development of Russian Capitalism', paper to the international conference Marx and the challenges of the 21st century, Havana, 5–8 May 2003, http://www.nodo50.org/cubasigloXXI/congreso/clarke_10abr03.pdf

Coggan, P. 2002, 'Goodbye, Easy Money', *Financial Times*, 27 July.

Cohen, B. and H. Shin 2003, 'Measuring Liquidity Black Holes', in A. Persaud (ed.), *Liquidity Black Holes: Understanding, Quantifying and Managing Financial Liquidity Risk*, London: Risk Book.

Colecchia, A. and P. Schreyer, 2002, 'The Contribution of Information and Communication Technologies to Economic Growth in Nine OECD Countries', *OECD Economic Studies*, 34(1).

Commander, S. and Ch. Mummsen, 2000, 'The Growth of Non-monetary Transactions in Russia: Causes and Effects in P. Seabright (ed.) *The Vanishing Rouble*, Cambridge: Cambridge University Press.

Commons, J., 2003, *Institutional Economics. Its Place in Political Economy*, New Brunswick and London: Transaction Publishers.

Congdon, T., 1988, *The Debt Trap*, Oxford: Basil Blackwell.

Corbridge, S., 1993, 'Discipline and Punish: The New Right and the Politics of the International Debt Crisis', in G. Riley, (ed.) *The Politics of Global Debt*, Basingstoke: Palgrave Macmillan.

Corsetti, G., P. Pesenti and N. Roubini, 1999, 'Paper Tigers? A Model of the Asian Crisis', *European Economic Review*.

Counterparty Risk Management Policy Group (CRMPG), 2005, *Toward Greater Financial Stability: A Private Sector Perspective*, Report, 27 July; www.crmpolicygroup.org

Cox, R. and T. Sinclair, 1996, *Approaches to World Order*, Cambridge: Cambridge University Press.

CRMPG, 2005, *Towards Greater Financial Stability: A Private Sector Perspective*, Report, 27 July, Counterparty Risk Management Policy Group www.crmpolicygroup.org

Crockett, A., 2003, Central Banking under Test, in 'Monetary Stability, Financial Stability and the Business Cycle: Five Views', BIS Paper No. 18, September.

Crotty, J. and G. Dymski, 2001, 'Can the Global Neo-liberal Regime Survive Victory in Asia?', in P. Arestis and M. Sawyer (eds) *Money, Finance and Capitalist Development*, Cheltenham: Edward Elgar.

Crotty, J. and K. Lee, 2002, 'A Political Economy Analysis of the Failure of Neo-liberal Restructuring in Post-crisis Korea', *Cambridge Journal of Economics*, 26: 667–78.

Dadush, U., D. Dasgupta and D. Ratha, 2000, 'The Role of Short-term Debt in Recent Crises', *Finance and Development*, December, 37(4): 54–7.

Dasgupta, D., M. Uzan and D. Wilson (eds), 2001, *Capital Flows with-out Crisis? Reconciling Capital Mobility and Economic Stability*, London: Routledge.

Davidson, P., 1992, *International Money and the Real World*, Basingstoke, London: Macmillan.

Davidson, P., 2001, 'If Markets are Efficient, Why Have There Been So Many International Financial Market Crises since the 1970s?', in P. Arestis *et al.* (eds), *What Global Economic Crisis?* Basingstoke: Palgrave.

Davidson, P., 2004, 'The Future of the International Financial System', *Journal of Post-Keynesian Economics*, 26(4).

Davis, P., 2003, Towards a Typology for Systemic Financial Instability, 12 November, *Financial Stability Review*, No. 2 of the Austrian National Bank.

de Goede, M., 2001, 'Discourses of Scientific Finance and the Failure of LTCM', *New Political Economy*, 6(2): 149–70.

de Goede, M., 2005, *Virtue, Fortune and Faith. A Genealogy of Finance*, London, Minneapolis: University of Minnesota Press.

Detragiache, E., 1996, 'Rational Liquidity Crises in Sovereign Debt Market: In Search of a Theory', *IMF Staff Papers*, 43(3).

Diaz, A. and F. Carlos, 1985, 'Goodbye Financial Repression, Hello Financial Crash', *Journal of Development Studies*, December.

Dodd, N., 1994, *The Sociology of Money. Economics, Reason and Contemporary Society*, Oxford, Cambridge: Polity/Blackwell.

Dodd, R., 2002, 'The Role of Derivatives in East Asian Financial Crisis', in J. Eatwell and L. Taylor (eds) *International Capital Markets. Systems in Transition*, Oxford: Oxford University Press.

Drucker, P., 1986, 'The Changed World Economy', *Foreign Affairs*, Spring, 64(4).

Dubinin, S., 1997, Interview to Radio Svoboda, 17 July.

Dumenil, G. and D. Levy, 2001, 'Costs and Benefits of Neoliberalism. A Class Analysis', *Review of International Political Economy*, 8(4): 578–607.

Dunbar, N., 2000, *Inventing Money. The Story of LTCM and the Legends Behind It*, Chichester, New York: John Wiley.

Duncan, R., 2005, *The Dollar Crisis*, New York: John Wiley and Sons.

Dymski, G., 2003, 'The International Debt Crisis', in J. Michie (ed.) *The Handbook of Globalisation*, Cheltenham: Edward Elgar.

Eatwell, J. and L. Taylor, 2000, *Global Finance at Risk*, Oxford: Polity Press.

Eatwell, J. and L. Taylor (eds), 2002, *International Capital Markets. Systems in Transition*, Oxford: Oxford University Press.

Eatwell, J., 2004, 'Useful Bubbles', *Contributions to Political Economy*, 23: 35–47.

Edwards F., 1999, 'Hedge Funds and the Collapse of LTCM', *Journal of Economic Perspectives*, 13(2).

Eichengreen, B. and R. Hausmann, 2002, 'How to Eliminate Original Financial Sin', *Financial Times*, 21 November.

Eichengreen, B. and K. Mitchener, 2003, 'The Great Depression as a credit boom gone wrong', BIS Working Paper No. 137, September.

Eichengreen, B. and R. Portes, 1987, 'The Anatomy of Financial Crises', in R. Portes and A. Swoboda (eds), *Threats to International Financial Stability*, Cambridge: Cambridge University Press.

Eichengreen, B., 1999, *Towards a New Financial Architecture: A Practical Post-Asian Agenda*, Washington D.C.: Institute for International Economics.

Eichengreen, B., 2002, *Financial Crises and What to Do About Them*, Oxford: Oxford University Press.

Ericson, R., 1999, 'Comment on an Accounting Model of Russia's virtual economy', *Post-Soviet Geography and Economics*, 40(2).

Ershov, M., 2000, *Valytno-Finansovye Mekhanismy v Sovremennom Mire*, Moscow: Ekonomika.

Fama, E.F., 1970, 'Efficient Capital Markets: A Review of Theory and Empirical Work', *Journal of Finance*, 25: 383–417.

Fay, C.K. and K.S. Jomo, 2001, 'Financial Intermediation and Restraint', in K.S. Jomo and Shymala Nagaraj (eds) *Globalization versus Development*, Basingstoke: Palgrave.

Federal Council, 1999, 'Zaklychenie vremennoi komissii Soveta Federacii po rassledovaniy prichin, obstojatelstv I posedstvii prinjatija reshenii pravitelstva Rossii I centralnogo banka Rossiiskoi Federacii to 17 avgusta 1998 goda', *Sovet Federacii Rossii*, Moscow 25 February, mimeo.

Feldstein, M., 1999, 'A Self-help Guide for Emerging Markets', *Foreign Affairs*, Match/April, 78(2).

Felix, D., 1999, 'Open Economy Minsky-Keynes and Global Financial Crises', presented at the 9th Annual Hyman Minsky Conference on Financial Structure, Jerome Levy Economics Institute, April 21–23.

Felix, D., 2003, 'The Past as Future? The Contribution of Financial Globalization to the Current Crisis of Neo-Liberalism as a Development Strategy', Washington University in St. Louis, September, 2003.

Ferguson, R., 2003, 'Should Financial Stability be an Explicit Central Bank Objective?', BIS Paper No. 18, Monetary Stability, Financial Stability and the Business Cycle: Five Views, Basel: BIS.

Fernandez, F., 1999, 'Liquidity Risk: New Approaches to Measurement and Monitoring', Securities Industry Association.

Ffench-Davis, R. and R. Studart, 2003, 'The Regional Fallout of Argentina's Crisis', in *The crisis that was Not Prevented: Argentina, the IMF and Globalisation*, FoNDAD, January 2003, www.fondad.org

Fidler, S. and V. Boland, 2002, 'Debt Mountains Threaten Avalanche', *Financial Times*, 31 May.

Fifield, A., 2004, 'The Economy: Time to Write Off Some Debt?', *Financial Times*, 1 December.

Fine, B., C. Lapavitsas and D. Milonakis, 1999, 'Addressing the World Economy: Two Steps Back', *Capital and Class*, No. 67.

Finnerty, J., 1992, 'Financial Engineering', in P. Newman *et al.*, *The New Palgrave Dictionary of Money and Finance*, London: Macmillan.

Fisher, S., 1998, 'The Russian Economy at the Start of 1998', Washington D.C.: International Monetary Fund, January 9 (http://www.imf.org/external/np/speeches/1998/010998.htm).

FitchRating, 2004, 'CDS Market Liquidity: Show Me the Money', *Corporate Finance*, 15 November, www.fitchratings.com

Flemming, J., 1982, 'A Comment on Minsky's Financial Instability Hypothesis', in Ch. Kindleberger, and J-P. Laffargue, 1982, *Financial Crises. Theory, History and Policy*, Cambridge: Cambridge University Press.

Fortin, C., 2000, 'Practical Proposals. The UN System and Financial Regulation', in W. Bello, N. Bullard and K. Malhotra, *Global Finance. New Thinking on Regulating Speculative Capital Flows*, London and New York: Zed Books.

Fortune, 2002, 'System Failure', 24 June.

Fratianni, M. and J. Pattison, 2002, 'International Standards, Crisis Management and Lenders of last Resort in the International Financial Architecture', in M. Fratianni, P. Savona, J. Kirton (eds) *Governing Global Finance, New Challenges, G7 and IMF Contributions*, Aldershot: Ashgate.

Freeland, C., 2000, *The Sale of the Century*, London: Little, Brown and Co.

Frieden, J., 1981, 'Third World Indebted Industrialization: International Finance and State Capitalism in Mexico, Brazil, Algeria and South Korea', *International Organization*, 35(1): 407–31.

Friedman, M. and A. Schwartz, 1963, *A Monetary History of the US, 1867–60*, Princeton: Princeton University Press.

Froud, J., S. Johal, C. Haslam and K. Williams, 2001, 'Accumulation under Conditions of Inequality', *Review of International Political Economy*, 8(1): 66–95.

Gaddy, C. and B. Ickes, 1998, 'Russia's Virtual Economy', *Foreign Affairs*, 77(5).

Gaddy, C. and B. Ickes, 1999, 'An Accounting Model of the Virtual Economy in Russia', *Post-Soviet Geography and Economics*, 40(2).

Galbraith, J., 1955, *The Great Crash of 1929*, London: Hamilton.

Galbraith, J.K., 1994, *The World Economy Since the Wars*, London: Sinclair-Stevenson.

Garber, P., 2000, *Famous First Bubbles: The Fundamentals of Early Manias*, Cambridge, Mass.: MIT Press.

Geither, T., 2005, 'Overview of the US Financial System', Remarks at the Bond Markets Association's Annual Meeting, New York, 20 April.

Germain, R., 1997, *The International Organization of Credit: States and Global Finance in the World Economy*, Cambridge: Cambridge University Press.

Giddens, A., 1991, *Modernity and Self-Identity*, Cambridge: Polity.

Gilpin, R., 2000, *Global Political Economy*, Princeton: Princeton University Press.

Glaziev, S., 1998, *Genocide*, Moscow: Terra.

Glaziev, S., 2000, 'Vozmozhen li v Rossii novyi finansovyi krisis?', *Vopsosy Ekonomiki*, March.

Gnos, C. and L-P. Rochon, 2004, 'Reforming the International Financial and Monetary System: from Keynes to Davidson and Stiglitz', *Journal of Post-Keynesian Economics*, 26(4): 613–29.

Godement, F., 1999, *The Downsizing of Asia*, London, New York: Routledge.

Goldfrain, I. and R. Valdes, 1997, 'Capital Flows and the Twin Crises: The Role of Liquidity', *Working Paper 97-87*, International Monetary Fund, July.

Goldsmith, R., 1982, 'A Comment on Minsky's Financial Instability Hypothesis', in Kindleberger, Ch., Laffargue, J-P. *Financial Crises. Theory, History and Policy*, Cambridge: Cambridge University Press.

Golub, P., 2004, 'From Globalisation to Militarism: The American Hegemonic Cycle and System-wide Crisis', in I. Assassi, D. Wigan and K. van der Pijl (eds) *Global Regulation. Managing Crises After the Imperial Turn*, Basingstoke: Palgrave Macmillan.

Goodhart, Ch. and G. Illing, 2002, *Financial Crises, Contagion and the Lender of Last Resort. A Reader*, Oxford: Oxford University Press.

Grabel, I. 1999, 'Rejecting Exceptionalism. Reinterpreting the Asian Financial Crises', in J. Michie, J. Smith (eds) *Global Instability. The Political Economy of World Economic Governance*, London: Routledge.

Grabel, I., 2000, 'The Asian Financial Crisis. What Went Wrong?', in R. Baiman, H. Boushey, D. Saunders (eds), *Political Economy and Contemporary Capitalism. Radical Perspectives on Economic Theory and Policy*, Armonk, London: M.E. Sharpe.

Grahl, J. and P. Teague, 2000, 'The Regulation School, the Employment Relation and Financialization', *Economy and Society*, 29(1) (February), 160–78.

Granville, B., 1999, 'Bingo or Fiasco? The Global Financial Situation is Not Guaranteed', *International Affairs*, 75(4): 713–28.

Gray, H. and J. Gray, 1994, 'Minskian Fragility in the International Financial System', in G. Dymski and R. Pollin (eds), *New Perspectives in Monetary Economics*, Ann Arbor: University of Michigan Press.

Gray, J., 1998, *False Down. The Delusions of Global Capitalism*, London: Granta Books.

Greider, W., 1997, *One World, Ready or Not: The Manic Logic of Global Capitalism*, London: Penguin Books.

Griesgraber, J.M. and B. Gunter, 1996, *The World's Monetary System*, London: Pluto.

Griffith-Jones, S. and O. Sunkel, 1989, *Debt and Development Crises in Latin America*, Oxford: Clarendon Paperbacks.

Griffith-Jones, S., 1998, *Global Capital Flows. Should They Be Regulated?* Basingstoke: Macmillan.

Griffith-Jones, S. and J. Kimmis, 1999, 'Stabilising Capital Flows to Developing Countries', in J. Michie and J. Smith (eds) *Global Instability. The Political Economy of World Economic Governance*, London: Routledge.

Grossman, S. and M. Miller, 1988, 'Liquidity and Market Structure', *Journal of Finance*, 43(3): 179–207.

Gruben, W., 2001, 'Mexico: The Trajectory to the 1994 Devaluation', in L. Armijo (ed.) *Financial Globalisation and Democracy in Emerging Markets*, Basingstoke: Palgrave.

Gustafson, T., 1999, *Capitalism Russian-Style*, Cambridge: Cambridge University Press.

Guttman, R., 1994, *How Credit-Money Shapes the Economy*, New York: M.E. Sharpe.

Ha, Y-C. and T. Kim, 2003, 'Lessons from the Asian Economic Crisis: A View from South Korea', *Cambridge Review of International Affairs*, 16(1), April.

Haggard, S. and A. McIntyre, 1998, 'The Political Economy of the Asian Economic Crisis', *Review of International Political Economy*, 5(3).

Haley, M., 2001, 'Emerging Market Makers: The Power of institutional Investors', in L. Armijo (ed.), *Financial Globalisation and Democracy in Emerging Markets*, Basingstoke: Palgrave.

Halligan, L., 2005, 'The Debt Pandemic', *New Statesman*, 24 October.

Harmes, A., 1998, 'Institutional Investors and the Reproduction of Neo-liberalism', *Review of International Political Economy*, 5(1): 92–121.

Hart, K., 2001, *Money in the Unequal World*, London, New York: Textere Publishing.

Hart-Landsberg, M. and P. Burkett, 1999, 'East Asia in Crisis', *Monthly Review*, June.

Harvey, D., 1990, *The Condition of Postmodernity. An Enquiry into the Origins of Cultural Change*, Cambridge and Oxford: Blackwell.

Harvey, D., 1999, *The Limits to Capital*, London: Verso.

Heise, M., R. Schneider, D. Milleker and C. Broyer, 2005, 'Global Liquidity Glut: Problem or Growth Driver?', *Economy and Markets*, July.

Helleiner, E., 1994, *States and the Re-emergence of Global Finance*, Ithaca and London: Cornell University Press.

Helleiner, E., 2005, 'The Strange Story of Bush and the Argentine Debt Crisis', *Third World Quarterly*, 26(6).

Henderson, J., 1999, 'Uneven Crises: Institutional Foundations of East Asian Economic Turmoil', *Economy and Society*, 28(3): 327–68.

Henwood, D., 1997, *Wall Street*, London: Verso.

Hewison, K., 2000, 'Thailand's Capitalism Before and After the Economic Crisis', in Richard Robison, Mark Beeson, Kanishka Jayasuriya and Hyuk-Rae Kim (eds) *Politics and Markets in the Wake of Asian Crisis*, London: Routledge.

Higgott, R., 1998, 'The Asian Economic Crisis: A Study in the Politics of Resentment', *New Political Economy*, 3(3).

Hilferding, R., 1981 *Finance Capital*, London: Routledge and Kegan Paul.

Hirst, P. and G. Thompson, 1999, *Globalisation in Question*, Oxford: Polity Press.

Hoffman, D., 2002, *The Oligarchs. Wealth and Power in the New Russia*, New York: Public Affairs.

Horne, J. and D. Nahm, 2000, 'International Reserves and Liquidity: A Reassessment', Department of Economics, Macquarie University, http://www.econ.mq.edu.au/research/2000/5-2000.pdf

Horowitz, S. and Heo, Uk (eds), 2001, *The Political Economy of International Financial Crisis*, Oxford, New York: Rowman & Littlefield.

Hughes, D., 2003, 'Flexible and Efficient Investments or Weapons of Mass Destruction?', *The Business*, 6/7 July 2003, p. 23.

Hunter, W., G. Kaufman and T. Krueger (eds), 1999, *The Asian Financial Crisis: Origins, Implications, and Solutions*, Boston: Kluwer Academic Publishers.

IIF, 1999, *Capital Flows to Emerging Market Economies*, 25 April, Washington D.C.: Institute for International Finance.

IMF, 1998, *World Economic Outlook* and *International Capital Markets*, Washington D.C.: International Monetary Fund.

IMF, 1999a, *International Capital Markets – Developments, Prospects and Key Policy Issues*, Washington D.C.: IMF, September.

IMF, 1999b, 'Global Liquidity', Box 4.4, *World Economic Outlook*, Washington D.C.: International Monetary Fund, October.

IMF, 2001a, *Emerging Market Financing Quarterly*, February, Washington D.C.: International Monetary Fund.

IMF, 2001b, *International Capital Markets*, Washington D.C.: International Monetary Fund.

IMF, 2002a, *Global Financial Stability Report*, Chapter 4, Washington D.C.: International Monetary Fund.

IMF, 2002b, 'Eye of the Storm', *Finance and Development*, 39(4), Washington D.C.: International Monetary Fund.

IMF, 2004a, *Global Financial Stability Report*, Washington D.C.: International Monetary Fund.

IMF, 2004b, *The Russian Federation. Statistical Appendix, Country Statistics*, Washington D.C.: International Monetary Fund.

IMF, 2005a, *Global Financial Stability Report*, Washington D.C.: International Monetary Fund, April.

IMF, 2005b, *World Economic Outlook*, Washington D.C.: International Monetary Fund.

IMF, 2006, *Regional Economic Outlook, Asia and the Pacific*, Washington D.C.: International Monetary Fund, May.

Isenberg, D., 1994, 'Financial Fragility and the Great Depression: New Evidence on Credit Growth in the 1920s', in G. Dymski and R. Pollin (eds) *New Perspectives in Monetary Economics. Explorations in the Tradition of H. Minsky*, Ann Arbor: University of Michigan Press.

Itoh, M. and C. Lapavitsas, 1998, *Political Economy of Money and Finance*, London and Basingstoke: Macmillan.

Johnson, Ch. 1998, 'Economic Crisis in East Asia: The Clash of Capitalisms', *Cambridge Journal of Economics*, 22(6): 653–61.

Jopson, B., 2006, 'Mutual Respect Might Replace Convergence', FT International Accountancy supplement, *Financial Times*, March 6, pp. 1–2.

Josephson, M., 1934 [1962], *The Robber Barons*, New York, London: Harvest Books.

Kahler, M. 1998, 'Introduction', in M. Kahler (ed.) *Capital Flows and Financial Crises*, Manchester: Manchester University Press.

Kaminksy, G. and C. Reinhart, 1998, 'The Twin Crises: The Causes of banking and Balance of Payments Problems', *American Economic Review*, 89: 473–501.

Kapstein, E., 1996, 'Shockproof: The End of Financial Crisis', *Foreign Affairs*, 75(1): 2–8.

Kapstein, E., 2006, 'Architects of Stability? International Cooperation among Financial Supervisors', BIS Working Paper No. 199, February, Basel: Bank for International Settlements.

Kaufman, H., 1998, 'The New Financial World: Policy Shortcoming and Remedies', in J. Fuhrer and S. Schuh (eds), *Beyond Shocks: What Causes Business Cycles?*, Conference Series, No. 42, June, Federal Reserve Bank of Boston.

Kenen, P., 2001, *The New International Financial Architecture. What's New, What's Missing*, Institute for International Economics.

Keynes, J.M., 1930, *A Treatise on Money*, London: Macmillan.

Keynes, J.M., 1931, 'The Consequences to the Banks of the Collapse of Money Values', in *Essays in Persuasion*, Vol. IX of the Collected Writings of John Maynard Keynes, Macmillan, St. Martins Press, for the Royal Economic Society.

Keynes, J.M., 1936, *The General Theory of Employment, Interest and Money*, London: Macmillan.

Kheifets, B., 2001, 'Russia's External Debt: New Management Strategy', www.wider.unu.edu/conference/conference-2001-2/poster%20papers/Kheifet.pdf

Kindleberger, C., 1988, *The International Economic Order: Essays on Financial Crisis and International Public Goods*, Brighton: Wheatsheaf.

Kindleberger, C., 1993, *A Financial History of Western Europe*, Oxford: Oxford University Press.

Kindleberger, Ch. and J-P. Laffargue, 1982, Introduction, in Ch. Kindleberger and J-P. Laffargue (eds) *Financial Crises. Theory, History and Policy*, Cambridge: Cambridge University Press.

Kindleberger, Ch., 1986, *Keynesianism vs. Monetarism and Other Essays in Financial Theory*, London: George Allen.

Kindleberger, Ch., 1996, *Maniacs, Panics and Crashes*, London: Macmillan.

King, J.E., 1995, 'Hyman Minsky: The Making of a Post Keynesian', Discussion Paper No. a.95.20.

King, M., 2001, 'Who Triggered the Asian Financial Crisis?', *Review of International Political Economy*, 8(3): 438–66.

Kirshner, J., 2003, 'Money is Politics,' *Review of International Political Economy*, 10(4).

Kiuchi, T., 2002, 'Japan, Asia and the Rebuilding of the Financial Sector', in M. Fratianni *et al.* (eds), *Governing Global Finance*, Aldershot: Ashgate.

Klebnikov, P., 2000, *Godfather of the Kremlin*, London, New York: Harcourt.

Knafo, S., 2006, 'The Gold Standard and the Origins of the Modern International System', *Review of International Political Economy*, 13(1): 78–102.

Knight, M., 2005, 'Challenges to Financial Stability in the Current Global Macroeconomic Environment', 6 September 2005, Speech at the IMF.

Kolodko, G., 2001, 'Globalization and Catching-up: From Recession to Growth in Transition Economies', *Communist and Post-Communist Studies*, 34: 279–322.

Kommersant, 1998, 'Kredit IMF yshel k Sorosy', No. 28, 29 July.

Korosteleva, J. and C. Lawson, 2005, 'The Belarusian Case of Transition: Whither Financial Repression?', Department of Economics & International Development, Working Paper, University of Bath.

Kregel, J., 1998a, 'Derivatives and Global Capital Flows: Applications to Asia', Jerome Levy Economics Institute, Working Paper No. 246.

Kregel, J., 1998b, 'East Asia is not Mexico: The Difference between Balance of Payments Crises and Debt Deflation', in K.S. Jomo (ed.) *Tigers in Trouble: Financial Governance, Liberalisation and Crises in East Asia*, London: Zed Books.

Kregel, J., 2000, 'The Brazilian Crisis: From Inertial Inflation to Fiscal Fragility', Levy Institute Working Paper No. 294, February, www.levy.org.

Kregel, J., 2001, 'Yes, "It" Did Happen Again – The Minsky Crisis in Asia', in R. Bellofiore and P. Ferris (eds), *Financial Keynesianism and Market Instability. The Economic Legacy of Hyman Minsky*, Vol. 1, Cheltenham: Edward Elgar.

Krueger, A., 2003, 'The IMF's View on the Restructuring of Sovereign Debt', *Financial Stability Review*, No. 3. Banque de France, November.

Krugman, P., 1979, 'A Model of Balance of Payments Crisis', *Journal of Money, Credit and Banking*, Vol. 11, August, pp. 311–25.

Krugman, P., 1997, 'Currency Crises', paper prepared for NBER conference, October, www.mit.edu/krugman/www/crises.html

Krugman, P., 1998, 'What Happened to Asia?', MIT Working Paper, January, http://web.mit.edu/krugman/www/DISINTER.html

Krugman, P., 2000, *The Return of Depression Economics*, London: Penguin.

Krugman, P. (ed.), 2002, *Currency Crises*, Chicago, London: University of Chicago Press.

Krugman, Paul R. and Maurice Obstfeld, 1997, *International Economics: Theory and Practice*, New York: Addison-Wesley.

Kurtzman, J., 1993, *The Death of Money*, New York, London: Little, Brown and Co.

Lagana, M., M. Perina, I. von Koppen-Mertes and A. Persaud, 2006, 'Implications for Liquidity From Innovation and Transparency in the European Corporate Bond Market', European Central Bank, Occasional Paper No. 50, August.

Lane, D., 2000, 'What Kind of Capitalism for Russia?', *Communist and Post-Communist Studies*, 33: 485–504.

Langley, P., 2002, *World Financial Orders: An Historical International Political Economy*, London and New York: Routledge.

Large, A., 2005, 'Financial Stability: Managing Liquidity Risk in a Global System', *Financial Stability Review*, December. London: Bank of England.

Lash, S. and J. Urry, 1994, *Economies of Signs and Space*, London: Sage.

Lauridsen, L., 1998, 'Thailand: Causes, Conduct, Consequences', in K.S. Jomo (ed.) *Tigers in Trouble: Financial Governance, Liberalization and Crisis in East Asia*, London: Zed Books.

Ledeneva, A., 1998, *Russia's Economy of Favours: Blat, Networking and Informal Exchange*, Cambridge and New York: Cambridge University Press.

Lee, H. and M. McNulty, 2003, 'East Asia's Dynamic Development Model and the Republic of Korea's Experiences', World Bank Policy Research Working Paper 2987, March.

Levy-Garboua, V. and B. Weumuller, 1979, *Macroeconomie Contemporaine*, Paris.

Leyshon, A. and N. Thrift, 1997, *Money/Space. Geographies of Monetary Transformation*, London: Routledge.

Liew, L., 1998, 'Political Economy Analysis of the Asian Financial Crisis', *Journal of the Asia Pacific Economy*, 3(3): 301–30.

Lipietz, A., 1983, *The Enchanted World. Inflation, Credit and the World Crisis*, London: Verso.

Lo, D., 2001, 'Consensus in Washington, Upheaval in East Asia', in B. Fine, C. Lapavitsas and J. Pincus (eds) *Development Policy in the 21ˢᵗ Century*, London, New York: Routledge.

Lowenstein, R., 2002, *When Genius Failed. The Rise and Fall of LTCM*, London: Fourth Estate.

Mackenzie, D., 2007, 'Globalisation, Efficient Markets, and Arbitrage', in L. Assassi, A. Nesvetailova, D. Wigan (eds) *Global Finance in the New Century*, Basingstoke: Palgrave Macmillan.

Magdoff, F., 2006, 'The Explosion of Debt and Speculation', *Monthly Review*, November, 58(6): 1–23.

Malhotra, K., 2000, 'Renewing the Governance of the Global Economy', in W. Bello, N. Bullard and K. Malhotra (eds) *Global Finance. New Thinking on Regulating Speculative Capital Flows*, London and New York: Zed Books.

Malkiel, B., 1987, 'Efficient Market Hypothesis', in J. Eatwell, M. Milgate and P. Newman (eds) *The New Palgrave: A Dictionary of Economics*, London: Macmillan.

Martinez, G., 1998, 'What Lessons Does the Mexican Crisis Hold for Recovery in Asia?', *Finance and Development*, 35(2): 6–9.

Mayer-Serra, C., 2001, 'Mexico: Foreign Investment and Democracy', in L. Armijo (ed.) *Financial Globalisation and Democracy in Emerging Markets*, Basingstoke: Palgrave.

McKinnon, R., 1973, *Money and Capital in Economic Development*, Washington D.C.: Brookings Institution.

McLeod, R., 2001, 'Lessons from Indonesia's Crisis', in D. Dasgupta, M. Uzan and D. Wilson (eds) *Capital Flows without Crisis? Reconciling Capital Mobility and Economic Stability*, London: Routledge.

Mehrling, P., 1999, 'The Vision of Hyman Minsky', *Journal of Economic Behaviour and Organization*, 39: 129–58.

Mehrling, P., 2001, 'Minsky, Modern Finance and the Case of LTCM', in R. Bellofiore and Piero Ferris (eds) *Financial Keynesianism and Market Instability. The Economic Legacy of Hyman Minsky*, Vol. 1, Cheltenham: Edward Elgar.

Mennicken, A., 2000, 'Figuring Trust: The Social Organisation of Credit Relations', in *Ökonomie und Geselllschaft*, Jahrbuch 16, Marburg: Metropolis Verlag.

Miller, M., 1986, 'Financial Innovation: The Last Twenty Years and the Next', *The Journal of Financial and Quantitative Analysis*, Vol. 21, No. 4, pp. 459–71.

Minsky, H., 1975, *John Maynard Keynes*, New York: Columbia University Press.

Minsky, H., 1977, 'A Theory of Systemic Fragility', in E. Altman and A. Sametz (eds) *Financial Crises: Institutions and Markets in a Fragile Environment*, New York: John Wiley and Sons.

Minsky, H., 1982a, *Can 'It' Happen Again?*, New York: M.E. Sharpe.

Minsky, H. 1982b, 'The Financial Instability Hypothesis: Capitalist Processes and the Behavior of the Economy', in Ch. Kindleberger and J-P. Laffargue, *Financial Crises, Theory, History and Policy*, Cambridge: Cambridge University Press.

Minsky, H., 1986, *Stabilizing an Unstable Economy*, New Haven, Conn.: Yale University Press.

Minsky, H., 1991a, 'Financial Crises: Systemic or Idiosyncratic', *Working Paper No. 51*, Jerome Levy Economics Institute, Bard College, April.

Minsky, H., 1991b, 'The Transition to a Market Economy: Financial Options', *Working Paper No. 66*, Jerome Levy Economics Institute, November.

Minsky, H., 1993, 'Finance and Stability: The Limits of Capitalism', *Working Paper No. 93*, Jerome Levy Economics Institute of Bard College.

Mishkin, F., 1996, 'Understanding Financial Crisis: A Developing Country Perspective', NBER Working Paper series, No. 5600, May.

Mishkin, F., 1999, 'Global Financial Stability: Framework, Events, Issues', *Journal of Economic Perspectives*, 13(4): 3–20.

Mishkin, F. and P. Strahan, 1999, 'What Will Technology Do to Financial Structure?', NBER Working Paper No. 6892, January, Cambridge, MA: National Bureau for Economic Research.

Montgomerie, 2006, 'Giving Credit Where It is Due: Public Policy and Household Indebtedness in Anglo-America', *Policy and Society*, 25(3), December.

Montgomerie, J., 2007, 'The Alchemy of Banks: The Consumer Credit Card Industry After Deregulation', in L. Assassi, A. Nesvetailova and D. Wigan (eds). *Global Finance in the New Century*, Basingstoke: Palgrave Macmillan.

Monthly Review, 2001, 'The New Economy: Myth and Reality', *Editorial*, April, 52(11).

Monthly Review, 2002, 'The New Face of Capitalism: Slow Growth, Excess Capital and a Mountain of Debt', *Editorial*, April, 53(11).

Mortimer-Lee, P., 1990, 'Globalization and Economic Policy', in R. O'Brien, I. Iversen (eds) *Finance and the International Economy*, Oxford: Oxford University Press.

Myers, S. and R. Rajan, 1998, 'The Paradox of Liquidity', *Quarterly Journal of Economics*, 113(3), August, 733–71.

Neftci, S., 2002, 'Synthetic Assets, Risk Management, and Imperfections', in J. Eatwell and L. Taylor (eds) *International Capital Markets. Systems in Transition*, Oxford: Oxford University Press.

Nesvetailova, A., 2006, 'Fictitious Capital, Real Debts: Systemic Illiquidity in the Financial Crises of the late 1990s', *Review of Radical Political Economics*, 38(1), January.

Nidhiprabha, B., 1998, 'Economic Crisis and the Debt Deflation Episode in Thailand', *ASEAN Economic Bulletin*, 15(3).

Nitzan, J., 1998, 'Differential Accumulation: Towards a New Political Economy of Capital', *Review of International Political Economy*, 5(2).

Nitzan, J., 2001, 'Regimes of Differential Accumulation', *Review of International Political Economy*, 8(2).

Novodvorskaja, V., 2000, 'Dialogi. A. Panikin i V. Novodvorskaja', Moscow: Solidarnost.

O'Hara, M., 2004, 'Liquidly and Financial Markets Stability', Working Paper No. 55, National Bank of Belgium, May.

O'Hara, P., 2003, 'Deep Recession and the Financial Instability or a New Long Wave of Economic Growth for US Capitalism? A Regulation School Approach', *Review of Radical Political Economics*, 35(1), Winter, 18–43.

Obstfeld, M., 1986, 'Rational and Self-Fulfilling Balance of Payments Crises', *American Economic Review*, Vol. 76, March, 72–81.

Obstfeld, M., 1994, 'The Logic of Currency Crises', *Cahiers Economiques et Monetaires*, 43: 189–23.

Obstfeld, M., 1998, 'The Global Capital Market: Benefactor or Menace?', *Journal of Economic Perspectives*, 12(4).

Obstfeld, M. and A. Taylor, 2004, *Global Capital Markets. Integration, Crisis and Growth*, Cambridge: Cambridge University Press.

OECD, 2002, 'The Global Financial Architecture in Transition', *The OECD Observer*, Paris: OECD.

Orhangazi, O., 2002, 'Turkey: Bankruptcy of Neoliberal Policies and the Possibility of Alternatives', *Review of Radical Political Economics*, 34: 335–41.

Pacelle, M., 1998, 'LTCM Partnership May get $50 million Fee Despite a Near-Collapse', *Wall Street Journal*, December 24, p. C1.

Palan, R., 1998, 'Trying to Have Your Cake and Eating It: How and Why the State System has Created Offshore', *International Studies Quarterly*, 42(4): 625–44.

Palan, R., 2002, 'Tax Havens and the Commercialization of State Sovereignty', *International Organization*, 56(1): 151–76.

Palan, R., 2003, *The Offshore World*, Ithaca and London: Cornell University Press.

Palley, T., 1999, 'International Finance and Global Deflation', in J. Michie, J. Smith (eds) *Global Instability. The Political Economy of World Economic Governance*, London: Routledge.

Palma, G., 1998, 'Three and a Half Cycles of "Manias, Panic, and [Asymmetric] Crash": East Asia and Latin America Compared', *Cambridge Journal of Economics*, 22(6).

Palma, G., 2002, 'The Magical Realism of Brazilian Economics', in J. Eatwell and L. Taylor (eds) *International Capital Markets. Systems in Transition*, Oxford: Oxford University Press.

Papadimitriou, D. and R. Wray, 1999, 'Minsky's Analysis of Financial Capitalism', Working Paper No. 275, the Jerome Levy Economics Institute.

Patomaki, H., 2001, *Democratizing Globalization: The Leverage of the Tobin Tax*, London, New York: Zed Books.

Perotti, E., 2002, 'Lessons from the Russian Meltdown: The Economics of Soft Legal Constraints', *International Finance*, 5: 3, 359–99.

Persaud, A., 2002, 'Liquidity Black Holes', Discussion Paper No. 2002/31, WIDER institute UN University.

Persaud, A. and J. Nugee, 2007, 'Redesigning Financial Regulation', in L. Assassi, A. Nesvetailova and D. Wigan (eds) *Global Finance in the New Century, Deregulation and Beyond*, Basingstoke: Palgrave.

Pettifor, A., 2003, 'Coming Soon: The New Poor', *New Statesman*, 1 September.

Pettis, M., 1996, 'The Liquidity Trap', *Foreign Affairs*, November/December.

Pettis, M., 2001, *The Volatility Machine. Emerging Economies and the Threat of Financial Collapse*, Oxford: Oxford University Press.

Pettis, M., 2003, 'Reengineering the Volatility Machine How the IMF Can Help Prevent Financial Crises', *World Policy Journal*, Fall.

Phatra Research Institute, 1997, *The Way Out of Economic Crisis*, Working Paper.

Phongpaijit, P. and C. Baker, 1995, *Thailand Economy and Politics*, Kuala Lumpur: Oxford University Press.

Pollin, R., 1996, 'Contemporary Economic Development in Historical Perspective', *New Left Review*, No. 219, pp. 109–18.

Popov, V., 2001, 'Currency Crisis in Russia in a Wider Context', in D. Dasgupta, M. Uzan and D. Wilson (eds) *Capital Flows without Crisis? Reconciling Capital Mobility and Economic Stability*, London: Routledge.

Portes, R., 1998, 'An Analysis of Financial Crisis: Lessons for the International Financial System', Federal Reserve Bank of Chicago, IMF conference, Chicago, 8–10 October.

Prachuabmoh, N., 1998, *Facts About the Economic Crisis* [In Thai], Bangkok: Ministry of Finance.

Prakash, A., 2001, 'The East Asian crisis and the Globalisation Discourse', *Review of International Political Economy*, 8(1): 119–46.

Puplava, J., 2002, 'Was That Really a Recession?', *Storm Watch: The Last Wave*, 12 April, www.usagold.com/gildedopinion/puplava/20020412.html

Pyo, H., 2001, 'The Financial Crisis in Korea and its Aftermath', in D. Dasgupta, M. Uzan and D. Wilson (eds) *Capital Flows without Crisis? Reconciling Capital Mobility and Economic Stability*, London: Routledge.

Radaev, V., 2000, 'Return of the Crowds and Rationality of Action a History of Russian "Financial Bubbles" in the mid-1990s', *European Societies*, 2(3): 271–94.

Radelet, S. and Sachs, J., 1998, 'The Onset of the East Asian Financial Crisis', NBER Working Paper No. 6680, August.

Rajan, R., 2002, 'Capital Account Crises, Liquidity Enhancing Measures and Monetary Cooperation in East Asia', University of Adelaide, Australia, February.

Rajan, R., 2005, 'Has Financial Development Made the World Riskier?', University of Chicago Business School, September.

Reddaway, P. and D. Glinski, 2001, *The Tragedy of Russia's Reforms. Market Bolshevism against Democracy*, Washington: US Institute for Peace.

Rennstich, J., 2002, 'The New Economy, the Leadership Long Cycle and the Nineteenth K-wave', *Review of International Political Economy*, 9(1): 150–82.

Rifkin, J., 2000, *The Age of Access. How the Shift form Ownership to Access is Transforming Capitalism*, London, New York: Penguin Books.

Rima, I., 2002, 'Venture Capitalist Financing: Contemporary Foundations for Minsky's "Wall Street"' Perspective', *Journal of Economic Issues*, June, 36(2): 407–14.

Rivera-Batiz, F. and L. Rivera-Batiz, 1994, *International Finance and Open Economy Macroeconomics*, New York, Oxford: Macmillan.

Robinson, N., 1999, 'The Global Economy, Reform and Crisis in Russia', *Review of International Political Economy*, 6(4).

Robison, R., M. Beeson, K. Jayasuriya and H. Kym, 2000 (eds), *Politics and Markets in the Wake of the Asian Crisis*, London: Routledge.

Rogoff, K., E. Prasad, S-J. Wei and M. Kose, 2003, 'Effects of Financial Globalization on Developing Countries', IMF Occasional papers.

Rowbotham, M., 2000, *Goodbye America! Globalisation, Debt and the Dollar Empire*, Charlbury: Jon Carpenter.

Rud'ko-Selivanov, V., 1998, 'Finansovyi I realnyi sektory: poisk vzaimodeistvija', *Voprosy Ekonomiki*, No. 5.

Saber, N., 1999, *Speculative Capital and Derivatives. The Invisible Hand of Global Finance*, London, Edinburgh: Pearson Education.

Sachs, J., 1997, 'Nature, Nurture and Growth', *The Economist*, 12 June.

Sakwa, R., 2000, 'State and Society in Post-Communist Russia', in N. Robinson (ed.) *Institutions and Political Change in Russia*, London: Macmillan.

Savona, P., 2002, 'On Some Unresolved Problems of Monetary Theory and Policy', in M. Fratianni, P. Savona and J. Kirton (eds) *Governing Global Finance, New Challenges, G7 and IMF Contributions*, Aldershot: Ashgate.

Schwartz, A., 1986, 'Real and Pseudo Financial Crises', in F. Capie and G. Wood (eds) *Financial Crises and the World Banking System*, London: Macmillan.

Shaw, E., 1973, *Financial Deepening in Economic Development*, New York: Oxford University Press.

Sheng, A., 2003, 'Asia and the Crisis of Money', Fernand Braudel Institute of Economics, Paper No. 19.

Shiller, R., 2000, *Irrational Exuberance*, Princeton, NJ: Princeton University Press.

Shiller, R., 2003, *The New Financial Order: Risk in the 21st Century*, Princeton: Princeton University Press.

Shleifer, A., 2000, *Inefficient Markets. An Introduction to Behavioural Finance*, Oxford, New York: Oxford University Press.

Shmelev, N., 1998, 'Krizis vnytri krizisa' [Crisis within the Crisis], *Voprosy Ekonomiki*, No. 10.

Siamwalla, A. and O. Sopchokchai, 1998, 'Responding to the Thai Economic Crisis', Bangkok: TDRI.

Sinclair, T., 2005, *The New Masters of Capital: American Bond Rating Agencies and the Politics of Creditworthiness*, Ithaca, NY and London: Cornell University Press.

Singh, A., 2000, *Global Economic Trends and Social Development*, UN Research Institute for Social Development, Occasional paper 9.

Singh, K., 2000, *Taming Global Financial Flows. A Citizen's Guide*, London, New York: Zed Books.

Skene, G., 1992, *Cycles of Inflation and Deflation. Money, Debt and the 1990s*, Westport, Conn., London: Praeger.

Slavic Research Centre, 1999, 'Financial-Industrial Groups-Continuity and Change in the Russian Corporate Development', Hokkaido University.

Smee, J., 2004, 'The IMF and Russia in the 1990s', Working Paper WP/04/155, Washington D.C.: International Monetary Fund.

Smith, J., 1935, 'Liquid Claims and National Wealth', Review article, *Journal of the American Statistical Association*, 30(191), September, 639–42.

Smithin, J. and B. Wolf, 1999, 'A World Central Bank?', in J. Michie and J. Smith (eds) *Global Instability. The Political Economy of World Economic Governance*, London: Routledge.

Smout, C., 2001, Speech to the 'Euromoney' Forex Forum, 16 May, London: Bank of England, http://www.bankofengland.co.uk/publications/speeches/2001/speech127.htm

Soederberg, S., 2002, 'On the Contradictions of the New International Financial Architecture', *Third World Quarterly*, 23(4): 607–20.

Soederberg, S., 2005, *The Politics of the New International Financial Architecture*, London, New York: Zed Books.

Solnik, S., 1998, *Stealing the State. Control and Collapse in Soviet Institutions*, Cambridge MA, London: Harvard University Press.

Solomon, E., 1997, *Virtual Money*, New York, Oxford: Oxford University Press.

Soros, G., 1997, 'Avoiding a Breakdown: Asia's Crisis Demand a Rethink of International Regulation', *Financial Times*, 31 December.

Soros, G., 2000, Interview to Journalist Mark Schapiro on Tuesday, September 5, 2000. http://www.simulconference.com/clients/sowf/interviews/interview3.html

Steinherr, A., 2000, *Derivatives – The Wild Beast of Finance: A Path to Effective Globalisation?*, New York: John Wiley and Sons.

Stiglitz, J., 1996, 'Some Lessons from the East Asian Miracle', *World Bank Observer*, 11(2).

Stiglitz, J., 1998, 'More Instruments and Broader Goals: Moving Toward the Post-Washington Consensus', WIDER Annual Lecture, UNU World Institute for development Economics Research.

Stiglitz, J. and A. Bhattacharya, 1999, 'Underpinnings for a Stable and Equitable Global Financial System', paper prepared for the Eleventh Annual Bank Conference on Development Economics, April 28–30.

Stiglitz, J. and B. Greenwald, 2003, *Towards a New Paradigm in Monetary Economics*, Cambridge: Cambridge University Press.

Stiglitz, J., 2002, *Globalization and Its Discontents*, London: Allen Lane.

Stiglitz, J., 2003, 'Dealing with Debt: How to Reform the Global Financial System', *Harvard International Review*, Spring, 25(1).

Stiglitz, J., 2004, *The Roaring Nineties*, London: Penguin Books.

Strange, S., 1997, *Casino Capitalism*, Manchester: Manchester University Press.

Strange, S., 1998, *Mad Money*, Manchester: Manchester University Press.

Sum, N.-L., 1999, 'A Material-Discursive Approach to the "Asian Crisis": The Breaking and Remaking of the Production and Financial Orders', in P. Masino (ed.) *Rethinking Development in East Asia*, London: Curzon.

Summers, L.H. and V.P. Summers, 1989, 'When Financial Markets Work Too Well: A Cautious Case For A Securities Transactions Tax', *Journal of Financial Services*, 3: 163–88.

Summers, L., 1998, Building an International Financial Architecture for the 21st century, prepared for the Cato Institute's 16th Annual Monetary Conference, October 22, 1998, Washington D.C.

Surin, 1998, 'Dependency Theory's Reanimation', *Cultural Logic*, 1(2).

Sutela, P., 1998, 'The Role of Banks in Financing Russian Economic Growth', *Post-Soviet Geography and Economics*, 39(2): 96–124.

Sutliff, T., 1925, 'Revival in All Industries Exceeds Most Sanguine Hopes', *New York Herald Tribune*, January 2, p. 1.

Sweezy, P., 1994, 'The Triumph of Financial Capital', *Monthly Review*, 46(2): 1–11.

Tabb, W., 1998, 'The East Asian Financial Crisis', *Monthly Review* 50(2).

Tabb, W., 1999, *Reconstructing Political Economy: The Great Divide in Economic Thought*, London: Routledge.

Tabb, W., 2001, 'New Economy...Same Irrational Economy', *Monthly Review*, 52(1).

Takatoshi Ito, 1999, 'Capital Flows in Asia', NBER Working Paper Series, No. 7134, Cambridge, Mass.: National Bureau of Economic Research, May.

Taylor, L., 1998, 'Capital Market Crises: Liberalisation, Fixed Exchange Rates and Market-driven Destabilisation', *Cambridge Journal of Economics*, 22: 663–76.

Tett, G., 2005, 'More Opacity is Dangerous in Financial Markets', *Financial Times*, 20 October.

The Economist, 1998, 'On the Rocks. How did Asia's Supposedly Watertight Economies Sink?', *A Survey of East Asia*, 5 March.

The Economist, 2002, 'Inflection Point?', October 17.

The Economist, 2002, 'Bubble and Squeak', *A Survey of World Economy*, 26 September.

The Economist, 2002, 'Bubble Trouble. And What Policymakers Should Do About It', *Survey of International Finance*, 16 May.

The Economist, 2003, 'The Weakest Link', *Survey of Asian Finance*, 6 February.

The Economist, 2005, 'In Come the Waves', 18 June.

The Economist, 2005, 'Subprime Real Estate', 18 August.

Tivakul, A., 1995, 'Globalization of Financial Markets in Thailand and their Implications for Monetary Stability', in *Bank of Thailand Quarterly Bulletin*, 35(2).

Tobin, J., 1965, 'Money and Economic Growth', *Econometrica*, 33: 671–84.

Toporowski, J., 1993, *The Economics of Financial Markets and the 1987 Crash*, Aldershot: Edward Elgar.

Toporowski, J., 1999, 'Monetary Policy in an Era of Capital Market Inflation', Working Paper No. 279, Jerome Levy Economics Institute, August.

Toporowski, J., 2000, *The End of Finance. The Theory of Capital Market Inflation, Financial Derivatives and Pension Fund Capitalism*, London, New York: Routledge.

Toporowski, J., 2001, 'Financial Derivatives, Liquidity Preference, Competition and Financial Inflation', in P. Arestis and M. Sawyer (eds) *Money, Finance and capitalist Development*, Cheltenham: Edward Elgar.

US Treasury, 1999, 'Strengthening the International Financial Architecture', Report of G7 Finance Ministers to the Köln Economic Summit Cologne, 18–20 June.

van der Pijl, K., 1998, *Transnational Classes and International Relations*, London: Routledge.

van Wincoop, E. and K. Yi, 2000, 'Asian Crisis Post-mortem: Where Did The Money Go and Did the US Benefit?', *Economic Policy Review*, September, New York: Federal Reserve Bank of New York.

Velasco, A., 1999, 'Financial Crises in Emerging Markets', *NBER Research Papers*, www.nber.org/reporter/fall99/velasco.html

Visano, B., 2002, 'Financial Manias and Panics: A Socioeconomic Perspective', *The American Journal of Economics and Sociology*, October.

Wade, R., 1998, 'From "Miracle" to "Cronyism": Explaining the Great Asian Slump', *Cambridge Journal of Economics*, 22: 693–706.

Wade, R., 1990, *Governing the Market*, Princeton, NJ: Princeton University Press.

Wade, R. and F. Veneroso, 1998a, 'The Gathering World Slump and the Battle Over Capital Controls', *New Left Review*, 228.

Wade, R. and F. Veneroso, 1998b, 'The Resources Lie Within', Invited essay, *The Economist*, 7 November.

Wall Street Journal, 1998, 'Asia's Credit Crunch is Sending it Back to the Age of Barter', April 6.

Warburton, P., 2000, *Debt and Delusion*, London: Penguin Books.

Ward, A., 2003, 'Economy: The End of a Dream – Or a Cause for Thought?', *Financial Times*, 17 November 2003.

Warr, P., 2001, 'Capital Mobility and the Thai crisis', in D. Dasgupta, M. Uzan and D. Wilson (eds) *Capital Flows Without Crisis? Reconciling Capital Mobility and Economic Stability*, London: Routledge.

Warr, P., 2005, 'Boom, Bust and Beyond', in *Thailand Beyond Crisis*, London: RoutledgeCurzon.

Weafer, C., 2004, 'Economic Reforms: With Actions or Slogans?', *Russian Investment Review*, 1 November.

Webber, M., 2001, 'Finance and the Real Economy: Theoretical Implications of the Financial Crisis in Asia', *Geoforum*, 32: 1–13.

Whalen, C., 2002, 'Money Manager Capitalism: Still Here, but Not Quite as Expected', *Journal of Economic Issues*, June, 36(2): 401–6.

White, W., 2006a, 'Procyclicality in the Financial System: Do We Need a New Macrofinancial Stabilisation Framework?', BIS Working Paper No. 193, January, Basel: BIS.

White, W., 2006b, 'Is Price Stability Enough?', BIS Working Paper No. 205, April, Basel: BIS.

Whittle, G., 2000, 'Russian Leader Faces £3bn Questions', *London Times*, 25 July.

Wibulsawasdi, C., 1996, 'How Should Central Banks Respond to the Challenges Posed By the Global Integration of Capital Markets?', *Bank of Thailand Quarterly Bulletin*, 36(1).

Wigan, D., 2006, 'Futurity, Financial Derivatives and Risk', paper to the ISA Convention, San Diego, California, March.

Wolfson, M., 1994, *Financial Crises. Understanding the Postwar US Experience*, New York, London: M.E. Sharpe.

Wolfson, M., 2000, 'Neo-liberalism and the International Financial Instability', *Review of Radical Political Economics*, 32(3): 369–78.

Wolfson, M., 2002, 'Minsky's Theory of Financial Crises in a Global Context', *Journal of Economic Issues*, June, 393–400.

Wood, G., 1999, 'Great Crashes in History: Have They Lessons for Today?', *Oxford Review of Economic Policy*, 15(3): 98–109.

Woodruff, D., 1999, *Money Unmade, Barter and the Fate of Russian Capitalism*, Ithaca and London: Cornell University Press.

Woodruff, D., 2000, 'Rules for Followers: Institutional Theory and the New Politics of Economic Backwardness in Russia', *Politics and Society*, 28(4).

Woodward, D., 2001, *The Next Crisis? Direct and Equity Investment in Developing Countries*, London, New York: Zed Books.

World Bank, 1993, *The East Asian Miracle*, New York: Oxford University Press.

World Bank, 1998/99, *Global Economic Prospects and Developing Countries: Beyond Financial Crisis*, Washington D.C.: World Bank.

World Bank, 2000, *Reforming Public Institutions and Strengthening Governance. A World Bank Strategy*, Washington D.C.: World Bank, November.

World Bank, 2002a, *Transition: Ten Years*, Washington D.C.: World Bank.

World Bank, 2002b, *Global Economic Prospects and the Developing Countries*, Washington D.C.: World Bank.

Wray, R., 1999, 'The 1966 Financial Crisis: Financial Instability or Political Economy?', *Review of Political Economy*, 11(4): 415–26.

Wray, R., 2004, 'The Fed and the New Monetary Consensus. Can the Symbiosis Last?', Levy Institute, Public Policy Brief No. 80, December.

Yavlinsky, G., 1998, 'Russia's' Phony Capitalism', *Foreign Affairs*, 77(3): 67–79.

Young, A., 1994, 'Lessons from the East Asian NICs: A Contrarian View', *European Economic Review*, 38: 964–73.

Young, A., 1995, 'The Tyranny of Numbers: Confronting the Statistical Realities of the East Asian Growth Numbers', *The Quarterly Journal of Economics*, 110: 641–80.

Young, B., 2002, 'Asian Financial Crisis and Social Reproduction', *New Political Economy of Development*, Conference Paper, Sheffield, UK July 4–6.

Zagashvili, V., 1999, 'Intergarcija Rossii v mirovoe khozjastvo', Mirovaja Ekonomika i Mezhdynarodnye Otnochenija, No. 7, 22–9.

Zakaria, F., 1994, 'Culture is Destiny. A Conversation with Lee Kuan Yew', *Foreign Affairs*, March/April, 73(2): 109–26.

Zelizer, V., 1994, *The Social Meaning of Money*, New York: Basic Books.

Name Index

Subject Index